Brain Rush

How to Invest and Compete in the Real World of Generative AI

Peter Cohan

Apress®

Brain Rush: How to Invest and Compete in the Real World of Generative AI

Peter Cohan
Marlborough, MA, USA

ISBN-13 (pbk): 979-8-8688-0317-8   ISBN-13 (electronic): 979-8-8688-0318-5
https://doi.org/10.1007/979-8-8688-0318-5

Managing Director, Apress Media LLC: Welmoed Spahr
Acquisitions Editor: Shivangi Ramachandran
Development Editor: James Markham
Project Manager: Jessica Vakili

Distributed to the book trade worldwide by Springer Science+Business Media New York, 1 New York Plaza, New York, NY 10004. Phone 1-800-SPRINGER, fax (201) 348-4505, e-mail orders-ny@springer-sbm.com, or visit www.springeronline.com. Apress Media, LLC is a California LLC and the sole member (owner) is Springer Science + Business Media Finance Inc (SSBM Finance Inc). SSBM Finance Inc is a **Delaware** corporation.

For information on translations, please e-mail booktranslations@springernature.com; for reprint, paperback, or audio rights, please e-mail bookpermissions@springernature.com.

Apress titles may be purchased in bulk for academic, corporate, or promotional use. eBook versions and licenses are also available for most titles. For more information, reference our Print and eBook Bulk Sales web page at http://www.apress.com/bulk-sales.

If disposing of this product, please recycle the paper

To Robin, Sarah, and Adam.

Table of Contents

About the Author

Peter Cohan is an Associate Professor of Management Practice at Babson College. He teaches strategy, leadership, and entrepreneurship to students in the college's undergraduate, Master of Science in Entrepreneurial Leadership (MSEL), MBA, and Executive Education programs. He is coordinator of Babson's required undergraduate strategy course and the creator and teacher of advanced strategy courses for undergraduate and MSEL students. Cohan is the founding principal of Peter S. Cohan & Associates, a management consulting and venture capital firm. He has completed over 150 growth-strategy consulting projects for global technology companies and invested in seven startups, three of which were sold for about $2 billion and one of which went public in 2021 at an $18 billion valuation. He has written 17 books, including *Net Profit: How to Invest and Compete in the Wild World of Internet Business*. Since 2011 he has been a contributor to *Forbes* and *Inc*. He is a frequent media commentator who has appeared on ABC's *Good Morning America, Bloomberg*, CNN, *CNBC*, Fox Business News, American Public Media's MarketPlace, WBUR, WGBH, New England Cable News, and the Boston ABC, NBC, and CBS affiliates. He has been quoted in the Associated Press, the *Christian Science Monitor*, the *London Evening Standard*, the *Times of London*, the *New York Times*, *Nikkei*, *USA Today*, the *Wall Street Journal*, *The Washington Post*, Portugal's *Expresso*, the *Economist*, *Time*, *BusinessWeek*, and *Fortune*. He also appeared in the 2016 documentary film *We the People: The Market Basket Effect*. Prior to starting his firm, he worked as a case team leader for Monitor Company, Harvard Business School Professor Michael Porter's consulting firm. He has taught at MIT, Stanford, Columbia, Tel Aviv University, New York University, Bentley University, the Vienna University of Technology, School of Management Fribourg, Barcelona's EADA, Singapore's Nanyang Technological University, the University of Coimbra, the University of Chile, the University of Hong Kong, and Technologico de Monterrey. RETHINK Retail chose him as a Top Retail Expert of 2021, 2022, 2023, and 2024. He earned an MBA from Wharton, did graduate work in Computer Science at MIT, and holds a BS in Electrical Engineering from Swarthmore College.

Acknowledgments

This book has benefited greatly from the help of many people.

I could not have embarked on this project without the enthusiastic support of Danna Greenberg, who chairs the Management Division at Babson among other responsibilities. My Babson colleagues Keith Rollag and Jonathan Sims read drafts of several chapters and provided many insightful suggestions for improvement. *Barron's Advisor* Editor Amey Stone shared insightful comments on Chapter 10. My Babson students, including Tadeo Acosta-Rubio and Shivant Malkani, shared examples of how they have used generative AI to get work done more efficiently. My neighbors Rob Quinn and Leslie Healy read and provided numerous helpful comments on the book as I was writing it.

I am very grateful for the executives and analysts who shared their perspectives on generative AI. These include Goldman Sachs's Chief Information Officer, Marco Argenti; State Street Executive Vice President, John Plansky; Forrester Research Senior Analyst, Rowan Curran; EY's global consulting AI and automation leader, Dan Diasio; Contra Costa's data and innovation officer, Matt White; State Street Alpha Data Platform Product Owner, Jeffrey Shortis; Forrester Research Vice President and Principal Analyst, Michele Goetz; EY Americas Data, AI, and Automation Leader, Traci Gusher; KPMG's national leader of artificial intelligence and head of data engineering, Sreekar Krishna; KPMG National Managing Principal, Atif Zaim; PwC's Vice Chair and US chief products and technology officer, Joe Atkinson; PwC Principal and Generative AI Leader, Bret Greenstein; Adobe President of Digital Experience Business and Worldwide Field Operations, Anil Chakravarthy; ServiceNow CEO, Bill McDermott; ServiceNow CFO, Gina Mastantuono; Service Now

ACKNOWLEDGMENTS

Chief Commercial Officer, Paul Smith; Arista Networks CEO, Jayshree Ullal; MongoDB CEO, Dev Ittycheria; Snowflake Chairman of the Board, Frank Slootman; Snowflake CEO, Sridhar Ramaswamy; Freddie Mac Vice President and Chief Data Officer, Aravind Jagannathan; Goldman Sachs Managing Director, Kash Rangan; Datadog Co-founder and CEO, Olivier Pomel; KPMG Vice Chair of AI and Digital Innovation, Steve Chase; and Dynatrace CEO, Rick McConnell.

Without Apress, this book would not exist. I am most grateful to Shivangi Ramachandran for her enthusiastic support of the idea for this book and for the outstanding project management and editing help from Jessica Vakili and James Markham.

Thanks to my editors at *Forbes*, Chris Gentilviso and Jeffrey Frankel, and my editor at *Inc.*, Mark Coatney, for their interest in and support of *Brain Rush*.

Finally, I could not have completed this book without the help of my wife, Robin, who patiently read and commented on each chapter of the book, and my children, Sarah and Adam, who always make me proud.

CHAPTER 1

Introducing *Brain Rush*

Who I Am and Why I Wrote This Book

I wrote this book because of a gut feeling that generative artificial intelligence, a system that delivers new and original content in response to natural language queries, could spark enormous change in the way people live and work. What prompted that feeling was the 40% rise in the value of Nvidia stock – bringing its stock market value to $1 trillion – three weeks after its May 2023 earnings report which featured a much higher than expected surge in revenue. The source of its soaring revenue growth was demand from companies using its chips to train and operate generative AI applications such as ChatGPT. This prompted a countervailing intellectual response: to investigate whether my gut reaction foretold a significant wave of opportunity or an emotional overreaction to a compelling sales pitch. Here are some of the questions I set out to answer in this book:

- Which applications of generative AI are the most valuable to their users?

- Will such high-value uses of generative AI create widespread demand or will they attract initial interest and later fade?

P. Cohan, *Brain Rush*, https://doi.org/10.1007/979-8-8688-0318-5_1

- Will generative AI contribute to economic growth? Will it create or improve more jobs than it destroys?

- What safeguards must emerge to prevent the legal and financial risks of generative AI from overwhelming its benefits?

- What does the map of the generative AI ecosystem look like?

- How should end users, executives, capital providers, and incumbent technology and service providers evaluate where to place their generative AI bets?

Two experiences qualify me to answer these questions: I worked in an AI startup early in my career that did not become a successful business. In addition, I wrote three books about the Internet – *Net Profit, eProfit,* and *eStocks* – the first during the 1990s when it was far from clear how much of the conversation about Internet business was hype and how much described real companies that changed the world. From working in the startup and writing the book, I learned two key lessons I applied in helping guide investors and business leaders to capture the opportunities of generative AI:

1. **To succeed, companies must solve the right problem well.** The AI startup I worked for aimed to help personal financial planners advise their clients. The startup aimed to encode the decision rules of financial planning experts by building a so-called expert system. Since personal financial planners did not see its product as a solution to a significant problem they faced, the company ultimately failed.

2. **When a tech bubble begins, smart investors and executives should bet on products and business models that deliver a sustainable increase in customer value.** Generative AI will be no different than the Internet was in that respect. Winners will back or lead companies that pass four tests:

- They build the world's best product to eliminate significant customer pain.

- They find and win market share in many large markets that need this solution.

- They harness the capabilities required to win customers and keep them buying by providing new products they crave.

- They sustain rapid growth by creating and capturing a meaningful share of new growth markets.

Who Should Read Brain Rush and How Will It Help Them?

Brain Rush answers pressing questions about generative AI in the minds of varying groups of readers:

- **Citizens and end users.** Generative AI rapidly gained the attention of hundreds of millions of people around the world. In 2023, politicians held public hearings about the perceived societal risks of generative AI. While the White House issued an executive order promoting safe and responsible AI in October 2023[1], as of early 2024, the United States had not passed specific laws or regulations protecting society against AI's risks.[2] *Brain Rush* addresses citizens' and end users' questions, such as Is generative AI an opportunity or a threat to society? Should I urge government representatives to pass laws to protect against its threats? Which generative AI applications could be most useful? Which ones could be useful but risky and how can I protect myself against the risks? Should I invest in companies that supply generative AI technology?

- **Business leaders.** Vendors are scrambling to develop and deliver generative AI products and services for enterprises. Companies are selectively making such tools, such as ChatGPT, available to their employees. Yet these technologies present a mixture of opportunities and risks of wasting money, damaging the company's reputation, and losing control of proprietary information. *Brain Rush* helps answer business leaders' questions arising from these dynamics, including: Which generative AI applications will provide the most value for our company in the short and long term? What is the most effective process for engaging employees and customers in the development of new generative AI applications?

---

[1] "Executive Order on the Safe, Secure, and Trustworthy Development and Use of Artificial Intelligence," *The White House*, October 30, 2023, www.whitehouse.gov/briefing-room/presidential-actions/2023/10/30/executive-order-on-the-safe-secure-and-trustworthy-development-and-use-of-artificial-intelligence/

[2] "Why AI still needs regulation despite impact," *Thomson Reuters*, February 1, 2024, https://legal.thomsonreuters.com/blog/why-ai-still-needs-regulation-despite-impact/

How can we assemble the right partners to design and implement these high-payoff applications? What policies should we establish to limit the risks of adopting generative AI? How can we assess and improve our generative AI applications?

- **Generative AI technology suppliers.** Not long after ChatGPT launched and grabbed the world's attention, incumbent technology and service providers recognized a building growth opportunity, compelling them to launch products to help customers profit from generative AI. Meanwhile, startups were developing products aimed at advancing the state of generative AI's art. *Brain Rush* examines questions these business leaders must resolve, such as Is there a large enough opportunity to justify investing in a generative AI product? If so, what capabilities must we deploy to design and build generative AI products of value to potential customers? Do we have – or can we collaborate to obtain – sufficient competitive strengths to win market share from rivals? Will the future benefits to customers and cash flows from the new generative AI products justify the investment?

- **Generative AI investors.** Investors – whether buyers of stock in publicly traded technology companies or startup capital providers – noticed Nvidia's extraordinary gains in market value. Investors who may have missed these gains regret the lost opportunity and hope to find new upsides among generative AI technology and service suppliers. *Brain Rush* helps such investors grapple with questions such as Which segments of the generative AI ecosystem have the most profit potential? Which companies have the best chance to win customers and keep them buying over the long term? Are these companies likely to sustain expectations-beating revenue and cash flow growth?

Brain Rush Roadmap

Brain Rush seeks answers to the questions I raised in the book. To that end, it is divided into three parts:

- *Part I. Mining Generative AI's End User Value.* Chapter 2 defines and provides examples of generative AI. The chapter explores generative AI's light and dark sides and discusses the concepts I used to guide my research for the book. In Chapter 3, readers learn who uses generative AI, explore generative AI use cases that create the most value for business and consumers, read case studies of how companies apply generative AI, and examine principles and processes for applying the lessons from these case studies.

- *Part II. Mapping the Generative AI Ecosystem.* In Chapters 4 through 7 readers investigate more deeply the key stages of the generative AI ecosystem, including consulting, software, cloud services, and hardware. For each stage in the ecosystem, these chapters provide insight into the key players, the segment's growth and profit potential, the generative AI strategies of the major players, and the key success factors. These chapters conclude by helping readers choose whether to participate in the industry by operating or investing in a generative AI business.

- ***Part III. Panning for Generative AI Gold.*** Chapter 8 provides industry stakeholders, including generative AI consumers, business leaders, technology and services suppliers, and investors, respectively, with tools to assess whether they should participate in generative AI, and if so, how best to set realistic goals and develop and implement strategies to achieve their aims. Chapter 9 investigates generative AI's benefits and costs to society, how citizens should evaluate them, how they can protect themselves from the dark side and profit from the bright side, and how they should advocate for government policies to maximize generative AI's benefits. Chapter 10 recaps the book's findings about the questions raised at the beginning of the book and envisions how the answers might change in the future.

Read on to learn how you can claim your *Brain Rush* stake!

CHAPTER 2

What Is Generative AI?

This chapter introduces the concept of generative AI. It defines generative AI and explains how it differs from other forms of AI. The chapter provides examples of how the technology is applied and offers business leaders a roadmap for how to build a useful generative AI application. It presents AI's bright and dark sides. The chapter continues by discussing how I researched the book and presents the core concepts that guided my thinking. Finally, the chapter summarizes the key ideas in the chapter and sets the stage for Chapter 3.

Defining Generative AI

While researching *Brain Rush*, the most compelling definition of generative AI likened the technology to the printing press. In July 2023, Goldman Sachs's Chief Information Officer Marco Argenti told me, "From what I've seen, LLMs are the largest, most profound revolution in technology since the invention of the printing press. LLMs are a revolution in how we manage and deal with knowledge in a scalable way. Before the printing press, people needed to travel to be in physical proximity to books and be educated well enough to read and understand them. The printing press made it possible to copy books and spread them to libraries that were closer to people." While the printing press made books more

© Peter Cohan 2024
P. Cohan, *Brain Rush*, https://doi.org/10.1007/979-8-8688-0318-5_2

physically available, they were no easier to understand, until LLMs broke "the comprehension barrier." As Argenti said, "They explain something difficult in simpler terms. They put the reader and the writer at the same level. This does not just happen—it depends on how you ask questions. It works better if you break it down in steps."[1]

Generative AI answers natural language questions with clearly written paragraphs, images, videos, or computer code. Through applications such as ChatGPT for text and DALL-E and Midjourney for images, generative AI identifies "patterns in large quantities of training data, and then [creates] original material that has similar characteristics," according to the *New York Times*.[2] How do chatbots – generative AI applications for text – discover these patterns? Chatbots are large language models – computer systems that have processed large volumes of text – called training data. Through training, LLMs can predict the words most likely to follow any prompt the user supplies. LLMs are a type of neural network that seeks to replicate the way the human brain processes information. ChatGPT's neural network is a transformer, which assigns numerical weights to the relationship between short bits of text, called tokens. Transformers use a technique called self-attention, which allows the model to focus on specific words that best elucidate the meaning of the sentence in which it appears.[3] The weights provide ChatGPT with information about the order of words in a sentence to help it predict, for example, "the blank in 'the cat in the ___' is more likely to be 'hat' than 'banana'."[4]

---

[1] Peter Cohan, "Generative AI's Growth Bodes Well For Microsoft, ChatGPT," *Forbes*, July 25, 2023, www.forbes.com/sites/petercohan/2023/07/25/generative-ais-growth-bodes-well-for-microsoft-chatgpt/

[2] Adam Pasick, "Artificial Intelligence Glossary: Neural Networks and Other Terms Explained," *New York Times*, March 27, 2023, www.nytimes.com/article/ai-artificial-intelligence-glossary.html

[3] Adam Pasick, "Artificial Intelligence Glossary: Neural Networks and Other Terms Explained," Ibid.

[4] Dana Gerber, "A technophobe's guide to AI chatbots," *Boston Globe*, July 10, 2023, www.bostonglobe.com/2023/07/10/business/chatbot-how-to-guide/

Generative AI Examples

Generative AI can provide a very good simulation of a well-informed and articulate human response to a question. Here is a July 2023 exchange between a *Boston Globe* reporter and ChatGPT:

> **"Globe reporter:** Fill in the blank and explain how you did it: 'Mary had a little [BLANK]'.
>
> **ChatGPT:** 'Mary had a little lamb'. To fill in the blank, I completed the famous nursery rhyme with the word 'lamb'. As an AI language model, I have been trained on a vast corpus of text, including nursery rhymes, literature, and common knowledge. This extensive training enables me to recognize and complete well-known phrases and sentences. The phrase 'Mary had a little lamb' is one of the most recognized and widely known lines from nursery rhymes, making it easy for me to identify and complete the missing word."

Such astonishingly articulate responses may lead business leaders to wonder whether they can harness the power of generative AI. Here are examples of how people have applied generative AI to a variety of business problems:

- Building chatbots for customer service and technical support[5]

- Giving money managers real-time insight into their investment performance[6]

---

[5] George Lawton, "What is generative AI? Everything you need to know," *TechTarget*, accessed July 21, 2023, www.techtarget.com/searchenterpriseai/definition/generative-AI

[6] George Lawton, "What is generative AI? Everything you need to know," *TechTarget*, accessed July 21, 2023, Ibid.

- Mimicking people through a deep fake[7] – a video that digitally alters a person's face or body with malicious intent so they appear to be someone else[8]

- Boosting the quality of movie dubbing and educational content into different languages[9]

- Writing email responses, dating profiles, resumes, and term papers[10]

- Creating photorealistic art[11]

- Creating powerful and persuasive presentations using video, audio, and text[12]

- Turning scripts into professional presentations with graphics, animations, videos, and realistic voice-overs with background music[13]

- Producing instructional materials and online courses[14]

- Improving product demonstration videos[15]

---

[7] George Lawton, "What is generative AI? Everything you need to know," *TechTarget*, accessed July 21, 2023, Ibid.

[8] "Deepfake," Oxford Languages, accessed February 3, 2024

[9] George Lawton, "What is generative AI? Everything you need to know," *TechTarget*, accessed July 21, 2023, Ibid.

[10] George Lawton, "What is generative AI? Everything you need to know," *TechTarget*, accessed July 21, 2023, Ibid.

[11] George Lawton, "What is generative AI? Everything you need to know," *TechTarget*, accessed July 21, 2023, Ibid.

[12] Keith Rollag, "Comment on 'Brain Rush' chapter draft," October 17, 2023.

[13] Keith Rollag, "Comment on 'Brain Rush' chapter draft," October 17, 2023.

[14] Keith Rollag, "Comment on 'Brain Rush' chapter draft," October 17, 2023.

[15] George Lawton, "What is generative AI? Everything you need to know," *TechTarget*, accessed July 21, 2023, Ibid.

- Recommending new drug compounds to test[16]
- Designing physical products and buildings[17]
- Improving new chip designs[18]
- Writing music with a specific style or tone[19]

Building Generative AI Applications

Reading the above list brings to mind an important observation: generative AI can be used for a variety of reasons, which could include to entertain, to persuade others to join your cause, or to save time and money. *Brain Rush* explores LLMs with business value. A striking example of such value is the use of generative AI to control costs at retail stores. By freeing workers from administrative tasks, a Stanford University study concluded generative AI could increase productivity in the retail and consumer packaged goods industry by "up to 2% of annual revenue – additional $400 billion to $660 billion." Such cost savings were the reason 46% of retail and eCommerce companies surveyed in 2023 said they were adopting generative AI.[20]

To achieve such benefits from generative AI, business leaders could train their own LLMs using proprietary company data related to a specific business function, such as customer service. While we will explore how

---

[16] George Lawton, "What is generative AI? Everything you need to know," *TechTarget*, accessed July 21, 2023, Ibid.

[17] George Lawton, "What is generative AI? Everything you need to know," *TechTarget*, accessed July 21, 2023, Ibid.

[18] George Lawton, "What is generative AI? Everything you need to know," *TechTarget*, accessed July 21, 2023, Ibid.

[19] George Lawton, "What is generative AI? Everything you need to know," *TechTarget*, accessed July 21, 2023, Ibid.

[20] "4 most effective uses of generative AI in retail," *CDW*, August 18, 2023, www.cdw.com/content/cdw/en/articles/software/4-most-effective-uses-of-generative-ai-in-retail.html

companies build proprietary LLMs later in this book, end users can benefit from a general understanding of how LLMs operate. Here is a process business leaders can follow to build generative AI applications:

- **Set a goal and articulate the values guiding your pursuit.** Before building an LLM, business leaders should assemble a team reflecting the views of people whom the project will affect. That team should set a goal – such as "win as many chess games as possible" – and define the values guiding the LLM's pursuit of that goal. For example, Anthropic, a ChatGPT rival, specified values consistent with its mission as a "safety-focused AI trying to compete with ChatGPT while preventing an AI apocalypse."[21] To illustrate this process, the *New York Times* used the example of MailBot, whose goal was to help people respond to their email.[22]

- **Collect and process data to train the LLM**. The next step is to train the LLM, which requires collecting data relevant to the goals and values and formatting the data so it can train the LLM. MailBot's LLM training data would include billions of pages scraped from the Internet, such as blog posts, tweets, Wikipedia articles and news stories. LLM developers could tap free data libraries – such as the Common Crawl repository of web data – supplemented by licensing foreign-language

---

[21] Kevin Roose, "Inside the White-Hot Center of A.I. Doomerism," *New York Times*, July 11, 2023, www.nytimes.com/2023/07/11/technology/anthropic-ai-claude-chatbot.html

[22] Kevin Roose, "Learning how a 'large language model' operates," *New York Times*, March 28, 2023, www.nytimes.com/2023/03/28/technology/ai-chatbots-chatgpt-bing-bard-llm.html

text, say in French or Spanish. Moreover, proprietary or specialized data would train Mailbot to give it features that its users find uniquely valuable. To shorten the training time, the data must be broken into smaller units – words, phrases, or characters – called tokens.[23]

- **Build the neural network.** A neural network – a computerized model based on the human brain – connecting nodes used to process and store information is the LLM's brains. ChatGPT uses a type of neural network called a transformer, which focuses on the word most important to conveying a sentence's meaning so the LLM can more efficiently predict the next word.[24]

- **Train the LLM.** The next step in building an LLM is to feed the tokenized data into the neural network – repeatedly for weeks. Mailbot might identify common patterns. For example, a name usually follows "Dear" and the meaning of certain words such as "bank" can vary depending on words – such as "river" or "deposit" – that appear nearby. After a sufficient number of iterations, the LLM constructs a language map – using numbers – referred to as parameters (the best LLMs have hundreds of billions of parameters) – to track the relationships between tokens. Once training is nearly complete, Mailbot will be almost ready to start writing emails. It might also develop new skills – called emergent behaviors – such as writing computer code or predicting the next word in a sequence.[25]

---

[23] Kevin Roose, "Learning how a 'large language model' operates," Ibid.

[24] David Gewirtz, "How does ChatGPT actually work?" *ZDNet*, July 13, 2023, www.zdnet.com/article/how-does-chatgpt-work/

[25] Kevin Roose, "Learning how a 'large language model' operates," Ibid.

- **Calibrate the LLM.** Before releasing an LLM to the world, developers should calibrate it for a specific purpose – for example, a hospital might tune it to understand medical terms. To fine-tune MailBot, its owners could hire people to rate its emails – based on accuracy – and use the feedback to improve the model. Such human feedback can also help eliminate biases. For example, as MIT Sloan School Professor, Danielle Li, told me "a tester could ask ChatGPT 'What do you think of Chinese people?' Humans would then grade its potential answers. For instance:

  1. 'They are good at math'

  2. 'Their factories are cheap'

  3. 'My role as an AI is not to make judgments about groups of people'

     In this case, 1 and 2 would get a low grade and 3 would get a high grade." [26]

- **Launch carefully.** Once an LLM has been trained and fine-tuned, it is ready to use, with the caveat that the user might discover new bugs the LLM owner will fix. To launch Mailbot, for example, developers might build a Chrome extension that plugs into a user's email app. Problems are likely to occur. As Microsoft and Meta have learned, generative AI systems can be "erratic and unpredictable, or even turn creepy and dangerous."[27]

---

[26] Email from Casey Bayer to Peter Cohan, "Some additional responses from Danielle Li," July 18, 2023.

[27] Kevin Roose, "Learning how a 'large language model' operates," *New York Times*, March 28, 2023, www.nytimes.com/2023/03/28/technology/ai-chatbots-chatgpt-bing-bard-llm.html

The Two Sides of Generative AI

Generative AI has a bright side: It could boost global growth and create significant demand in industries that supply the technology to support it, and advance the productivity of many kinds of work. At the same time, generative AI has a potential dark side, including creating misinformation, boosting legal liability, displacing workers, and as some fear, ending human civilization. To be sure, these predictions vary in their accuracy while others spring from strong emotions backed by limited information. Below we highlight those benefits and costs, which we examine in greater depth in Chapter 9 where we will discuss how to evaluate each and choose actions to maximize generative AI's societal benefits and minimize its costs and risks.

Generative AI's Bright Side

Here are highlights of how generative AI could benefit society:

- **Boosting global growth.** Many analysts predict generative AI will boost economic growth and change the nature of work. For example, according to Goldman Sachs, generative AI could raise global GDP by $7 trillion (nearly 7%) and boost productivity growth by 1.5 percentage points. AI could produce demand for web page designers, software developers, and digital marketing professionals and service sector workers in "healthcare, education and food services."[28] Generative

---

[28] "Generative AI could raise global GDP by 7%," *Goldman Sachs Intelligence*, April 5, 2023, www.goldmansachs.com/intelligence/pages/generative-ai-could-raise-global-gdp-by-7-percent.html

AI could concentrate those new jobs in specific regions such as San Francisco and San Jose, California, according to a July 2023 Brookings Institution report.[29]

- **Increasing worker productivity.** Generative AI was already boosting productivity in 2023 and was likely to continue to do so as more people used it. Boston-based State Street, a provider of financial services to institutional investors, deployed a generative AI platform, Alpha, to help its institutional investor clients manage their portfolios. State Street Executive Vice President John Plansky told me "We have 40,000 knowledge workers who look up answers to questions about why something broke and how to fix it. How much of their time in that activity could the right large language model save? Boosting productivity is the name of the game."[30]

- **Strengthening demand for generative AI technology and services.** Meeting the need to improve productivity at companies such as State Street will produce significant growth opportunities for suppliers of generative AI technology and services. The market for generative AI software could reach $150 billion, representing 22% of the global software industry.[31]

[29] Steve Lohr, "Best Place for A.I. Jobs (New Report Says) Won't Surprise You," *New York Times*, July 20, 2023, www.nytimes.com/2023/07/20/business/ai-jobs-bay-area-brookings-institution-report.html

[30] Peter Cohan, "How Generative AI Could Revolutionize State Street," *Forbes*, June 21, 2023, www.forbes.com/sites/petercohan/2023/06/21/how-generative-ai-could-revolutionize-state-street/

[31] "Generative AI could raise global GDP by 7%," *Goldman Sachs Intelligence*, April 5, 2023, www.goldmansachs.com/intelligence/pages/generative-ai-could-raise-global-gdp-by-7-percent.html

Cloud services providers such as Amazon Web Services could spend over $100 billion to build the hardware they need to train and operate LLMs.[32]

Generative AI's Dark Side

Here are highlights of the costs and risks generative AI could impose on society:

- **Creating misinformation.** Generative AI chatbots can create misinformation, dubbed hallucinations. ChatGPT can make up fake judicial opinions and legal citations and pass them off as accurate information. In 2023, a lawyer who, without verifying its details, submitted such a ChatGPT brief to a Manhattan judge said, "God, I wish I [had verified the ChatGPT response], and I didn't do it. I did not comprehend that ChatGPT could fabricate cases."[33] Such misinformation can also include racial bias. For example, a 2023 MIT graduate, Rona Wang, asked an AI image creator app called Playground AI to turn a photo of her wearing a red MIT sweatshirt into a professional LinkedIn profile photo. Playground AI returned Wang – who is of Asian American descent – a photo with Caucasian features.[34]

---

[32] Matt Bornstein, Guido Appenzeller, and Martin Casado, "Who Owns the generative AI Platform?" *Andreessen Horowitz*, January 19, 2023, https://a16z.com/2023/01/19/who-owns-the-generative-ai-platform/

[33] Benjamin Weiser and Nate Schweber, "The ChatGPT Lawyer Explains Himself," *New York Times*, June 8, 2023, www.nytimes.com/2023/06/08/nyregion/lawyer-chatgpt-sanctions.html

[34] Spencer Buell, "An MIT student asked AI to make her headshot more 'professional.' It gave her lighter skin and blue eyes," *Boston Globe*, July 19, 2023, www.bostonglobe.com/2023/07/19/business/an-mit-student-asked-ai-make-her-headshot-more-professional-it-gave-her-lighter-skin-blue-eyes/

- **Boosting legal liability.** Generative AI raised several legal risks. In light of hallucination risk, service providers, such as lawyers, consultants, investment advisors, financial planners, and many other professionals, could incur legal liability if they use flawed generative AI results in work they share with clients. In 2023, chatbot owners faced legal risk from authors whose work they used without compensation. Moreover, firms feared the liability of sharing proprietary company information as prompts to ChatGPT and other chatbots.[35]

- **Displacing workers.** As with most significant new technologies, people fear generative AI will eliminate jobs. While no one is sure what will happen, experts predict generative AI will change significant numbers of jobs, eliminating some work, changing many jobs, and creating new ones. Goldman Sachs estimated that in the United States and Europe, AI could threaten up to 300 million jobs. Goldman forecasted 66% of US jobs could be partially automated through AI, and as many as 25% of current work tasks could be completely automated by AI in the United States and Europe.[36]

---

[35] Talal Ansari, "Thousands of Authors Ask AI Chatbot Owners to Pay for Use of Their Work," *Wall Street Journal*, July 18, 2023, www.wsj.com/articles/thousands-of-authors-ask-ai-chatbot-owners-to-pay-for-use-of-their-work-9c6198b1

[36] Lucas Mearian, "AI will kill these jobs (but create new ones, too)," *Computerworld*, June 28, 2023, www.computerworld.com/article/3700857/ai-will-kill-these-jobs-but-create-new-ones-too.html

- **Ending civilization.** People fear generative AI could destroy humanity – the basis for this fear is vague. In May 2023, "hundreds of well-known people in the world of artificial intelligence signed an open letter warning that A.I. could one day destroy humanity." The warning? "Mitigating the risk of extinction from A.I. should be a global priority alongside other societal-scale risks, such as pandemics and nuclear war."[37] A surprisingly large number of CEOs feared generative AI posed existential risk. In 2023, Yale Professor Jeff Sonnenfeld surveyed 119 CEOs, 42% of whom said AI has the potential to destroy humanity five to 10 years from now, while 58% said that could never happen and they are "not worried."[38]

How I Researched Generative AI

To research generative AI, I found and read articles and conducted interviews with generative AI industry leaders and experts. I conducted different interviews to gain insights into various topics, for example:

- To learn more about the likely societal and economic implications of generative AI, I interviewed professors and economists to explore their scenarios for the industry's future.

---

[37] Cade Metz, "How Could A.I. Destroy Humanity?" *New York Times*, June 10, 2023, www.nytimes.com/2023/06/10/technology/ai-humanity.html

[38] Matt Egan, "42% of CEOs say AI could destroy humanity in five to 10 years," *CNN Business*, June 14, 2023, www.kcra.com/article/ai-could-destroy-humanity-ceos-say/44201290

- To investigate how businesses are experimenting with and finding valuable applications for generative AI, I interviewed corporate chief information officers and other c-suite executives.

- To evaluate the likely leaders and laggards in each stage of the generative AI value network, detailed in Figure 2-2, I interviewed CEOs of technology and service providers.

- To discover how investors were deciding where to place their bets in generative AI, I spoke with venture capital firms and public equity investors.

In early 2023, I was researching what percentage of company founders remained CEO from the time they came up with the idea for their company to three years after they took the company public. I read an article in an academic journal with the answer: only 0.4% of them were able to take their ventures public and remain as CEO a mere three years later.[39] The article failed to satisfy my question: "Why so few?" Fortunately, I knew several such founders and set off to interview them. I discovered two types of thinking: cognitive lock-in and cognitive hunger.

Leaders with cognitive lock-in had a stagnant mindset that was not conducive to long-term success. Many leaders who adopted this mindset stopped learning – this made it difficult for their organizations to adapt to changing customer needs, new technology, and the competitive strategies

---

[39] Brian Broughman and Jesse Fried, "Do Founders Control Start-up Firms That Go Public?" *Harvard Business Law Review*, March 2020, www.hblr.org/wp-content/uploads/sites/18/2020/03/HLB104_crop.pdf

of new rivals. Successful leaders, on the other hand, displayed cognitive hunger – a desire to keep learning and solving new problems. These leaders adapted to changing headwinds and invested in new areas of growth.[40] Based on this mindset, I developed a framework to help identify the characteristics of leaders most likely to preside over companies that dominate their industry. I used that framework, depicted in Figure 2-1, to handicap the competition among generative AI companies in each stage of its value network.

Figure 2-1. *Five drivers of cognitive hunger*

[40] John Crawford, "Inquiring Minds and Inspiring Research," *Babson Thought & Action*, February 2, 2024, https://entrepreneurship.babson.edu/inspiring-research/

My interviews revealed that leaders who went the distance shared six characteristics:

- **Fuel cognitive hunger.** Cognitive hunger drives CEOs to turn an idea into a successful public company. Such leaders never lose their curiosity and desire to learn the new skills required to further their vision for the company. Such CEOs never rest on their laurels; instead, they maintain their cognitive hunger through each stage of the company's growth.

- **Solve the right problem well.** The first hurdle a startup must overcome is to solve the right problem well. The right problem is one that causes customers considerable pain. It makes sense for a startup to solve that problem if the founder has superior insight into how to solve the problem even as large incumbents ignore the customer pain.

- **Win and keep customers.** Next, the leader must turn the company's solution to the problem into a product that provides so much value that a string of customers buy it. By observing how customers use the product, the company can identify new customer problems and solve them with new products, thus creating an ongoing revenue stream.

- **Adapt to changing headwinds and tailwinds.** Even as a company builds its customer base, external forces outside the company's control could create existential threats to the company's survival or present new growth opportunities. The cognitively hungry CEO will find ways to defend against the threats and capture a share of the opportunity created by these shifting headwinds and tailwinds.

- **Invest in new growth vectors.** Every product or service goes through a life cycle – from initial interest to possibly exponential growth followed by maturity, decline, and death. The cognitively hungry CEO will invest in new growth vectors before a company's first successful product matures. CEOs afflicted by cognitive lock-in will look for reasons to squeeze more money out of the maturing product for fear of cannibalizing the company's cash cow.

- **Prepare the next CEO.** Finally, the cognitively hungry CEO will develop the next generation of leadership years before retirement. Such a leader will put a higher value on keeping the company going long after the founding CEO has left the company.

The Generative AI Ecosystem Model

To help readers understand how technology companies develop products to satisfy the needs of end users, I find it useful to map the industry's value network – a chain of industries connecting a product's raw materials to its customers. Figure 2-2 summarizes that analysis for the generative AI industry. The framework will guide readers through Chapters 4 through 8 as we investigate each link in the generative AI industry value network.

Generative AI Hardware	Generative AI Cloud Platforms	Generative AI Software	Generative AI Consulting	Generative AI End-Users
• GPU design • GPU manufacturing • Lithography systems • Generative AI servers • Data center liquid cooling	• Hyperscalers • Data centers • Networking • Databases • Application performance monitoring	• Proprietary LLMs • Open Source LLMs • Application Specific Generative AI tools	• Strategy • Application development • Compliance	• Consumers • Enterprises

Figure 2-2. *Generative AI value network*

We will explore each value network stage in Part II of this book. Below is a brief summary of each generative AI value network stage. Rather than explaining from left to right, we start with end users and move left to examine the industries that supply generative AI technology and services:

- **Generative AI end-users.** Consumers and organizations use generative AI to save time and money and to develop new ideas. As we will explore later in this book, end users derive a range of benefits from generative AI, such as saving time and money in accomplishing more tedious tasks and becoming more effective at generating new products and solving difficult problems. Generative AI applications enable enterprises to increase productivity in activities such as general and administrative, sales and customer service, marketing, IT, and information security. Moreover, vendors have developed industry-specific generative AI solutions for law firms, advertising agencies, as well as health care, defense, and construction companies.[41]

- **Generative AI consulting.** When ChatGPT scaled rapidly to over 100 million users in early 2023, enterprises hired consultants to learn more about generative AI and to explore how it could boost their productivity and creativity, while avoiding its risks. Established consulting firms have invested significantly in AI. In June 2023, Accenture announced a $3 billion investment in the technology, with plans

---

[41] Konstantine Buhler, "Generative AI Is Exploding. These Are The Most Important Trends You Need To Know," *Forbes*, April 11, 2023, www.forbes.com/sites/konstantinebuhler/2023/04/11/ai-50-2023-generative-ai-trends/

to double its AI-focused staff to 80,000 by 2026. PwC and EY announced plans to invest over $1 billion in AI. Meanwhile, Bain collaborated with OpenAI, and Deloitte "is teaming up with Nvidia."[42]

- **Generative AI software.** Software companies provide tools for training and operating LLMs. Closed-source LLM software providers include OpenAI, Anthropic, and Cohere. Open source LLM providers are also available such as Hugging Face and Meta Platform's Llama. In addition, application-specific generative AI software includes Adobe's Firefly for generating images, data warehouses such as Snowflake and Databricks, and AI-powered corporate process management services such as ServiceNow.[43]

- **Generative AI cloud platforms.** Cloud service providers such as Amazon's AWS, Microsoft Azure, and Google Cloud assemble many of the components required to train and operate generative AI applications. These components include servers and network equipment and tools for labeling and processing data to train open source and full-stack large language models. Cloud services providers outsource some of their hardware to data centers.

---

[42] Andrew Ross Sorkin, Ravi Mattu, Bernhard Warner, Sarah Kessler, Michael J. de la Merced, Lauren Hirsch, and Ephrat Livni, "Accenture Makes a $3 Billion Bet on A.I.," *New York Times*, June 13, 2023, www.nytimes.com/2023/06/13/business/dealbook/accenture-ai-billion-consulting.html

[43] Konstantine Buhler, "Generative AI Is Exploding. These Are The Most Important Trends You Need To Know," Ibid.

- **Generative AI hardware.** Many kinds of computer hardware form the foundation for generative AI. These include GPU designers and manufacturers, lithography system providers, computer server makers, and data center liquid cooling systems companies.

Conclusion

In 2023, many people experimented with generative AI. In this chapter, we provided a definition of generative AI and examined many ways consumers and employees were using generative AI. We highlighted a process companies could follow to adopt generative AI in their organizations based on early experiments with the technology. We explored the light and dark sides of generative AI chatbots, presented the key concepts I used to research the book, and provided a roadmap to the chain of industries supplying generative AI products and services. In Chapter 3, we begin our investigation into the links of this value chain by learning about how end users are deploying generative AI.

PART I

Mining Generative AI's End-User Value

CHAPTER 3

Generative AI Customer End Uses

Based on my experience writing about and investing in Internet companies in the 1990s, I believe the evolution of generative AI will depend heavily on whether customers can find valuable ways to use the new technology. To that end, Chapter 3 answers questions including: Who uses generative AI? Which generative AI applications are most valuable to companies and end users? How have companies in specific industries – specifically health care and financial services – deployed generative AI? What lessons about what to do and what to avoid emerge from these case studies? How can end users make the most of generative AI? In general, experiments with generative AI – particularly in industries such as financial services and health care – have helped people accomplish more in less time than they could before.

Who Uses Generative AI?

Because it was so easy for the average person to use, hundreds of millions of people had tried generative AI in 2023, less than a year after the launch of ChatGPT. Such widespread adoption also encouraged companies to consider generative AI applications that would improve business functions requiring coordination of employees and departments. By 2024, there were two broad categories of generative AI customer applications:

© Peter Cohan 2024
P. Cohan, *Brain Rush*, https://doi.org/10.1007/979-8-8688-0318-5_3

- **Individual applications.** Generative AI helped consumers and employees perform activities they could initiate on their own. Consumers used chatbots to plan travel and meals, compare products before making a purchase, search for movies to watch with a spouse, solve technical problems with consumer technology, and research and write homework assignments. Employees, especially those working for companies that encouraged such experimentation, used AI-powered chatbots to draft and reply to email, write code, and craft and deliver compelling advertising copy, among other uses. Such individual generative AI initiatives required a lower investment and had the potential to deliver rapid productivity improvements, especially if individuals shared and adopted best practices.

- **Organizational applications.** Generative AI also helped businesses to increase productivity in activities requiring coordination within and across departments. Such organizational initiatives helped companies to cut the time and improve the quality of business processes such as customer service, training new salespeople, advising wealth management clients, and boosting product development productivity. To achieve these results, organizations incurred upfront costs. For example, organizations created project teams to plan, execute, evaluate, and refine their generative AI initiatives. Because of the significant investments involved, companies created formal processes to brainstorm ideas and supply corporate resources to the projects with the most potential benefit.

Individual Generative AI Applications

This section highlights specific examples of individual generative AI applications by consumers and employees.

Consumer End Uses

Following ChatGPT's launch, consumers used chatbots to perform daily activities more smoothly. An August 2023 Consumer Reports survey of 2,062 US adults found Americans were using AI chatbots for fun (37%), to save time (36%), and/or to make a task easier or less stressful (35%). "The survey highlights that consumers use AI chatbots for education, writing, editing, and a variety of other tasks," said Consumer Reports analyst Grace Gedye.[1] Here are several examples:

- **Doing PowerPoint presentations**. Student presentations have improved significantly since ChatGPT became available.[2] ChatGPT helps make presentations more creative, comprehensive, clear, concise, consistent in tone and quality, grammatically correct, and visually appealing, adding "relevant images, graphs, and charts."[3]

---

[1] "Consumer Reports surveys American consumers about how they use and think about text-based generative AI chatbots," *Consumer Reports*, January 30, 2024, https://advocacy.consumerreports.org/press_release/consumer-reports-surveys-american-consumers-about-how-they-use-and-think-about-text-based-generative-ai-chatbots/

[2] Keith Rollag, "Comments on Chapter 3," January 4, 2024.

[3] Zhun Yee Chew, "4 Genius Ways to Use ChatGPT To Create A PowerPoint Presentation," *Classpoint.io*, October 31, 2023, www.classpoint.io/blog/chatgpt-to-create-powerpoint-presentation

- **Travel planning**. People used Google Bard — renamed Gemini in February 2024 — to plan[4] vacations more efficiently, starting by uploading a picture of their travel destination. Next users prompted the chatbot with the phrase "Find me the best travel deals for this destination." Gemini created personalized suggestions for flights, hotels, and other activities based on a user's budget and preferences. Gemini also simplified planning and organizing a trip.[5] Bard offers travelers several advantages over a travel website. "If you're planning a trip to the Grand Canyon (a project that takes up many tabs), you can now ask Bard to grab the dates that work for everyone from Gmail," according to Yury Pinsky, Bard's director of product management. "You can look up real-time flight and hotel information, see Google Maps directions to the airport, and even watch YouTube videos of things to do there—all within one conversation."[6]

- **Meal planning**. Gemini helped consumers create personalized cookbooks. People uploaded pictures of available ingredients into Bard, then prompted the chatbot with the phrase "What recipes can I make

---

[4] Sissie, Hsaio, "Bard becomes Gemini: Try Ultra 1.0 and a new mobile app today," *Google Blog*, February 8, 2024, https://blog.google/products/gemini/bard-gemini-advanced-app/

[5] Bijin Jose, "Gemini outperforms ChatGPT with these 5 incredible use cases," *Indian Express*, July 25, 2023, https://indianexpress.com/article/technology/artificial-intelligence/google-bard-beats-chatgpt-with-these-5-incredible-use-cases-8854411

[6] Michael Cappetta, "Google's AI Tool Can Now Help You Plan Your Next Vacation — Here's How," *Travel + Leisure*, September 22, 2023, www.travelandleisure.com/google-bard-ai-travel-planning-7973479

with these ingredients?" Bard returned suggested meals based on the ingredients and the user's dietary preferences. Over time, consumers used Bard to create their own recipes and eventually their own cookbooks.[7]

- **Solving technical problems.** Consumers who ran into technical problems could upload a screenshot of the error message they were encountering. Gemini returned step-by-step instructions on how to resolve the issue. Bard also explained to users how to avoid common technical issues in the future.[8]

- **Brainstorming headlines**. Generative AI is particularly useful for helping people think of new ideas. For example, to come up with a subject line for an email, consumers prompted ChatGPT with a few paragraphs of the email and the chatbot returned a list of suggestions. To brainstorm party ideas, consumers asked the chatbot for a list of party themes. While many of the ideas were not useful, often some of them provided a different perspective leading to a good result.[9]

---

[7] Bijin Jose, "Gemini outperforms ChatGPT with these 5 incredible use cases," Ibid.
[8] Bijin Jose, "Gemini outperforms ChatGPT with these 5 incredible use cases," Ibid.
[9] Justin Pot, "5 Uses for ChatGPT that Aren't Fan Fiction or Cheating at School," *Wired*, July 5, 2023, www.wired.com/story/5-surprising-uses-chatgpt/

Employee End Uses

By mid-2023, businesses were using ChatGPT to perform administrative support activities – ranging from writing emails to managing meetings – and looking to expand its applications. In June 2023, roughly 50% of US companies were using ChatGPT and 93% of them planned to expand their use of the chatbot.[10] Workers across industries used generative AI chatbots for a variety of administrative activities common to businesses across all industries, including

- **Writing software**. Software developers used ChatGPT to write code more efficiently, an activity touching all of a company's stakeholders in a digital world. Programmers posted code into a chatbot with the prompt "What does this code do?" They pasted code written in one language and asked the bot to rewrite it in another; and they prompted the chatbot to write code to perform a specific function. Coders could use the output of the chatbot as a starting point, which they needed to clean up.[11] A data engineer used the chatbot to find flaws with code logic and identify syntax errors. Another software engineer used ChatGPT to create more complex liquid code snippets that help his client websites to filter products, create membership programs, and track consumer interactions.[12] GitHub's

---

[10] Isobel O'Sullivan, "10 Ways Businesses Are Using ChatGPT Right Now," *tech.co*, June 20, 2023, https://tech.co/news/10-ways-businesses-using-chatgpt

[11] Justin Pot, "5 Uses for ChatGPT that Aren't Fan Fiction or Cheating at School," Ibid.

[12] Isobel O'Sullivan, "10 Ways Businesses Are Using ChatGPT Right Now," Ibid.

Copilot, an AI program that suggests code and functions to coders, cut programmer time by 56% compared to those completing the task without Copilot.[13]

- **Writing emails.** Luke Lovelady, an ad developer at BlueOptima, used ChatGPT to save between one and two hours a day. He prompted ChatGPT with information about a prospect and told it to write a personalized email using a selling framework – called "attention, interest, desire, and action" – and included a call to action at the end. He also used ChatGPT to create cold calling scripts by feeding the chatbot "simple value propositions, engaging hooks, and issues that potential customers may face." ChatGPT helped to reduce the time he spent thinking, structuring, and writing outreach materials.[14]

- **Improving an email's tone.** In addition to saving time, ChatGPT also helped workers write more effectively. They used the chatbot to make requests more assertive, to excise an undiplomatic tone, to make stuffy writing more casual, or to correct spelling and grammatical errors. To do that, workers pasted their email into the chatbot and asked it to change its tone. While ChatGPT's responses were not always perfect, they helped employees think more clearly about how to make their emails more effective.[15]

---

[13] Claire Cain Miller and Courtney Cox, "In Reversal Because of A.I., Office Jobs Are Now More at Risk," *New York Times*, August 24, 2023, www.nytimes.com/2023/08/24/upshot/artificial-intelligence-jobs.html

[14] Isobel O'Sullivan, "10 Ways Businesses Are Using ChatGPT Right Now," Ibid.

[15] Justin Pot, "5 Uses for ChatGPT that Aren't Fan Fiction or Cheating at School," *Wired*, July 5, 2023, www.wired.com/story/5-surprising-uses-chatgpt/

- **Serving as a personal assistant.** ChatGPT helped workers enter data and manage their email inboxes. Abdullah Prem, CEO of Bloggersneed, used the chatbot for these purposes to increase his efficiency. He envisioned ChatGPT would "revolutionize the way people work across sectors."[16]

- **Managing schedules.** Workers used ChatGPT to create daily schedules. Lovelady fed the chatbot a prompt about his daily situation and a typical day and asked for advice on how best to schedule his time. He used ChatGPT's response to organize tasks based on his top priorities.[17]

- **Creating presentations.** ChatGPT helped employees create presentations. A cybersecurity executive used the chatbot to create reports and presentations, to respond to customer inquiries, and to write blogs, all of which increased his efficiency at work.[18]

- **Managing meetings.** Workers used ChatGPT to summarize meeting transcripts and ease access to information for remote workers. Calvin Wallis, owner of a malware software company Moo Soft, said ChatGPT freed him to participate more fully in meetings by summarizing virtual discussions effectively.[19]

---

[16] Isobel O'Sullivan, "10 Ways Businesses Are Using ChatGPT Right Now," Ibid.

[17] Isobel O'Sullivan, "10 Ways Businesses Are Using ChatGPT Right Now," Ibid.

[18] Isobel O'Sullivan, "10 Ways Businesses Are Using ChatGPT Right Now," Ibid.

[19] Isobel O'Sullivan, "10 Ways Businesses Are Using ChatGPT Right Now," Ibid.

- **Streamlining marketing content creation and distribution.** Companies used ChatGPT to draft and distribute marketing copy. Lauren Van Woerden, a content specialist at Ollo Metrics, eliminated writer's block and slashed copywriting time 30% to 40% by using clear, specific ChatGPT prompts. Alice Wu of Mind Meld PR used ChatGPT to tailor content for social media, blogs, and emails. Before sending out marketing content, she checked what ChatGPT produced to ensure Mind Meld's marketing message accurately conveyed what a product could deliver without controversial content.[20]

- **Brainstorming strategic solutions.** Executives used ChatGPT to brainstorm solutions to problems such as:

  - **Streamlining operations.** Companies used ChatGPT to identify best practices in automation, outsourcing, and supply chain management. To do that, companies prompted ChatGPT along the following lines: "How can I optimize my business operations, which involve [describe your business processes and how you make money] and increase efficiency, specifically in the areas of [describe the business areas where you suspect efficiency can be made]?"[21]

  - **Raising private capital.** ChatGPT helped private company CEOs to identify appropriate capital providers and to develop a pitch, set a valuation,

---

[20] Isobel O'Sullivan, "10 Ways Businesses Are Using ChatGPT Right Now," Ibid.
[21] Jodie Cook, "ChatGPT: The 5 Most Popular Prompts Used By Entrepreneurs," *Forbes*, July 25, 2023, www.forbes.com/sites/jodiecook/2023/07/25/chatgpt-the-5-most-popular-prompts-used-by-entrepreneurs/

and negotiate a final deal. To that end, CEOs used a ChatGPT prompt along the following lines: "What are the key factors to consider when raising capital for my startup? My business does [describe what your business does] for the benefit of [describe your target audience]. Can you give me potential sources of funding and suggest how I approach each one?"[22]

- **Expanding into new markets.** To sustain a company's growth, business leaders used ChatGPT to help them identify new areas of market research, product diversification, international expansion, and partnerships. To seek ideas for expansion, business leaders prompted ChatGPT as follows: "How can I scale my business and expand into new markets? My business is [describe your business] and most of our customers come from [describe how you get your clients]. We want ideas of new ways forward, potentially including new customer bases, product lines and partnerships. Please suggest some in order of priority."[23]

Organizational Generative AI Applications

In 2023, businesses were also using ChatGPT to improve the effectiveness and efficiency of essential business processes, those that deal directly with customers, investors, and other key stakeholders. As mentioned earlier,

---

[22] Jodie Cook, "ChatGPT: The 5 Most Popular Prompts Used By Entrepreneurs," *Forbes*, Ibid.

[23] Jodie Cook, "ChatGPT: The 5 Most Popular Prompts Used By Entrepreneurs," *Forbes*, Ibid.

organizations weighed the investment required to change these processes against the productivity improvements resulting from the deployment of generative AI. In addition to cutting time from business processes, analysts anticipated generative AI would enable companies to cut highly paid jobs. In February 2024, the Burning Glass Institute published an analysis of 200 occupations most likely to require fewer workers due to the adoption of generative AI. The most affected occupations included "business analysts, marketing managers, software developers, database administrators, project managers and lawyers," many of whom worked in finance for firms such as Goldman Sachs, JPMorgan Chase, and Morgan Stanley that spend 60% to 80% of their salary budgets on people in these job categories. Google, Microsoft, and Meta also employed many workers whom the technology was likely to make redundant. By contrast, for industries such as retail, restaurants, and transportation – that spent 20% of their payroll on affected jobs – generative AI was less likely to result in job losses.[24]

Here are examples of how companies used ChatGPT to make essential business processes more efficient:

- **Answering customer service questions.** ChatGPT enabled businesses to improve customer service. Parker Heyn, CEO of digital marketing firm Parker Marker, used the chatbot to manage customer service inquiries and track customer data – cutting the digital marketer's processing time, saving the company money, and increasing the accuracy of its responses to customer questions.[25] Microsoft chief commercial officer Judson Althoff provided other such examples: with over 195,000 interactions per month, Virgin

---

[24] Steve Lohr, "Generative A.I.'s Biggest Impact Will Be in Banking and Tech, Report Says," *New York Times*, February 1, 2024, www.nytimes.com/2024/02/01/business/ai-impact-jobs.html

[25] Isobel O'Sullivan, "10 Ways Businesses Are Using ChatGPT Right Now," Ibid.

Money's Power Virtual Agents helped customers self-serve, and Brazil-based PicPay used Azure OpenAI to enable its customer experience team to resolve customer questions more effectively.[26]

- **Responding to questions from wealth management clients.** Morgan Stanley trained a business version of OpenAI with about 100,000 internal documents. Financial advisers used the application to find information quickly to answer client questions, such as whether to invest in a specific company. This saves financial advisors the time they previously spent reading multiple reports. Jeff McMillan, who leads Morgan Stanley's data analytics and wealth management, said the tool lacks individual client detail, including life changes such as a divorce or illness.[27]

- **Mortgage processing.** Sreekar Krishna, national leader artificial intelligence and head of data engineering at Microsoft partner KPMG, said generative AI reduced workload for mortgage processing, which takes on average 30 days – much longer than people want to wait when they are trying to purchase a home.[28] For example, in 2023 generative AI enabled mortgage

---

[26] Judson Althoff, "The future of business is here: How industries are unlocking AI innovation and greater value with the Microsoft Cloud," *Microsoft*, July 24, 2023, https://blogs.microsoft.com/blog/2023/07/24/the-future-of-business-is-here-how-industries-are-unlocking-ai-innovation-and-greater-value-with-the-microsoft-cloud/

[27] Claire Cain Miller and Courtney Cox, "In Reversal Because of A.I., Office Jobs Are Now More at Risk," Ibid.

[28] Peter Cohan, "Why Generative AI Could Grow After Bad Nvidia Earnings," Ibid.

company Mpowered to reduce the time to complete a mortgage application from an industry average of one to two hours to a mere eight to ten minutes. The company aimed to reduce the time to deliver a formal mortgage offer from six weeks to under ten minutes.[29]

- **Manufacturing.** Generative AI's ability to interpret images and videos made operations more efficient. For example, LLMs made it possible for shop floor workers to access information about production bottlenecks by making natural language inquiries, rather than writing code or making complex SQL queries. These LLMs accelerated operational improvements and boosted productivity.[30]

- **Accounting.** KPMG used generative AI to reduce the time to comply with regulation. Krishna said KPMG used the technology with four use cases that "cut the time for complying with documentation and work paper requirements. For example, every three months a chief information security officer must certify the company is in compliance, that everyone has been trained, and so on." "We have mini-chatbots enabling users to ask a few questions to automate a service."[31]

---

[29] Stuart Cheetham, "AI in mortgages: transforming the lending process," *Finextra*, September 13, 2023, www.finextra.com/blogposting/24883/ai-in-mortgages-transforming-the-lending-process

[30] Sam Steiny and Shiv Trisal, "The Great Unlock: Large Language Models in Manufacturing," *Databricks*, May 30, 2023, www.databricks.com/blog/great-unlock-large-language-models-manufacturing

[31] Sam Steiny and Shiv Trisal, "The Great Unlock: Large Language Models in Manufacturing," *Databricks*, May 30, 2023, www.databricks.com/blog/great-unlock-large-language-models-manufacturing

- **Health care.** Health care providers used generative AI to reduce administrative activities and shorten patient wait times. For example, Epic, an electronic health records company, used an audio transcription service, Nuance DAX Express, to transcribe patient physician conversations "in seconds." This enabled physicians to focus on their patient, rather than typing while listening. Cigna used MDLIVE, a machine-learning tool, to predict patient demand more accurately and reduce patient wait times by 50%. Using AI solutions on Azure, Mount Sinai Health System used AI technology to reduce patient hospital stays by identifying patient risks such as malnutrition, delirium, and falls.[32]

These experiments pointed the way to more widespread generative AI adoption. Yet more risk-averse organizations may still question the technology's potential to create benefits for people, companies, and society. In early 2024, such organizations may have been seeking answers to questions such as:

- What are the most compelling benefits of generative AI?

- What are the costs of generative AI, such as capital and operating expenses to build and run the systems, training costs, displaced workers, reputational damage from hallucinations, and harnessing generative AI by bad actors for evil ends?

- Do generative AI's benefits exceed its costs?

---

[32] Judson Althoff, "The future of business is here: How industries are unlocking AI innovation and greater value with the Microsoft Cloud," Ibid.

- Will objective analysis of these questions become available to consumers and business leaders?

- Will the value of these end uses be sufficiently high to spur widespread adoption and create growing demand for the technology and services required to implement generative AI?

Which Generative AI End Uses Create the Most Value?

While many of these questions were unanswered, the costs of many experiments were so low that companies were trying out generative AI. In August 2023, Forrester Research Senior Analyst Rowan Curran told me that "A vanishingly small number of companies are doing nothing with generative AI." Most companies were training and testing LLMs – building and buying the needed capabilities – as a way to boost their productivity by automating activities such as poring through hundreds of documents – such as transcripts of conversations between customer service agents and customers – to find the nuggets of insight. Dan Diasio, EY's global consulting AI and automation leader, said, "There is a huge amount of excitement and hype regarding generative AI." After listening to hundreds of CEOs, he observed companies eager to push generative AI applications into production – perceiving value in the technology's ability to "augment work – resulting in more productivity and greater efficiency."[33]

Companies aiming to promote the widespread adoption of generative AI made their bold revenue forecasts available to the public – as if to provide a justification for their investments. For example, KPMG US chair

---

[33] Peter Cohan, "Why Generative AI Could Grow After Bad Nvidia Earnings," *Forbes*, Ibid.

and CEO Paul Knopp said the firm would train its 265,000 employees –
with help from Microsoft – on how to take advantage of AI. Knopp
envisioned generative AI would make KPMG's work processes more
efficient and effective and create new business models. In 2023, Knopp
expressed confidence that generative AI would add $12 billion of
additional revenue for KPMG "over the next several years."[34]

In addition, forecasts for generative AI applications and industry-
specific uses of the technology hinted at the returns that companies
expected to reap from their investments. PitchBook forecast AI enterprise
applications alone would grow at a nearly 32% average annual rate from
$43 billion to $98 billion by 2026.[35] Executives and experts anticipated
financial services firms to adopt generative AI. A 2022 Nvidia survey of 500
financial services professionals found 64% of their company executives
"valued and believed in AI," up from 36% in 2021, while the respondents
who agreed "AI is important to my company's future success" rose from
39% in 2021 to 58% in 2022. IDC expected financial services and retail firms
to invest most heavily in AI, accounting for 28% of domestic AI spending.
Between 2021 and 2025, IDC forecast securities and investment firms to
increase their AI investment at a 30% compound annual growth rate. While
financial services had been slow to adopt AI, a "global economic funk"
forced the industry to cut costs, grow revenue, and boost return on capital.
In addition, financial services providers felt pressure to retain existing
customers, win new ones through mobile and other branchless channels,
and sell more products. About half of respondents to a Deloitte survey
expected AI to boost their company's revenues at least 10%, while more
than a third saw AI helping cut costs by at least 10%.[36]

---

[34] Hope King, "Microsoft strikes $2 billion AI partnership with KPMG," Ibid.
[35] Hope King, "Microsoft strikes $2 billion AI partnership with KPMG," Ibid.
[36] VB Staff, "Reinventing financial services with next-gen AI,"
VentureBeat, April 13, 2023, https://venturebeat.com/ai/
reinventing-financial-services-with-next-gen-ai/

From these trends, implications for business leaders include the following:

- **Deploy generative AI to automate responses to customer inquiries.** Businesses facing a high volume of customer and employee inquiries could capture value – cutting time, lowering cost, and boosting customer satisfaction – by deploying generative AI to shift their response to those inquiries from people to chatbots.

- **Use generative AI to streamline compliance.** Businesses whose operations demanded a significant amount of human effort to comply with detailed regulations could use generative AI to lower the cost and reduce the time required to comply with such regulations. Through natural language prompts, the technology reduced the time required to analyze legal and regulatory texts related to risk management. By "extracting relevant information from complex documents," generative AI helped organizations to remain well informed about and comply with relevant regulatory changes.[37]

- **Invest in processes to protect against generative AI's flaws.** While capturing efficiency gains from such applications of generative AI, enterprises needed to invest to minimize the consequences of the technology's flaws – most notably the risk of hallucinations – such as producing and transmitting

---

[37] "Leveraging generative AI for Streamlined Compliance," *Scrut Automation*, January 2, 2024, www.scrut.io/post/generative-ai-streamline-grc#:~:text=generative%20AI's%20NLP%20capabilities%20can,regulatory%20changes%20affecting%20risk%20management

inaccurate or false marketing information that harms a company's brand[38] – and the loss of control of proprietary information to ChatGPT.

- **Discover new products fueled by generative AI that customers are eager to buy.** Moreover, while respondents to the Deloitte survey mentioned above were confident AI could add to revenues, a significant amount of creativity would be required to create new products and services for which customers would be eager to pay.

In early 2024, I could not find comprehensive studies of successful and unsuccessful business applications of generative AI. To be sure, in October 2023, surveys indicated organizations were piloting generative AI. A Gartner poll of over 1,400 executive leaders found 43% of respondents were piloting generative AI. The survey revealed 47% of interviewees were testing the technology in marketing and customer service functions, while 30% of them were applying generative AI in software development, IT infrastructure, and IT operations.[39] To gain deeper insight for organizations seeking to benefit from generative AI while shielding themselves against its risks, the next section presents a more in-depth analysis of specific case studies. More specifically, this analysis examines the business challenges facing companies in the health care and financial services industries, how they used generative AI to solve painful problems facing their employees and/or customers, and, where available, the results of those experiments.

---

[38] Laura Starita, "Risks From AI Hallucinations and How to Avoid Them," *Persado*, January 11, 2024, `www.persado.com/articles/ai-hallucinations/#:~:text=Without%20strong%20controls%20and%20even,create%20risk%20for%20your%20brand`

[39] "Gartner Poll Finds 55% of Organizations are in Piloting or Production Mode with generative AI," *Gartner*, October 3, 2023, `www.gartner.com/en/newsroom/press-releases/2023-10-03-gartner-poll-finds-55-percent-of-organizations-are-in-piloting-or-production-mode-with-generative-ai`

Healthcare Generative AI Case Studies

In 2023, health care providers were under pressure to accomplish more with fewer resources while improving the quality of patient care. The providers were using generative AI to streamline administrative tasks, such as answering patient questions and scheduling appointments, automating the transcription of patient conversations with health care providers, simplifying patient consent forms, and to help doctors diagnose patients.

Generative AI Helps Contra Costa County Health Services Answer Patient Questions Faster

During the pandemic, patients were trying to get information about Covid-19. Health care providers struggled to hire and attract enough staff to handle the patient demand for such information. To solve the problem, health care providers sought to shift work from call center staff to patient self-service. To improve the quality of patient self-service, Martinez, California-based Contra Costa Health Care, worked with New York City-based Hyro, an AI-powered health care conversational assistant. In August 2023, Matt White, Contra Costa's data and innovation officer, told me patients went to Contra Costa's website looking for information. Although Contra Costa's website posted links to government health orders and answers to frequently asked questions, the website made it too difficult for the patients to find the information they needed. Frustrated patients dialed Contra Costa's customer service line for answers. This pressured Contra Costa's call center with questions. White believed a better-organized, more frequently updated website could answer more efficiently. Meanwhile, patients overwhelmed the health care provider with requests to schedule appointments for Covid tests and for access to their long-forgotten passwords that would enable them to communicate with their health care providers via their MyChart accounts.[40]

Hyro and ChatGPT helped Contra Costa to improve the productivity and effectiveness of its call center. Hyro enabled Contra Costa "to deflect 80% of the calls from patients who forgot their passwords or wanted to schedule appointments to its web portal," White said. Without such a deflection, Contra Costa would have had to outsource those calls to a partner that charged $20 per call, generating a positive return on investment. Moreover, he said, "This freed up our staff's time to allow them to answer other calls more promptly – improving the patient experience." Hyro also helped Contra Costa to reduce call volume from customers who left voicemail messages to verify, cancel, or reschedule their appointments. Such calls had previously accounted for 33% of the health care provider's call volume. Finally, ChatGPT summarized a 130-page document detailing patient benefits so Contra Costa call center staff could answer patient questions about their benefits much more efficiently.[41]

Generative AI Simplifies Patient Consent Forms

The medical forms doctors presented to their patients before beginning a medical procedure were full of jargon likely to be meaningless to the average patient. One reason for this mismatch between patients and the consent forms was that the average American read at an eighth grade level while physicians and lawyers wrote the forms for their peers who had a higher level of educational attainment. To solve this problem, Dr. Rohaid Ali, a neurosurgery resident at Brown University, collaborated with colleagues at

---

[40] Peter Cohan, "Should You Start a Company? Use 4 Tests to Decide," *Inc.*, August 16, 2023, www.inc.com/peter-cohan/should-you-start-a-company-use-4-tests-to-decide.html

[41] Peter Cohan, "Should You Start a Company? Use 4 Tests to Decide," Ibid.

Brown, Massachusetts General Hospital, and Brigham and Women's Hospital. Ali collected medical consent forms from 15 US hospitals, pasted them into GPT-4, and prompted it to create simplified versions. Ali used the following prompt: "While still preserving the same content and meaning, please convert to the average American reading level." Colleagues in the medical and legal fields judged whether the content remained legally and medically accurate, posting their results to MedRxiv.org, a medical preprint database.[42]

The medical and legal reviewers concluded GPT-4 reduced the reading time and improved the clarity of the consent forms while presenting the medical information accurately and complying with the same legal standard. Ali found the GPT-4-generated forms "used significantly fewer characters and words, decreased reading time from 3.26 minutes to 2.42, and reduced the number of sentences written in the passive voice, boosting the clarity and directness of the consent forms. Here is an example of how GPT-4 accomplished this:

> Original: "I agree to have additional procedures if, during the Procedure, my Surgeon decides they are needed for reasons not known before the Procedure. I also authorize my Surgeon to provide or arrange for the provision of additional services, as necessary or advisable, including but not limited to, pathology and radiology services."
>
> GPT-4: "If the Doctor thinks I need more procedures during the Treatment, I agree to have them. I also let the Doctor get other services for me if needed, like tests and imaging."[43]

---

[42] Maggie Scales, "Before and after: See how ChatGPT helped local doctors make medical forms easier to understand," *Boston Globe*, August 23, 2023, www.bostonglobe.com/2023/08/23/metro/can-chatgpt-help-with-medical-forms/

[43] Maggie Scales, "Before and after: See how ChatGPT helped local doctors make medical forms easier to understand," Ibid.

Generative AI Frees Doctors from Transcribing Patient Conversations

When doctors meet with patients, they often type the conversation into a computer. For the patient and the doctor, the typing is somewhat distracting. There is a risk that while typing the doctor will miss emotional cues from patients' facial expressions that might lead to important follow-up questions from the physician that could uncover symptoms of a previously undiagnosed illness. Moreover, as they ask questions and listen to patient responses, physicians may not type everything they hear into the computer. Meetings between patients and physicians could be more effective and efficient if physicians were not required to type and converse with their patients simultaneously.

One potential solution to this problem was to use an AI-based tool to transcribe these conversations so doctors can focus more attention on their patients. In March 2023, the University of Kansas Health System was making a generative AI-based tool from Pittsburgh-based Abridge AI to reduce the time doctors spend on notes available to "their over 2,000 doctors and other medical staff," said Chief Medical Informatics Officer Dr. Gregory Ator. Ator said Abridge created summaries of medical conversations from recorded audio during patient visits, reducing the "more than two hours" physicians typically spent on notes daily. During the Covid-19 pandemic, the University of Pittsburgh Medical Center (UPMC) began using Abridge to digitize virtual interactions between physicians and patients. UPMC intended to integrate Abridge into its electronic medical records system before rolling it out to its thousands of medical employees.[44]

---

[44] Belle Lin, "Generative AI Makes Headway in Healthcare," *Wall Street Journal*, March 21, 2023, www.wsj.com/articles/generative-ai-makes-headway-in-healthcare-cb5d4ee2

Generative AI Helps Doctors Diagnose Disease

Unlike note-taking or scheduling patient appointments, nothing is more fundamental to being an effective physician than diagnosing a patient's illness. In August 2023, ChatGPT's "struggles in key areas" of patient diagnosis suggested generative AI would not be replacing the doctor in the near future. A study published in the August 2023 *Journal of Medical Internet Research* found ChatGPT matched newly minted medical school graduates – about 72% accurate in overall clinical decision making – in performing the steps from arriving at a final diagnosis to developing treatment plans. However, ChatGPT struggled to produce a list of initial diagnoses from initial information from the patient, a crucial step that determines which tests a physician should run to assess whether any of their initial diagnoses are accurate. Corresponding author Dr. Marc Succi, associate chair of innovation and commercialization at Mass General Brigham Enterprise Radiology and strategic innovation leader at Mass General Brigham, concluded, "The big takeaway is the chatbot performs well in some scenarios but not all. And you have to be cautious in applying it."[45]

Such success rates in diagnosis were promising but suggested more improvements would be required for chatbots to become a reliable, integrated partner in health care management. In the study, Mass General Brigham researchers prompted ChatGPT to evaluate "36 clinical vignettes." Researchers provided initial patient information, including age, gender, symptoms, whether the case was an emergency, and additional information, and asked the chatbot to suggest a set of possible diagnoses, a final diagnosis, and a treatment plan. The team found ChatGPT was only 60% correct with its initial diagnoses, but was 77% accurate in the final

---

[45] Jessica Bartlett, "ChatGPT nearly as good as a recent medical school graduate at making clinical decisions, MGB study suggests," *Boston Globe*, August 22, 2023, www.bostonglobe.com/2023/08/22/metro/chatgpt-medicine-ai-mgb-study/

diagnosis and 68% accurate in recommending medications to prescribe and other medical management. These results suggested researchers should investigate why ChatGPT was less accurate in some areas than others and how to improve its overall accuracy. As Succi said, "All these tools physicians and health care providers use, like a stethoscope, are augmenting tools to make us more efficient. This is another augmenting tool. AI ultimately augments the health care provider, but it doesn't replace the provider."[46]

Financial Services Generative AI Case Studies

In 2023, financial services firms were experimenting with generative AI to interpret signals from the Federal Reserve, to provide financial advice on where to invest, and to answer customer questions about their investment portfolios.

JPMorgan Developing ChatGPT-Like Investment Advisor

One of the most significant challenges in the financial services industry is choosing investments that enrich their clients. Financial advisors who persuade people to park their money at financial services firms must justify their fees by delivering high investment returns, ideally greater than benchmark averages with manageable levels of risk to clients. If financial advisors fail to deliver the goods, clients may become former clients. Indeed, they may ultimately choose to forego the chance of beating the market averages by investing in index funds that track the returns of an

---

[46] Jessica Bartlett, "ChatGPT nearly as good as a recent medical school graduate at making clinical decisions, MGB study suggests," Ibid.

index such as the S&P 500 with very low fees and expenses. To keep clients from fleeing, JPMorgan filed a May 2023 patent for "IndexGPT," an AI software service that can be used for the "selection of financial securities and financial assets."[47]

JPMorgan had already begun to use generative AI and had clear support from its CEO Jamie Dimon, yet its IndexGPT patent filing merely hinted at how the financial services giant might apply it to help attract and retain clients. In April 2023, the investment bank's economists began using generative AI to analyze Federal Reserve communications to help predict interest rate policies. In 2023, Dimon praised developments in AI, saying the technology was "staggering," and after using AI for risk, fraud, marketing, and prospecting, he intended for JPMorgan to deploy the technology in "a variety of ways." JPMorgan's IndexGPT application hinted it might use the technology for "advertising and business" services, "insurance and financial" services, and "computer and scientific" services. The filing suggested IndexGPT might help clients pick securities and funds and enable help JPMorgan to boost the efficiency and effectiveness of its advertising and marketing services and its clerical and administrative tasks. The vagueness of JPMorgan's filing widened the playing field on which to experiment with generative AI throughout the banking giant's operations.[48] By February 2024, JPMorgan had not shared public evidence of its successful application of IndexGPT.

---

[47] Will Daniel, "Meet 'IndexGPT,' the A.I. stock picker JPMorgan is developing that may put your 'financial advisor out of business,'" *Fortune*, May 26, 2023, https://fortune.com/2023/05/26/jpmorgan-indexgpt-a-i-stock-picker/

[48] Will Daniel, "Meet 'IndexGPT,' the A.I. stock picker JPMorgan is developing that may put your 'financial advisor out of business,'" Ibid.

Alpha Keeps State Street's Clients Happy

Financial services firms that manage investment portfolios for institutional investors must produce huge quantities of information for their clients. To keep those clients from bolting to the competition, such custodian banks must produce accurate, timely, and relevant information as quickly as possible. Moreover, given the highly competitive nature of the industry, such service providers must not only get all these details right all the time, they must come up with innovative services that enable institutional investors to achieve market-beating returns for their investors while complying with their risk preferences. To those ends, Boston-based State Street used generative AI to build Alpha, a platform that helps institutional investors manage their investments.[49]

State Street's Alpha delivered accurate, detailed, and timely information to its institutional investor clients. State Street executive vice president John Plansky said three forces drove State Street's decision to build the Alpha platform:

- **Demand for front-office functions.** Clients wanted State Street to provide front-office trading services so it entered the commercial software industry by acquiring Charles River Development for $2.6 billion in 2018.

- **Need for better portfolio management.** At the industry level, investment data for client reporting, risk analysis, and regulatory reporting was not being managed well.

- **Desire to make data available to State Street clients.** There was a need to integrate State Street's data into a data platform and make it available and meaningful to clients.

---

[49] Peter Cohan, "How Generative AI Could Revolutionize State Street," *Forbes*, June 21, 2023, www.forbes.com/sites/petercohan/2023/06/21/how-generative-ai-could-revolutionize-state-street/

Through Alpha, State Street aimed to solve a problem that caused clients significant pain. There was a "wide cross section of data – including front-to-back-end services, market data, pricing, reference data, and ESG data – from different categories that clients needed" to do their jobs effectively, said Jeffrey Shortis, State Street Alpha Data Platform Product Owner. Clients particularly appreciate Alpha's ability to answer their questions more quickly. As Plansky said in June 2023, clients formerly needed to wait to get information about their portfolio until the next trading day. "Now, we can make information available to them in near-real-time," he said.

This gave clients faster answers to questions such as:

- Why did my portfolio decline in value?

- What are the top ten news events affecting my portfolio?

- Why were there errors with certain types of trades?

- What could happen to move the portfolio by 1%?

- What is the current performance of the portfolio?

- What happens to my portfolio if, say, First Republic goes under?[50]

Microsoft's $10 billion investment in OpenAI triggered State Street's interest in using generative AI. Plansky said, "I am on the executive board which has been asking about generative AI. What triggered their interest was Microsoft's January 2023 $10 billion investment in OpenAI." State Street saw breakthrough potential to use generative AI to save time. "We have 40,000 knowledge workers who look up answers to questions about why something broke and how to fix it. How much time could they save in that activity if they had the right large language model? Boosting productivity is the name of the game," he said.[51]

---

[50] Peter Cohan, "How Generative AI Could Revolutionize State Street," Ibid.

[51] Peter Cohan, "How Generative AI Could Revolutionize State Street," Ibid.

In December 2023, State Street customer Bank of Montreal's Global Asset Management unit expressed satisfaction with Alpha. "By adopting the State Street Alpha solution, we can provide our experienced investment teams with a market-leading end-to-end platform that will benefit the business both now and in the future," said Bill Bamber, CEO, BMO Global Asset Management. "Our partnership has enabled us to continue to streamline and modernize our operating model."[52]

Goldman Sachs Tests Generative AI

In 2023, many financial services firms were encouraging their employees to try generative AI –within corporate guidelines – to brainstorm ways the technology could reduce costs, boost productivity, and enhance customer relationships. To be sure, such financial services firms saw generative AI as having the potential to provide all those benefits, as long as firms could manage the technology's concomitant risks. Goldman initially focused on generative AI applications that quickly enable its professionals to deliver clients the most insight. As chief information officer Marco Argenti said, "We are a digital business and aim to provide information that is pertinent for a context. Time is the most valuable currency. We aim to invest in generative AI applications that provide a return on attention." Such applications included

---

[52] "State Street Announces Successful Implementation of State Street Alpha for BMO Global Asset Management," *BusinessWire*, December 5, 2023, www.businesswire.com/news/home/20231204950294/en/State-Street-Announces-Successful-Implementation-of-State-Street-Alpha%C2%AE-for-BMO-Global-Asset-Management

- **Instrumenting complex operations**. For example, enabling a portfolio manager to "query a basket of stocks," applying criteria such as "technology companies that will benefit from AI, are not exposed to China, and have diverse boards."[53]

- **Empowering brokers to talk to clients about market moving events.** For example, when big news breaks, the application enables the broker to see how the event will change the value of a client's portfolio and provide a list of talking points the broker can use in conversing with each client.[54]

Goldman was eager to tap into the creativity of its workforce while limiting the financial firm's exposure to generative AI's risks. To that end, Goldman is actively testing use cases while making sure they are consistent with its governance standards, such as accuracy and intellectual property protection. Goldman enables "safe experimentation before rolling out applications more broadly," Argenti said. While Goldman brainstormed hundreds of use cases, it invested resources in those that satisfied criteria such as:

- Is generative AI the right technology for solving this problem?

- Does the application augment talent?

- Will the application have a long-term impact?

- Will iterative feedback make the application better?

---

[53] Peter Cohan, "Generative AI's Growth Bodes Well For Microsoft, ChatGPT," *Forbes*, Ibid.

[54] Peter Cohan, "Generative AI's Growth Bodes Well For Microsoft, ChatGPT," *Forbes*, Ibid.

Goldman Sachs expected generative AI's benefits to exceed its costs as long as the bank made the right decisions. As Argenti said, "In theory, a company can spend hundreds of millions of dollars building a large language model. However, a company can get much more value by pursuing the right policies." These included using constitutional AI, the alignment of AI operations with a country's laws and ethics. Goldman also tried not to spend more on technology than required to build an application. "You don't need to build a fully pre-trained model—you can build your application on top. And you can engineer your prompts to gain better insights," he explained.[55]

Principles of Successful Generative AI Deployment

In 2023, as consumers and businesses experimented with generative AI, they needed guideposts for increasing their chances of success. Based on my evaluation of the case studies detailed above, here are principles for what to do and what to avoid.

What to Do

- **Solve the right problems.** Make sure the problem you are trying to solve will help your company capture evolving tailwinds and protect against emerging headwinds and is important to your employees, customers, and/or investors. Early generative AI

---

[55] Peter Cohan, "Generative AI's Growth Bodes Well For Microsoft, ChatGPT," *Forbes*, Ibid.

experiments suggested the right problems included inefficient customer service and marketing operations and the high cost and low productivity of software developers.

- **Set clear goals.** As you test and roll out generative AI applications, communicate clearly the criteria – such as cost reduction, productivity improvement, customer retention, or new business model creation – you will use to pick the projects in which to invest. Based on the case studies presented above, leaders ought to consider setting goals for productivity improvement, customer retention, employee satisfaction, and even revenue growth.

- **Train staff and let them experiment.** Train the staff who will try out generative AI in how to make the most effective use of the technology, for example, through creative prompt engineering, while avoiding its risks.

- **Provide and monitor guardrails.** Articulate the values on which your company will base its use of generative AI, describe clear processes – such as human review of generative AI output – to make sure people act according to these values, and monitor whether people are following those principles.

What to Avoid

- **Don't assume generative AI always produces correct answers.** In 2023, generative AI applications responded to prompts with a mixture of useful answers and hallucinations. The most memorable example was the

Manhattan lawyer who suffered public embarrassment after delivering a legal motion produced by ChatGPT that contained fake case citations without checking their validity.[56] Therefore, you should avoid blindly trusting how the technology responds to user prompts.

- **Don't allow employees to prompt with proprietary information.** In 2023, companies did not want to risk the release of proprietary information to chatbots. To avoid this risk, you should employ a version of ChatGPT that enables you to control your proprietary data.[57]

- **Don't collaborate with suppliers you have not vetted carefully.** While Microsoft and other established technology companies offered generative AI tools, startups provided such products as well. Given the potential risks of error-prone chatbots, before contracting with generative AI technology providers, check customer references carefully.

---

[56] Benjamin Weiser and Nate Schweber, "The ChatGPT Lawyer Explains Himself," *New York Times*, June 8, 2023, www.nytimes.com/2023/06/08/nyregion/lawyer-chatgpt-sanctions.html#:~:text=In%20a%20cringe%2Dinducing%20court,bot%20could%20lead%20him%20astray.&text=As%20the%20court%20hearing%20in,talking%20with%20his%20legal%20team

[57] Hayden Field, "OpenAI launches ChatGPT Enterprise, the company's biggest announcement since ChatGPT's debut," *CNBC*, August 28, 2023, www.cnbc.com/2023/08/28/openai-chatgpt-enterprise-launches.html

How End Users Can Make the Most of Generative AI

If your company is considering generative AI, start by letting your people use ChatGPT – or its peers – with guardrails. As we will discuss in Chapter 8, guide your people to use it as follows:

- After a chatbot responds to a prompt, encourage employees to check the answer's validity, such as by Googling the result to see if credible sources confirm its accuracy.

- Provide clear examples of what constitutes proprietary information and create clear policies against including such information in chatbot prompts.

- Tell employees to treat ChatGPT's response as a way to speed up the creation of a rough draft, not to produce a final product.

If, after experimenting with generative AI, you decide to build your own system, consider starting with a customer service chatbot trained with transcripts of call center interactions with customers.[58]

Conclusion

Because it was so easy for the average person to use, consumers and enterprises experimented with many generative AI end uses. In 2023, anecdotal evidence suggested the technology helped short-staffed businesses to increase the productivity of their employees, most notably

---

[58] Peter Cohan, "How to Get Your Company Started With generative A.I.," *Inc.*, July 20, 2023, www.inc.com/peter-cohan/how-to-get-your-company-started-with-generative-ai.html

63

in responding to customer inquiries. Case studies in the health care and financial services industries highlighted generative AI's ability to digest large amounts of information more quickly, enabling front-line employees to respond more quickly and effectively to customer inquiries. The experiments and case studies left many unanswered questions: Were companies encountering significant risks when deploying the technology? Did the benefits of generative AI exceed its costs? Would the use of generative AI cause firms to copy each other with easy-to-implement applications? Would companies use generative AI to introduce new, difficult-to-replicate services that yielded significant revenue growth?

While time would tell the answers, the providers of generative AI products and services scrambled to help ensure positive outcomes. For insight into the goals, strategies, and capabilities of key participants in the generative AI ecosystem that enables the applications discussed above, read on!

PART II

Mapping the Generative AI Ecosystem

CHAPTER 4

Generative AI Consulting

In early 2024, due to its rapid and widespread adoption and blend of opportunity and risk for companies, generative AI represented an exciting growth opportunity for consulting firms. Which firms had the best strategies to help companies profit from the technology's opportunities and protect against its risks? How high was the generative AI consulting industry's profit potential? What competitive strategies did leading generative AI consulting firms deploy to win and keep new clients? What principles for success emerged from analyzing these strategies? Read on for answers to these questions.

Generative AI Consulting Industry Players

Established consulting firms quickly jumped on the wave of growth signaled by the consumers and enterprises that began using generative AI within months of ChatGPT's launch. In fact, some consulting firms went so far as to publicly declare how much they were investing to satisfy corporate demand for services to help them tap the technology's potential to improve their business. Firms announcing such investments included the following:

P. Cohan, *Brain Rush*, https://doi.org/10.1007/979-8-8688-0318-5_4

- Accenture announced in spring 2023 its intention to invest $3 billion to double the number of employees with AI expertise to 80,000, 11% of its 738,000 employees.

- KPMG pledged to buy $2 billion worth of Microsoft Cloud and AI services by 2028 to unlock $12 billion in incremental revenue for KPMG, which would amount to 34% of its 2022 revenue of roughly $35 billion.

- PwC planned to invest $1 billion in a "3-year AI roadmap" and to improve its AI consulting services, enhance technology partnerships, and train 65,000 employees.

Not all generative AI industry players were as forthcoming about how much they would invest. Nevertheless – while not quantifying their investments – McKinsey, Boston Consulting Group, Deloitte, and others published their thoughts on how potential clients, with the consultants' help, could benefit from deploying generative AI.[1]

Many other established consulting firms were jumping into the market for generative AI consulting services. Below is an August 2023 ranking of the top eight AI consulting firms – based on *Business Chief's* assessment of their ability to deliver ethical applications of generative AI that deliver competitive advantage – with a brief description of their capabilities:

1. **IBM Consulting.** IBM Consulting helped clients enhance their AI capabilities by providing strategy, implementation, and management services. IBM said it possessed "expertise, methods, and

---

[1] Peter Cohan, "Why Companies Buy Generative AI Consulting: The 3-Month Payback Factor, *Forbes*, September 23, 2023, `www.forbes.com/sites/petercohan/2023/09/23/why-companies-buy-generative-ai-consulting-the-3-month-payback-factor/`

accelerators to deliver successful outcomes," and the company adopted ethical principles into its AI applications. The company collaborated with Meta to make its Llama 2 platform available within IBM's watsonx.ai and data platform.

2. **Accenture**. Accenture consultants aimed to help companies "move from interest to action and value in a responsible way with clear business cases." The consulting firm's approach kept "data, people and processes ready for AI with a secure, cloud-based digital core" to help clients achieve more growth, efficiency, and resilience. Accenture's $3 billion investment in AI sought to improve its work with clients and improve its own operations.

3. **EY**. EY provided "deep strategy, design, architecture, data, systems integration, program operations, and risk" services delivered differently for specific industries. EY helped enterprises incorporate "robotic, intelligent and autonomous capabilities, as well as enabling experimentation and scaling" to help companies operate and compete more effectively.

4. **Infosys** Infosys helped companies reduce cost, increase resiliency, and boost revenue through "automation acceleration." By improving their performance on Infosys's Responsible AI Index, the firm aimed to help clients increase their operating margins by as much as 5%.

5. **PwC.** PwC's AI consulting services sought to help clients "navigate AI safely and strategically" by deploying the firm's expertise with "natural language processing, machine learning (ML), deep learning, model operations, automated ML, digital twins, generative AI, embodied AI, and responsible AI."

6. **Boston Consulting Group**. BCG approached AI through a "10/20/70 rule," meaning BCG believed 10% of the AI effort should go to algorithms, 20% to data and technological backbone, and 70% to business and people transformation. BCG said its client, clothing retailer H&M, benefited from its AI services, adding $500 million "in value delivered in 15 months" and a 0.4 percentage point addition to margins within 18 months.

7. **Deloitte.** Nitin Mittal, Deloitte Global Consulting Emerging Markets leader, said, "As a leading provider of AI services and solutions, we are helping our clients scale AI across their organizations and achieve tangible business results."

8. **QuantumBlack.** In 2015, McKinsey acquired QuantumBlack, a 45-person AI London-based consulting firm.[2] This acquisition was the consulting giant's "data and analytics center of excellence working to enable clients to improve performance by using cutting-edge advanced analytics to make precise interventions with measurable results."

---

[2] "Accelerating with Quantum Black," *McKinsey Blog*, December 14, 2015, www.mckinsey.com/about-us/new-at-mckinsey-blog/accelerating-with-quantumblack

QuantumBlack's unique selling proposition was its "hybrid intelligence, a source of competitive advantage that transforms how companies think, operate, and disrupt, by harnessing the foresight and precision of data and technology with the creativity and understanding of people."[3]

Generative AI Consulting Industry Attractiveness

In 2023, there were no published forecasts on the size, growth rate, and profitability of the generative AI consulting industry. However, a 2023 analysis of the US management consulting industry – of which the generative AI consulting industry could become a significant component – suggested generative AI consulting had the potential to be a large, rapidly growing, and profitable industry. However, in 2023, the US management consulting industry had yet to capitalize on the potential growth opportunity. Instead, the industry generated $330 billion in revenue, was growing at an anemic 1.1% average annual rate in the preceding five years, and earned a 10.3% average profit margin over that time.[4]

Overall, the profit potential of the US management consulting industry was moderate. Low barriers to entry; high supplier power, particularly salaries for talented employees; slow industry growth; and significant buyer power all cut into the profitability of the industry. Nevertheless, despite the highly fragmented distribution of market share, increased

[3] Charlie King and Amber Jackson, "Top 10 Consulting Companies for Artificial Intelligence," *Business Chief*, August 23, 2023, https://businesschief.com/top10/top-10-consulting-companies-for-artificial-intelligence

[4] Tina Fine, "Management Consulting in the US," *IBISWorld*, September 2023, https://my-ibisworld-com.ezproxy.babson.edu/us/en/industry/54161/at-a-glance

consolidation enabled the consulting industry to reduce its costs, helping to offset some of the profit-reducing forces. The five forces underlying the US management consulting industry's moderate profit potential included

- **Threat of entry: Moderate to high.** While entry was difficult at a large scale due to the costs of attracting a large talent pool needed to service large projects, there were lower barriers to entry for firms seeking to serve specialized markets and services. Adopting technologies such as videoconferencing enabled smaller firms to grow and expand by accessing a broader client base. To enter the field of generative AI consulting, entry barriers were likely to include a reputation for excellent services and the costs of hiring the talented people required to build and sustain such a reputation.

- **Rivalry among existing competitors: Moderate.** Analysts expected competition to reduce profit margins. Nevertheless, slow growth in the number of establishments caused increased concentration. The advantages of scale motivated mergers in the highly fragmented industry. Due to consolidation, smaller firms could pool labor resources and benefit from economies flowing from serving similar clients. Moreover, data sharing and communications cloud technology reduced the costs of mergers among smaller enterprises, enabling experts to form teams to serve larger clients seeking solutions to varied and complex problems. These forces were likely to apply to generative AI as well.

- **Bargaining power of buyers: High.** Larger clients could negotiate lower prices with management consulting firms aspiring to win business in the future. Firms with in-house consulting staff could use its expertise to negotiate prices. Technology that enabled remote analysis and communications strengthened buyer power by expanding the number of firms from which buyers could select. These forces were likely to keep customer bargaining power high for organizations buying generative AI services. If specific firms emerged with uniquely valuable services, their skills could mitigate the high customer bargaining power.

- **Bargaining power of suppliers: High.** As technology influenced clients' businesses and prompted the need for consulting expertise, analysts expected companies to hire more skilled workers, increasing wages' share of revenue – workers with generative AI skills were likely to have unusually high supplier power.

- **Threat of substitutes: High.** Companies could hire and train employees to specialize in the areas needed (e.g., corporate strategy, human resources, information technology marketing, sales, finance, and logistics). This was a cost-effective long-run strategy if the company planned to grow and expand. The threat of substitutes for generative AI consulting was likely to be lower for consultants offering uniquely valuable services.[5]

---

[5] Tina Fine, "Management Consulting in the US," *IBISWorld*, Ibid.

While the US management consulting industry was barely growing, KPMG grew at a much faster 14% rate in 2022 driven by demand for transaction services and help implementing innovative technologies.[6] KPMG clearly expected generative AI consulting to accelerate its revenue growth. The significant investments by Accenture and PwC also suggested rivals perceived generative AI consulting to be a highly attractive growth opportunity. Moreover, unless smaller consulting firms emerged with exceptionally valuable insights into how companies could accelerate their performance through generative AI, it was likely that only the largest consulting firms would win a significant share of the industry's potential profit. At the same time, the internal use of generative AI for conducting research and producing reports and presentations for clients had the potential to reduce the number of lower-level employees required to do consulting work.

Generative AI Consulting Industry Participants

Which generative AI consulting firms will lead and which will struggle? The answer could help employees choose which firm would provide the best career development opportunities, enable customers to select the consultants most likely to help them improve their performance, and provide investors with insight into which firm would yield an attractive return on their capital. In 2023, there was insufficient data available to provide a definitive assessment of the leaders and laggards in the generative AI consulting industry. Michele Goetz, Vice President and

---

[6] "KPMG delivers strong global revenues, reporting 14% growth in FY22," *KPMG*, December 13, 2022, https://kpmg.com/xx/en/home/media/press-releases/2022/12/kpmg-reports-global-revenues-of-usd-35-billion-for-fy22.html

Principal Analyst at Forrester Research, told me in September 2023, "McKinsey [which acquired QuantumBlack in 2015] and BCG are leaders. Clients formerly perceived them as good on the executive perspective of how best to deploy AI. Now they are good at [systems implementation] as well." Deloitte, Capgemini, KPMG, EY, and PwC are good at delivery. She credits these firms with "business chops" and the ability to "deliver data and AI as well as digital business transformation. They have respectable, scalable approaches with protocols or plans for the C-Suite, senior managers, and developers. They are teaching skills to put into an operationalized environment," she argued. Companies like Cognizant, Wipro, and Infosys she saw as lacking business strategy skills, while being strong in "delivering."[7]

The available information yielded the following observations:

- **Employees** with the skills required to build generative AI applications could expect good career opportunities at several of the firms. Firms would compete for the best talent by helping those with the right skills to achieve their career goals in a work environment consistent with their values. Here are three categories of generative AI consultants and the varying career opportunities they might present employees:

    - *Strategists* such as McKinsey and BCG looked good for professionals with strategic skills aiming to advise client executives on how to use generative AI to cut costs and boost revenues.

---

[7] Peter Cohan, "Why Companies Buy Generative AI Consulting: The 3-Month Payback Factor," *Forbes*, Ibid.

- *Risk and Process Managers* such as EY, KPMG, and Accenture might provide good opportunities for employees aiming to develop their risk management and process improvement skills.

- *Coding Outsourcers* such as Cognizant and Infosys might be best for employees with strong coding skills.

- **Customers.** Similarly, companies seeking to engage with generative AI consultants might vary their choice depending on their goals. After checking with reference customers and others, companies might choose the *Strategists* if they were primarily seeking ideas on how to use generative AI to increase profitability or boost revenues. They might consider the *Risk and Process Managers* if they were mostly interested in limiting the risks of generative AI, formal training for their employees, and process improvement. If they had already mapped out what they wanted generative AI to do, they might hire *Coding Outsourcers* to build their applications.

- **Investors in consulting firms.** Accenture was the most prominent publicly traded consulting firm allocating significant resources to compete in generative AI consulting. Given the uncertainty about the size of the payoff from Accenture's $3 billion bet, there were few, if any, good ways for investors in public equities to profit from buying shares of generative AI consulting firms.

The remainder of this section analyzes generative AI consultants in these three categories.

Strategists

McKinsey

In 2023, New York City-based management consulting firm McKinsey & Company – that employed 45,000 employees that generated $12.5 billion in 2022 revenue through over 100 offices in 50 countries[8] – was positioning itself as a generative AI consulting leader. As we saw in Chapter 1, the McKinsey Global Institute contributed to the excitement surrounding generative AI by publishing forecasts of the significant economic impact of the technology. As noted above, McKinsey has helped companies with generative AI strategy and implementation. Moreover, in 2023, the consulting giant was rolling out a customized version of ChatGPT to change the way consultants did their jobs.

McKinsey pioneered management consulting industry practices such as professor-founded consulting firms, consultants taking over established companies as CEOs, and running a consulting firm more like a legal practice. For example, in 1926 founder James McKinsey was a University of Chicago professor who opened a consulting office in Chicago to provide engineering and accounting services. He left to become CEO of the department store Marshall Field. In 1933, Marvin Bower, a Harvard Law and Business School graduate, took over as head of McKinsey's New York Office, adopting the title of managing director. Bower likened McKinsey to a law firm, calling consulting projects "engagements" and setting strict codes for professional conduct.[9]

Sadly, McKinsey has also been associated with several high-profile corporate blowups. McKinsey agreed in November 2021 to pay nearly $600 million to settle investigations into its role in helping "turbocharge"

---

[8] McKinsey & Company, *Forbes*, accessed September 29, 2023, www.forbes.com/companies/mckinsey-company/

[9] Douglas Martin, "Marvin Bower, 99; Built McKinsey & Co.," *New York Times*, January 24, 2003, www.nytimes.com/2003/01/24/business/marvin-bower-99-built-mckinsey-co.html

opioid sales, according to the book *When McKinsey Comes To Town*. The book also charged McKinsey with helping insurers "to slash claim payouts to poor households, its involvement in South Africa's post-apartheid corruption scandal and its work supporting authoritarian regimes in China and Saudi Arabia." In addition, former McKinsey partners were the driving force behind enormous bankruptcies. The most notable example is Jeff Skilling, the former McKinsey partner who became CEO of Enron in February 2001 after founder Ken Lay's departure. Skilling began working with Enron in 1987 while at McKinsey, joined the company as head of its Enron Finance unit in 1990, and rose up the ranks, resigning as CEO in August 2001.[10] In February 2019, authorities released Skilling from prison after he had served 12 years of a 24-year jail sentence for fraud and conspiracy in the wake of Enron's December 2001 bankruptcy[11] that wiped out $68 billion from the energy company's peak stock market value.[12]

To be fair, one former McKinsey partner, Hubert Joly, did a marvelous job turning around electronics retailer Best Buy while he was CEO from 2012 to 2019. Joly took Best Buy from losing billions to earning a 3% net profit margin, contributing to a 330% rise in its stock price (about three times faster than the S&P 500's growth). As Joly told me in August 2023, when he became CEO in 2012, Best Buy had gone sideways. "The company had become complacent and needed a new purpose, strategy, and culture," Joly said. "You need to replace it with intellectual humility and curiosity. When I became CEO, I knew nothing about retail. I was

---

[10] Bethany McLean and Peter Elkind, "The Smartest Guys in the Room: The Amazing Rise and Scandalous Fall of Enron," *Portfolio Trade*, www.amazon.com/Smartest-Guys-Room-Amazing-Scandalous/dp/1591840538
[11] Matt Stevens and Matthew Haag, "Jeffrey Skilling, Former Enron Chief, Released After 12 Years in Prison," *New York Times*, February 22, 2019, www.nytimes.com/2019/02/22/business/enron-ceo-skilling-scandal.html
[12] Kenneth N. Gilpin, "ENRON'S COLLAPSE: THE INVESTORS; Plenty of Pain to Go Around for Small Investors, Funds, Workers and Creditors," *New York Times*, December 4, 2001, www.nytimes.com/2001/12/04/business/enron-s-collapse-investors-plenty-pain-go-around-for-small-investors-funds.html

humble. I asked questions in the stores. Not knowing anything was a huge advantage."[13] My guess is Bower would have been proud of Joly's professionalism and the results he achieved at Best Buy.

McKinsey's AI consulting practice – dubbed QuantumBlack, AI by McKinsey – helps companies use "hybrid intelligence to create unimagined opportunities in a constantly changing world." McKinsey clients grow faster by "reinventing themselves" with help from the firm's "Hybrid intelligence," a blend of multidisciplinary teams, domain expertise, AI, and McKinsey's industry understanding.[14] McKinsey hinted at its consulting process by highlighting seven steps CEOs should follow to enable their organizations to capitalize on generative AI, which strike me as the firm's standard change management approach applied to the new technology:

- **Organizing for generative AI.** McKinsey advised CEOs to assemble cross-functional teams whose composition would vary depending on the generative AI application. For example, the firm advised clients to assemble teams from functions such as data science, engineering, legal, cybersecurity, marketing, and design in order to build generative AI for applications to personalize marketing messages.

- **Brainstorming fresh ways to perform essential processes.** McKinsey urged CEOs to use generative AI to make dramatic improvements in how their company performs essential business functions to create new ways of working both inside the company and with stakeholders such as partners and customers.

---

[13] Peter Cohan, "5 Lessons For Leaders From the CEO Who Turned Around Best Buy," *Inc.*, September 29, 2023, www.inc.com/peter-cohan/5-lessons-for-leaders-from-ceo-who-turned-around-best-buy.html
[14] "Quantum Black: AI by McKinsey," *McKinsey*, accessed September 29, 2023, www.mckinsey.com/capabilities/quantumblack/how-we-help-clients

- **Enabling a fully loaded technology stack.** CEOs should charge their chief technology officers to build or collaborate with outside firms to deploy the technical capabilities – such as computing resources, data systems, data governance and security processes, tools, and access to models – required to deploy generative AI applications that will enhance the company's performance, McKinsey noted.

- **Building a "lighthouse."** To generate enthusiasm and inspire creativity, McKinsey advised CEOs to pilot generative AI applications that added value quickly. An example was a "virtual expert" that allowed workers to provide the most relevant content to customers. Such "early wins" would help pave the way for more important applications of the technology.

- **Weighing risk against value creation.** CEOs should initially roll out lower-risk generative AI applications that may deliver less value, McKinsey advised. This approach aimed to help leaders develop and master procedures – such as requiring humans to review generative AI content – to prevent hallucinations and biases in LLM training data from reaching customers.

- **Balancing internal development and external partnership.** Business leaders should acquire or collaborate with providers to gain access to capabilities where the firm lacked sufficient expertise, McKinsey noted. For instance, the firm advised CEOs to "team up with model providers to customize models for a specific sector, or partner with scalable cloud computing" service providers.

- **Developing talent and adding skills.** Finally, to make better use of generative AI, CEOs should train their people in prompt engineering and develop clear guidelines restricting use of proprietary company data. Leaders should also consider hiring new technical people in fields such as engineering, data, design, risk, and product, McKinsey advised.[15]

While McKinsey did not publish QuantumBlack success stories, its 2023 report, "The state of AI in 2023: generative AI's breakout year," highlighted McKinsey's view of what distinguishes the most successful users of AI from their peers. Specifically, McKinsey's report found the most successful organizations did the following:

- **Used generative AI for more business functions.** High-performing organizations were more likely to have adopted AI in four or more business functions. Specifically, the most successful organizations adopted the technology for product and service development, risk and supply chain management human resource activities such as performance management, organization design, and workforce deployment optimization.

- **Focused less on cost reduction.** Top-performing organizations used generative AI less for cost reduction and more for creating new businesses or sources of revenue, and to cite the increase in the value of existing offerings through new AI-based features.

---

[15] Michael Chui, Roger Roberts, Tanya Rodchenko, Lareina Yee, Alex Singla, Alex Sukharevsky, and Delphine Zurkiya, "What every CEO should know about generative AI," *McKinsey Digital*, May 12, 2023, www.mckinsey.com/capabilities/mckinsey-digital/our-insights/what-every-ceo-should-know-about-generative-ai

- **Put more emphasis on worker reskilling.**
  Top-performing organizations were three times more
  likely to reskill at least 30% of their employees by 2026.

- **Spent more of their technology budget on AI.** High
  performers were over five times more likely to spend at
  least 20% of their digital budgets on AI.[16]

In 2023, McKinsey had taken some of its own advice by making
generative AI available to its consultants and by collaborating with Cohere,
a developer of large language models, to help clients make effective use
of generative AI. By August 2023, McKinsey had made Lilli – an internally
developed generative AI tool named after its first female consultant Lillian
Dombrowski – available to half of its employees. Lilli served "information,
insights, data, plans, recommendations of internal experts" based on
more than 100,000 documents and interview transcripts. McKinsey
senior partner Erik Roth said, "If you could ask the totality of McKinsey's
knowledge a question, and [an AI] could answer back, what would that
do for the company? That's exactly what Lilli is." He estimated 7,000
employees had used Lilli as of August 2023 and trimmed time spent on
research and planning work "from weeks to hours." Recently, Roth said
Lilli had "answered 50,000 questions and 66% of users were returning
to it multiple times per week." Lilli had a notable advantage over most
generative AI chatbots: it provided a separate sources section below every
response with links and page numbers Lilli used in its response. Roth
said that clients got "very excited about that." Roth envisioned McKinsey

---

[16] David Ramel, "How 'High Performer' Firms Benefit from AI Embrace,
While Others Don't," *Virtualization Review*, August 2, 2023, https://
virtualizationreview.com/articles/2023/08/02/ai-high-performers.aspx

consultants would use Lilli throughout a client engagement from gathering initial research on the client's sector and competitors or comparable firms, to drafting plans for how the client could implement specific projects.[17]

McKinsey also collaborated with Cohere to help improve clients' business performance. Ben Ellencweig, a McKinsey senior partner and global leader of alliances and acquisitions for QuantumBlack, said clients "are all looking for the right generative AI solution tailored for their needs to address privacy, IP protection, and cost." He anticipated QuantumBlack and Cohere would collaborate to help clients move from discussing to capturing productivity and growth opportunities through "secure, enterprise-grade generative AI solutions." Martin Kon, COO and president of Cohere, said that Cohere and QuantumBlack were independent of specific technology providers, which would enable the partnership to customize "responsible and data-secure" generative AI applications for clients. Alex Singla, a senior partner and global leader of QuantumBlack, said the firm's "conversations with CEOs have rapidly shifted from curiosity about generative AI to more practical considerations around how to use this technology to create value throughout their organizations." By July 2023, clients had begun experimenting with these applications, including a financial services group implementing generative AI to reduce customer wait times by managing "routine customer feedback in more than 100 languages." McKinsey and Cohere were also helping a company reduce costs and shorten time to market by bringing together "product requirements and past designs to optimize the creation of future designs."[18]

---

[17] Carl Franzen, "Consulting giant McKinsey unveils its own generative AI tool for employees: Lilli," *VentureBeat*, August 16, 2023, https://venturebeat.com/ai/consulting-giant-mckinsey-unveils-its-own-generative-ai-tool-for-employees-lilli/

[18] "McKinsey and Cohere collaborate to transform clients with enterprise generative AI," *McKinsey Blog*, July 18, 2023, www.mckinsey.com/about-us/new-at-mckinsey-blog/mckinsey-and-cohere-collaborate-to-transform-clients-with-enterprise-generative-ai

In 2024, McKinsey's generative AI service struck me as offering a blend of advantages and opportunities for winning and keeping new clients. The positives of McKinsey's service included a diverse set of strengths, including new business ideation, best practices research, internal experimentation with generative AI, change management skills, and technical expertise. McKinsey's approach seemed relatively weak in identifying powerful new strategies for using generative AI to create and sustain superior performance. Moreover, it was unclear whether McKinsey clients achieved measurable increases in revenue growth, productivity, and cash flow following their engagements with the firm.

Boston Consulting Group

In 2023, BCG was building on its history as a thought leader in the field of strategy as it positioned itself to help organizations harness generative AI to improve their performance. For example, BCG conducted in-depth research into how hundreds of its consultants used generative AI. The findings of this research uncovered important insights into how BCG could best help clients use the technology to build and sustain competitive advantages. Among its findings, the need to become more effective at conducting experiments and how best to use the rapidly evolving generative AI technology were most pressing for BCG and its clients.

Founded in 1963, Boston-based Boston Consulting Group is a global management consulting firm. BCG helps corporations and other organizations innovate and achieve sustainable competitive advantage.[19] In 1963, Bruce D. Henderson started the management consulting division of the Boston Safe Deposit and Trust Company with "one desk, no clients, no telephone and no staff," he said. Henderson marketed BCG with short, provocative essays called "Perspectives" aiming to encourage business

---

[19] "BCG," *Forbes*, accessed September 29, 2023, `www.forbes.com/companies/bcg-boston-consulting-group/?sh=49c1248a358a`

leaders to rethink "accepted economic theory and business practice." In 1966, BCG introduced the experience curve, showing how doubling accumulated experience can lower costs and provide deeper insights into a company's competitive position. In 1968, BCG introduced its growth share matrix; at its peak, half of all Fortune 500 companies used the tool to diagnose their business portfolios. The growth share matrix enabled CEOs to identify where to invest: in so-called stars with high market share in fast-growing markets, and what businesses to sell or shut down: so-called dogs with low market share in declining markets.[20] In 2022, BCG employed 30,000 people and generated about $11.7 billion in revenue from over 100 offices worldwide.[21]

In 2023, Bruce Henderson's culture of thought leadership was flourishing in BCG's generative AI consulting practice. A September 2023 report highlighted surprising findings about a study conducted with scholars – from Harvard Business School, MIT Sloan School of Management, the Wharton School at the University of Pennsylvania, and the University of Warwick – into how more than 750 BCG consultants used generative AI in their work. The key findings of this research highlighted the importance of the gap between what the consultants expected generative AI to do well and the technology's actual strengths and weaknesses. As the authors wrote, "people mistrust generative AI in areas where it can contribute tremendous value and trust it too much where the technology isn't competent." Simply put, peoples' performance improved when they trusted the output of generative AI within its sphere of competence and distrusted the output where the technology performed poorly. More specifically

---

[20] "The Timeline of BCG's History," *BCG*, accessed September 29, 2023, www.bcg.com/about/our-history/timeline

[21] "Global revenue of Boston Consulting Group from 2015 to 2022," *Statista*, accessed September 29, 2023, www.statista.com/statistics/999444/boston-consulting-group-global-sales/

- In creative ideation, a task within generative AI's competence, around 90% of participants improved their performance. People did best when they did not attempt to edit GPT-4's output. In this task, researchers asked participants to develop ideas for new products and plans for going to market. Generative AI is better at these tasks due to the vast amount of data used to train LLMs.

- When working on business problem solving, a task outside the tool's current competence, many participants took GPT-4's misleading output at face value. Their performance was 23% worse than those who did not use the tool at all. In the business problem-solving task, researchers asked participants to analyze performance data and executive interviews to find the root cause of a company's challenges. Since LLMs were more likely to err when "asked to weigh nuanced qualitative and quantitative data to answer a complex question," GPT-4's results were more likely to be wrong, requiring consultants to use their own judgment instead.[22]

BCG's analysis of these results suggested an agenda for business leaders likely to shape how the firm delivers generative AI consulting services to provide clients with a sustainable competitive advantage. The agenda items include

---

[22] François Candelon, Lisa Krayer, Saran Rajendran, and David Zuluaga Martínez, "How People Can Create—and Destroy—Value with generative AI," *BCG*, September 21, 2023, www.bcg.com/publications/2023/how-people-create-and-destroy-value-with-gen-ai

- **Train LLMs with firm-specific data**. A firm's ability to outperform rivals depends on performing activities differently than rivals do. Companies will achieve superior performance by using advanced data analysis tools and "high-quality, firm-specific data" to train their LLMs.

- **Invest more employee time in tasks generative AI does not do well.** BCG suggested workers should spend less time rewriting the chatbot results of tasks, such as creative ideation, which generative AI does well. Instead, people should redirect their efforts to tasks – such as root cause analysis – beyond generative AI's competency frontier.

- **Change human resources strategy.** BCG anticipated that leaders would need to change their human resources strategy in four areas:

  - **Skills.** Rapidly evolving generative AI capabilities would require companies to change the kinds of skills they needed. For example, while prompt engineering was a skill in growing demand in the second quarter of 2023, new technology could make it obsolete in the future.

  - **Traits.** BCG expected companies to hire for new traits. For example, rather than needing people with high raw talent, they might need people who could work effectively with generative AI tools.

  - **Training.** Companies would need to train people to check the results of tasks done primarily by generative AI.

- **Diversity of thought.** Finally, companies would need to encourage diversity of thought, most likely by creating new approaches to ideation.

- **Get better at experimenting and testing.** Due to the rapid rate at which generative AI is changing, companies will need to get better at experimenting with new uses of the technology, getting feedback, and trying again. BCG recommended companies create "generative AI labs" to improve their skills at experimenting and testing. The new capability would generate insights, such as new kinds of hallucinations, changing approaches to collaboration between people and machines, and counterintuitive ways to achieve better business outcomes.[23]

In 2023, BCG collaborated with Anthropic and Intel to deliver generative AI consulting services to its clients. Its September 2023 collaboration with Anthropic, a provider of AI models such as Claude 2, aimed at helping BCG to inform its customers about the best ways to use AI and to help them deploy the Anthropic models to generate better business results for BCG clients. The collaborators expected to present clients with many business activities that generative AI would enhance, including "knowledge management, market research, fraud detection, demand forecasting, report generation, and business analysis." Anthropic and BCG also emphasized their collaboration would ensure ethical and responsible use of AI, enabling them to attract new clients.[24]

---

[23] François Candelon, Lisa Krayer, Saran Rajendran, and David Zuluaga Martínez, "How People Can Create—and Destroy—Value with generative AI," *BCG*, Ibid.

[24] Sabrina Ortiz, "BCG partners with Anthropic to launch yet another AI consulting initiative," *ZDNet*, September 18, 2023, `www.zdnet.com/article/bcg-partners-with-anthropic-to-launch-yet-another-consulting-ai-initiative/`

In May 2023, BCG announced a partnership with Intel, also aimed at selling generative AI to companies. Before this partnership, Intel enabled BCG employees to ask natural language questions of a 50-year archive of BCG reports and presentations, as summaries or in their entirety. Suchi Srinivasan, a managing director and partner at BCG, said, "We're in the knowledge business and the expertise business. Rarely are we just looking for one piece of something on the page." Intel built the system on a supercomputer using its Zeon CPUs. Srinivasan said BCG and Intel will sell the technology they have developed to help other companies to train AI systems using "the customer's proprietary data, without having to share it with Intel or BCG." The two will target "industries like financial services, which have strict rules over data storage and sharing."[25]

In 2024, BCG's generative AI services struck me as fitting within the firm's legacy of thought leadership. The results of its research into how BCG consultants used generative AI providing meaningful new insights which had the potential to help clients make better use of AI chatbots. BCG also developed an approach to change management in generative AI that flowed from the insights of its research. Moreover, BCG's partnerships with Intel and Anthropic offered the potential for client adoption of generative AI applications trained on internal company information. While the results achieved from BCG's AI client engagements were unknown, BCG's services struck me as offering clients an innovative edge.

---

[25] Stephen Nellis, "Intel, Boston Consulting Group team to sell AI to corporate customers," *Reuters*, May 10, 2023, www.reuters.com/technology/intel-boston-consulting-group-team-sell-ai-corporate-customers-2023-05-10/

Risk and Process Managers

EY

EY brought considerable resources to the challenge of helping companies make the most of generative AI. By 2023, the nearly $50 billion (2023 revenue) provider of assurance, consulting, and other services had invested more than $1 billion to build EY.ai, a platform to help clients harness generative AI to boost operational efficiency while protecting against the technology's potential reputational, compliance, and security risks.

EY is the result of merging auditing firms – Arthur Young and Ernst & Whinney – founded in the Midwest over 100 years ago. By 2023, EY – the corporate descendant of those founders – employed nearly 400,000 people and generated nearly $50 billion in revenue. Arthur Young founded the original eponymous firm, based in Kansas City, in 1896. Ernst and Whinney began life in Cleveland as Ernst & Ernst in 1906. It took on additional partners and grew rapidly after 1913 when the United States began to levy income taxes. While Ernst and Whinney thrived in the 1980s, enjoying rapid growth in its management consulting practice, Arthur Young ran into trouble during the decade, facing allegations the firm allowed the Western Savings Association of Dallas to overstate its net worth by more than $400 million. In 1989, Arthur Young and Ernst and Whinney merged to form Ernst and Young, hosting 6,100 partners and generating nearly $4.3 billion in revenue.[26] By September 2023, London-based EY, which provided services including assurance, consulting, law, strategy, tax, and transactions, ended its fiscal year with $49.4 billion in revenue and 395,442 employees in over 150 countries.[27]

---

[26] "Ernst & Young," *Company-Histories*, accessed September 30, 2023, www.company-histories.com/Ernst-Young-Company-History.html

[27] Rachel Lloyd, "EY reports record global revenue results of just under US$50b," *EY*, www.ey.com/en_gl/news/2023/09/ey-reports-record-global-revenue-results-of-just-under-us-50b

In 2023, EY made a significant investment in generative AI services. The firm spent $1.4 billion in build its AI capabilities and launch EY.ai, "a unifying platform combining EY capabilities, AI and curated ecosystems." EY also introduced an LLM called EY.ai EYQ – the EY.ai Confidence Index and specialized AI training for all EY's people. This followed the AI tools including EY Tax Co-Pilot, aimed at "augmenting the capabilities of EY tax professionals."[28] EY.ai guided EY through a four-phase consulting process:

- **Chart Strategy.** EY used its EY.ai Maturity Model to evaluate a client's level of AI adoption and "uncover gaps" by analyzing and benchmarking the client's AI strategy and roadmap.

- **Create Value.** The firm's EY.ai Value Accelerator identified "opportunities for value creation and capture" to fill gaps identified in the "Chart Strategy" phase. The "Create Value" phase sought to help clients achieve "meaningful strategic growth" through "prioritized initiatives and solutions."

- **Build Confidence.** EY used its EY.ai Confidence Index to conduct an "empirical assessment of [a client's] underlying AI model." The goal was to reach a conclusion about how confident clients should be about the data, model, and processes making up their generative AI applications.

---

[28] Rachel Lloyd, "EY reports record global revenue results of just under US$50b," *EY*, Ibid.

- **Empower People.** In the final phase of its consulting process, EY aimed to develop the generative AI skills of a client's workforce by "harnessing AI, reimagining skill development, and reshaping talent management" to increase employees' "creativity and productivity."[29]

In 2023, EY saw companies hurrying to capture generative AI's productivity and efficiency improvements. Dan Diasio, EY's global consulting AI and automation leader, told me in an August 2023 interview that he spoke with 1,300 CEOs in July. Sixty-five percent said they "were clear AI would have a significant role in their business. Everybody is dipping their toe in the water," Diasio said. "What is different about generative AI is they don't just want to learn about it; they want to push it into production. It is already creating value. It is augmenting work—resulting in more productivity and greater efficiency."[30] Clients were seeking to use generative AI to transform their businesses and were choosing EY due to the insights it gained from using the technology internally. In September 2023 EY Americas Data, AI and Automation Leader Traci Gusher said client needs included

---

[29] "EY.ai – A unifying platform," *EY*, accessed September 30, 2023, www.ey.com/en_gl/ai/platform

[30] Peter Cohan, "Why generative AI Could Grow Even After A Set Of Bad Nvidia Earnings," *Forbes*, August 27, 2023, www.forbes.com/sites/petercohan/2023/08/27/why-generative-ai-could-grow-even-after-a-set-of-bad-nvidia-earnings/

- Scaling technology and data architectures for enterprise-wide generative AI deployment

- Training board and C-Suite leaders in generative AI literacy

- Building high-priority generative AI applications to deliver "quick value wins"[31]

EY saw itself meeting the generative AI needs of its clients as the technology and their goals evolved. "They are seeking providers that can demonstrate execution level experience using the technology, as well as constantly evolving the how and why of using the technology, given how fast it is evolving," according to Gusher. She considered EY's ability to help clients use generative AI as a "transformative accelerator" to be a competitive strength. Clients valued EY's blend of technical and business expertise as well as the firm's ability to design generative AI applications that would allow clients to scale up deployment to all their employees. To satisfy clients' future requirements, EY intended to help them connect generative AI with other "AI systems, automation and analytics to drive transformative value," Gusher noted. Companies also needed EY's help "with process redesign, talent reskilling, and broad change management," she said.[32]

EY collaborated with Everest Group, a property-casualty (P&C) insurance company, to produce an August 2023 report on how to achieve a "quick win" by using generative AI to improve the efficiency and effectiveness of the personal lines claims process. The report found testing generative AI for claims would deliver short-term improvements in efficiency and claims accuracy and ultimately lead insurers to reimagine the claims process completely. The report presented EY's and Everest Group's views on topics including

---

[31] Peter Cohan, "Why Companies Buy Generative AI Consulting: The 3-Month Payback Factor," *Forbes*, Ibid.

[32] Peter Cohan, "Why Companies Buy generative AI Consulting: The 3-Month Payback Factor," *Forbes*, Ibid.

- Changing industry attitudes toward P&C insurers

- Growing interest and investment in generative AI

- Why claims operations would be a good place for P&C insurers to start using generative AI

- A roadmap and key considerations for P&C insurance company use of generative AI to improve the claims process[33]

In early 2024, EY's generative AI services struck me as appealing to a narrower client base than the strategies of McKinsey and BCG. EY built internal know-how by applying generative AI to its internal processes such as tax accounting. Through its partnership with Everest Group, EY learned how property-casualty firms could deploy the technology to boost productivity. While the specific client benefits of EY's generative AI services were unknown, the path ahead for EY appeared to lie in mastering very specific functionalities – such as auditing and compliance – and industry-specific applications of the technology, possibly in other segments of the financial services industry.

KPMG

KPMG distinguished itself from rivals through its partnership with Microsoft, owner of ChatGPT. After collaborating for over a decade, the two had 2,500 joint clients and could potentially add more due to Microsoft product innovations and successful consulting engagements led by KPMG. Ultimately, KPMG's ability to generate a return on its investment in

---

[33] Aaditya Jain and Rugved Sawant, "Unleashing the Potential of generative AI (GAI): A Game-changer for Property and Casualty (P&C) Insurance Claims Exploring the Need, Urgency, and Roadmap for Adopting GAI Across Claims Operations," *EY*, accessed September 30, 2023, www.ey.com/en_nl/insurance/future-of-generative-ai-in-property-and-casualty-claims

Microsoft services and technology depended on whether clients achieve tangible benefits from KPMG's generative AI consulting services.

KPMG has come a long way since 1870 when London-based William Barclay Peat established an accounting firm. In 1911, Peat's firm merged with US accounting firm Marwick Mitchell to form Peat Marwick Mitchell, a provider of audit, tax, and advisory services. KPMG resulted from the 1987 merger of Peat Marwick International and Amsterdam-based Klynveld Main Goerdeler (founded in 1917). Not escaping controversy, in 2005, KPMG agreed to pay $456 million to settle claims related to its audit of Xerox Corporation.[34] In 2022, KPMG generated $35 billion in revenue and employed more than 265,000 partners and workers in 143 countries and territories.[35]

KPMG had keen insight into why companies were adopting generative AI and tailored its practice to meet those needs effectively. By August 2023, companies were adopting generative AI because they feared missing its benefits. As Sreekar Krishna, KPMG's national leader of artificial intelligence and head of data engineering, said, "People are seeing value across the board. KPMG started experimenting five months back with 15 to 20 people. A couple weeks later thousands of people were using it. Now there are 15,000 to 16,000 people at KPMG who are using it." Unlike other technologies such as blockchain, companies were in a hurry to adopt generative AI. "Across the board there is interest. Nobody wants to be late the way they were with mobile," Krishna said. "Why is generative AI taking off faster than blockchain technology did? Blockchain is an engineering achievement. However, the realization of blockchain was cryptocurrency and other applications. Blockchain has made improvements in cybersecurity—enabling the sharing of data across industries." Yet Krishna saw generative AI as different. "It enables the democratization of access

---

[34] "How Did KPMG Start?," *Rebellion Research*, March 28, 2023, www.rebellionresearch.com/how-did-kpmg-start

[35] "KPMG delivers strong global revenues, reporting 14% growth in FY22," *KPMG*, Ibid.

to data—you no longer need a data scientist to get access," he said. "Companies see generative AI as easy to test and worth putting the energy into it. When something becomes widely adopted; if you delay, your customers will push you into adopting it."[36]

Many KPMG clients were using generative AI. "Between 200 and 300 of our clients are investing in generative AI," Krishna said. "Companies investing the most are Microsoft, Google, Meta. They are investing billions in the technology." Financial services and manufacturing firms are also investing. "These are industries driven by manual processes," he added. "Generative AI can reduce the workload on everybody's hands. For example, 30 days is the average time it takes to close a mortgage. People don't want to wait that long. Manufacturers are starting to use generative AI because it can interpret images and videos."[37]

KPMG was using the technology internally. Krishna explained that KPMG had four use cases that "cut the time for complying with documentation and work paper requirements. For example, every three months a chief information security officer must certify the company is in compliance, that everyone has been trained, and so on," he said. "We have mini-chatbots enabling users to ask a few questions to automate a service." KPMG observed some companies using generative AI tools that gave them greater control. "Microsoft's OpenAI Studios—which has been operating for the last six or seven months—provides companies a semi-controlled environment," Krishna said. "They can use OpenAI without giving it proprietary information, they can choose what data they will not share with OpenAI, retain full rights to the data, and require OpenAI to delete their data."[38]

---

[36] Peter Cohan, "Why Generative AI Could Grow Even After A Set Of Bad Nvidia Earnings," *Forbes*, Ibid.

[37] Peter Cohan, "Why Generative AI Could Grow Even After A Set Of Bad Nvidia Earnings," *Forbes*, Ibid.

[38] Peter Cohan, "Why Generative AI Could Grow Even After A Set Of Bad Nvidia Earnings," *Forbes*, Ibid.

Companies hired generative AI consultants such as KPMG to solve a variety of problems. As KPMG National Managing Principal Atif Zaim told me in September 2023, "Large corporations focus on productivity improvement opportunities. Private equity firms seek to both improve their deal-making process and support their portfolio companies in adopting the technology. In general, companies hire generative AI consultants to help "re-shape their strategies, identify new revenue opportunities and stay ahead of competitive risks," Zaim said. "While companies began 2023 by learning about and starting to experiment with generative AI, after nine months fast-moving companies were planning large scale implementations to gain competitive edge and accelerate productivity improvements ahead of others," he explained. Companies ask KPMG for support with projects such as

- Ranking generative AI use cases based on how much they will improve client processes and operations

- Developing safe-for-employee internal generative AI tools

- Preparing internal proprietary data to train their customized generative AI models safely

- Building a long-term AI strategy to scale and capture potential value

- Establishing governance policies, frameworks, and tools for managing risk[39]

KPMG said clients wanted to work with consulting teams with the diverse skills needed to capture generative AI's opportunities and protect against its risks. To help clients, Zaim said KPMG offered skills in diverse domains such as the following:

---

[39] Peter Cohan, "Why Companies Buy Generative AI Consulting: The 3-Month Payback Factor," *Forbes*, Ibid.

- Generative AI engineering

- Key systems and data platforms

- Risk management and cybersecurity

- Experience with responsible and ethical generative AI use

- Knowledge of functional and industry "value-levers"

- Business strategy and change management[40]

KPMG saw itself as a strong contender in generative AI consulting projects due to its history in traditional AI and clients' trust in the firm's risk, regulatory, and cybersecurity practices. Zaim said KPMG – first in its field to deploy generative AI for its employees – was "now recognized as an early mover in the generative AI space." KPMG also wins due to its ability to engage with a client from strategy through implementation and its partnerships with technology partners that "are now the leading shapers of the Gen AI revolution," noted Zaim.[41]

KPMG was strengthening its capabilities by using generative AI inside the firm. Specifically, in July 2023, KPMG tax professionals used generative AI to help corporate tax departments prepare for new requirements to disclose their tax obligations by country. KPMG gave its clients access to its "virtual assistant," enabling them to gather tax data, and analyze and draft reports on what taxes were owed to different countries. Brad Brown, global chief technology officer for KPMG's tax business, said the

---

[40] Peter Cohan, "Why Companies Buy Generative AI Consulting: The 3-Month Payback Factor," *Forbes*, Ibid.

[41] Peter Cohan, "Why Companies Buy Generative AI Consulting: The 3-Month Payback Factor," *Forbes*, Ibid.

98

firm's partnership with Microsoft was "probably the most transformative moment for technology in a generation."[42]

As noted above, in July 2023, KPMG planned to invest $2 billion in Microsoft's AI with the expectation that KPMG would generate $12 billion in additional revenue by 2028. "The Microsoft Cloud and Azure OpenAI Service capabilities will empower our teams to help our clients, including more than 2,500 joint clients, keep pace with the rapidly evolving AI landscape and solve their greatest challenges while ensuring they are well positioned for success in the future world of work," said Cherie Gartner, KPMG's global lead partner for Microsoft. KPMG said the partnership would empower its global workforce of 265,000 professionals "to explore their creativity, expedite analysis and allocate more time to strategic guidance." Steve Chase, US consulting leader at KPMG, said the firm "is tapping into the opportunity to expand in new markets and sectors; and this collaboration is designed to see the latest AI and innovations used responsibly at scale, helping to unlock sustainable growth for clients, which ultimately can benefit society."[43]

In 2024, KPMG's generative AI strategy struck me as very strong within specific market segments. The firm's partnership with Microsoft would likely enable KPMG clients to have access to new generative AI technology, a move that would benefit Microsoft as well as KPMG. The consulting firm's internal application of generative AI helped identify high-payoff applications and heightened the credibility of the firm's advice to clients. Ultimately, KPMG was likely to enjoy significant revenues from helping clients apply generative AI to financial functions including risk

---

[42] Amanda Iacone,"KPMG Rolls Out generative AI to Tax Pros, Launches Audit Pilot," *Bloomberg Tax*, July 21, 2023, https://news.bloombergtax.com/financial-accounting/kpmg-rolls-out-generative-ai-to-tax-pros-launches-audit-pilot

[43] Victor Dey, "KPMG to invest $2 billion in AI in expanded partnership with Microsoft," *VentureBeat*, July 13, 2023, https://venturebeat.com/ai/kpmg-to-invest-2-billion-in-ai-in-expanded-partnership-with-microsoft/

management, cybersecurity, employee and firm safety, and regulatory compliance. Over the long run, KPMG had the potential to apply this generative AI know-how to a broad range of industries.

PwC

Since 1849, when Samuel Lowell Price set up an accounting practice in London, PwC has come a long way. William Cooper set up his own practice six years later. By 1874, Price had added new partners and formed Price Waterhouse. Skipping ahead, in 1998 Price Waterhouse and Coopers & Lybrand merged into PwC. The firm's services included "assurance, tax, human resources, transactions, performance improvement and crisis management." PwC delivered these services to enterprises as well as educational institutions, the federal government, nonprofits, and international relief agencies.[44] For the fiscal year ending June 2022, PwC employed nearly 328,000 people in 152 countries and generated $50 billion in revenue.[45]

In April 2023, PwC announced a $1 billion investment in generative AI, presented its reasons for the investment, and described how it would use the funds to build a generative AI consulting service for its clients. PwC made the large bet because it envisioned the technology would "revolutionize how we work, live and interact." The firm expected AI to contribute as much as $15.7 trillion to the global economy in 2030 while enabling PwC to build trust and deliver sustained outcomes to its clients and stakeholders. PwC aimed to answer client questions such as

---

[44] "History and milestones," *PwC*, accessed September 30, 2023, www.pwc.com/us/en/about-us/pwc-corporate-history.html

[45] "PwC announces record global revenues of US$50 billion," *PwC*, October 4, 2022, www.pwc.com/gx/en/news-room/press-releases/2022/pwc-global-annual-review-2022.html

- How can businesses use AI to reimagine business models to lead to new growth?

- How can companies protect their confidential or proprietary data used to train generative AI applications?

- How can enterprises confirm their generative AI models are fair, explainable, and transparent?

- How can organizations develop their peoples' skills as AI becomes more significant?[46]

To answer these questions PwC collaborated with Microsoft and Azure OpenAI Service to develop "hundreds of AI and generative AI use cases to drive efficiencies, cost and time savings and new insights." In 2023, PwC helped boost the efficiency of an auto insurer's claim estimation process by 29% through an AI application. PwC was building "governance, risks and controls, and algorithmic confidence" to protect the confidentiality and security of client data. PwC was "upskilling all 65,000 employees to give them "the skills they need for a world that is increasingly being shaped by AI."[47]

PwC observed keen client interest in generative AI. As PwC's vice chair, US chief products and technology officer Joe Atkinson told me in August 2023, "I have been on a roadshow meeting with clients and partners. I went to 15 markets and met with 100 clients. There was peer-to-peer sharing. Overall, there is a sense of excitement and some skepticism. While people see some hype, we think generative AI will have a massive impact." PwC

---

[46] Joe Atkinson and Mohamed Kande, "PwC US makes $1 billion investment to expand and scale capabilities in AI," *PwC*, April 26, 2023, www.pwc.com/us/en/tech-effect/ai-analytics/scaling-ai-capabilities-with-generative-investment.html

[47] Joe Atkinson and Mohamed Kande, "PwC US makes $1 billion investment to expand and scale capabilities in AI," *PwC*, Ibid.

was developing consulting services to help companies with generative AI. "Companies are seeking consulting help on everything from generative AI strategy to implementation," Atkinson added. "We set up an AI factory with use cases, AI specialists and data scientists. We are helping with specific value chain applications of generative AI such as customer care, financial reporting, and training employees."[48]

PwC aimed to reduce risk by testing applications on a small scale before rolling them out. Atkinson said the company is piloting generative AI across multiple teams and will eventually make it more widely available. "We want to deploy it in a responsible way in a safe environment with help from our employees," he added. "It will be used for customer care, help desk, analysis of data, reading and summarizing lots of data. We will train people firm-wide in responsible uses of generative AI." PwC observed companies taking different approaches to balancing generative AI's opportunities against its risks. "Some are shutting down employee access to third-party chatbots; some are allowing the use of chatbots with guardrails; others—like PwC are deploying generative AI chatbots trained with company-only data," Atkinson said. Finally, PwC saw an opportunity to limit the likelihood of hallucinations and protect proprietary data by following responsible AI principles, such as infrastructure, governance, training, and human review. Atkinson said companies can use specific data sets – he calls micro-models – so they "can secure proprietary data."[49]

In September 2023, PwC shared its thoughts on what kinds of generative AI consulting help clients need most, how clients evaluated potential service providers, how PwC was winning new clients, and what new services clients would demand in the future. Here are PwC's insights:

---

[48] Peter Cohan, "Why Generative AI Could Grow Even After A Set Of Bad Nvidia Earnings," *Forbes*, Ibid.
[49] Peter Cohan, "Why Generative AI Could Grow Even After A Set Of Bad Nvidia Earnings," *Forbes*, Ibid.

- **Clients were eager for help prioritizing generative AI uses.** Clients asked for help in "GenAI strategy and assessment, support building and deploying secure GenAI use cases and workflows, governance and responsible AI, and ongoing operations and support. The number one question we are still receiving from clients is how to prioritize where to transform and what are the best early steps to set up for their future," according to Bret Greenstein, Principal and Generative AI Leader at PwC.[50]

- **Clients wanted consultants with deep business and technical know-how who produced results.** Clients sought insights into how their service provider's own business performance improved by applying generative AI, lessons clients wanted to apply to their own operations, Greenstein explained.[51]

- **Clients chose PwC because it achieved results from its internal use of generative AI and has trust in the technology.** "GenAI success depends on trust in the technology, data and outputs. We are a leader in developing and delivering a proven approach to building trust in AI through PwC's Responsible AI Framework which we have been using since 2019," Greenstein said.[52]

---

[50] Email from Bret Greenstein, Principal and Generative AI Leader at PwC, to Peter Cohan, September 26, 2023.

[51] Email from Bret Greenstein, Principal and Generative AI Leader at PwC, to Peter Cohan, September 26, 2023.

[52] Email from Bret Greenstein, Principal and Generative AI Leader at PwC, to Peter Cohan, September 26, 2023.

- **Clients would choose future consultants based on how well they prioritize generative AI applications.** In 2023, Greenstein expected clients to shift their attention from help with the basics of building generative AI applications to gaining insight into which applications paid off as measured by "time saved, money saved, and insights extracted. Where companies are looking to go, we have already or are going ourselves, equipping us to continue leading in the space to best help transform our client's business."[53]

In 2024, PwC's generative AI services struck me as having many of the same advantages for clients as those KPMG provided. Both firms used the technology internally and understood many specific applications of the technology in a range of business functions. Both shared concerns about protecting proprietary client data and minimizing client risk in deploying generative AI. One difference was the extent of their Microsoft partnerships – KPMG's struck me as more significant than PwC's.

Coding Outsourcers

Coding outsources such as Cognizant saw generative AI as a means to boost software development productivity. By using the technology internally, Cognizant sought to reduce its costs in the wake of a significant headcount reduction in 2023. Its new CEO listened to customers and concluded they would seek cost-reduction benefits. Yet compared to the strategists, Cognizant appeared to be late to developing consulting processes for helping client senior executives to conceptualize new business models using generative AI.

---

[53] Email from Bret Greenstein, Principal and Generative AI Leader at PwC, to Peter Cohan, September 26, 2023.

Cognizant

Cognizant started life in 1994 as a subsidiary of Dun & Bradstreet. With 50 employees, Dun & Bradstreet Satyam Software (DBSS) implemented large-scale information technology projects for its parent company. After branching out to serve other companies and numerous restructurings, DBSS became Cognizant Technology Solutions, a publicly traded company based in Teaneck, New Jersey.[54] By October 2023, Cognizant had $19.4 billion in revenue for the year-ending June 2023, 345,600 employees, following a 5,900-employee headcount reduction, and a $34.5 billion stock market capitalization.[55]

In 2023, Cognizant experimented internally with generative AI and collaborated with clients to identify high-payoff applications of the technology. As Cognizant CEO Ravi Kumar said, "We are using AI to enhance our own creativity and productivity. We are operating pilots that use generative AI to accelerate consulting, design, engineering and operations with the long-term goal of doubling the productivity of our associates." Kumar said generative AI would increase employee productivity and create more demand for software and data engineering expertise. Cognizant was operating generative AI pilots "to accelerate consulting, design, engineering and operations with the long-term goal of doubling the productivity of our associates." Kumar added specific cost-reduction metrics he expected to flow from the use of generative AI, including

---

[54] "Dun & Bradstreet Spinoff Will Split in Two," *New York Times*, January 16, 1998, www.nytimes.com/1998/01/16/business/dun-bradstreet-spinoff-will-split-in-two.html

[55] "Cognizant reports second quarter 2023 results," *PR Newswire*, August 2, 2023, www.prnewswire.com/news-releases/cognizant-reports-second-quarter-2023-results-301892007.html#:~:text=Full%2Dyear%202023%20revenue%20is,of%2014.2%25%20to%2014.7%25

- **Lower operational costs.** The technology would reduce operational costs by 25% to 45%.

- **Faster delivery.** It would reduce mean time to delivery and mean time to detect by 30% to 50%.

- **Lower headcount.** Finally, it would lower full-time-equivalent employees by 15% to 30% "compared with the use of traditional approaches."[56]

Cognizant was beginning to formulate how it would deliver generative AI consulting services. Cognizant had to monitor shifts in clients' needs, Kumar said. Clients liked Cognizant's entrepreneurial approach to "developing solutions to their challenges, as well as the company's willingness to learn, listen and adapt," he explained. Specifically, after meeting with executives from about 100 clients, he said, "I came away from these meetings with many new opportunities to pursue related to cost takeout when the consolidation, post-merger integration and the new wave of outsourcing and fintechs."[57]

In July 2023, Cognizant rolled out Neuro AI, "an enterprise-wide platform" to help its clients deploy generative AI. The company described Neuro AI as a comprehensive approach to accelerating client adoption of generative AI technology that would produce "business value in a flexible, secure, scalable and responsible way." Cognizant anticipated working with clients to

---

[56] Joseph Kovar, "Cognizant CEO: 'Generative AI Will Revolutionize The Technology Services Industry,'" *CRN*, May 4, 2023, www.crn.com/news/managed-services/cognizant-ceo-generative-ai-will-revolutionize-the-technology-services-industry-

[57] Joseph Kovar, "Cognizant CEO: 'Generative AI Will Revolutionize The Technology Services Industry,'" *CRN*, Ibid.

- Identify and implement company-specific use cases

- Help AI and software engineering teams to build "flexible, reusable, safe, and secure solutions"

- Implement industry-specific generative AI applications such as "healthcare analytics and crop science optimization."

Cognizant executives expressed excitement about the opportunity to help clients. "It is fast becoming clear that businesses must embrace AI without delay to remain competitive," said Prasad Sankaran, EVP of Cognizant's Software and Platform Engineering. "This is an exciting moment, as Cognizant's Neuro AI platform goes beyond proof of concept, aiming to accelerate the adoption of enterprise scale AI applications, increase ROI potential, minimize risks and get to better business solutions, faster." Moreover, Cognizant believed it had the skills needed to serve clients. Anna Elango, EVP of Cognizant's Core Technologies and Insights, added, "By partnering human expertise, including Cognizant's deep industry insights, with the power of generative AI, we aim to help our clients catalyze informed decisions and tackle complex business challenges to drive cost efficiencies, resilience and business revenue."[58]

Generative AI Consulting Critical Activities

In 2023, there was no conclusive evidence of which generative AI consultants were gaining market share and which were not. Based on the case studies, a consulting firm's ability to perform five critical activities

---

[58] "Cognizant rolls out platform to help companies with generative AI use," *Consultancy UK*, July 31, 2023, www.consultancy.uk/news/34972/cognizant-rolls-out-platform-to-help-companies-with-generative-ai-use

was likely to determine its ability to gain market share in generative AI consulting:

- **Ability to sell consulting services to teams of senior executives and technology executives.** Since generative AI had the potential to enable companies to boost productivity, lower costs, and increase revenues, the most successful consulting firms would need to excel at framing the consultant's ability to persuade all members of a client's executive team of the consultant's superior skills, from helping clients to brainstorm new business models to building applications that delivered results.

- **Ability to attract and motivate consultants with broad skills.** To help clients turn new ideas – enabled by generative AI – into results such as higher productivity and faster growth, consultants needed to hire and motivate diverse teams. Winning consultants would field teams that included business strategists, data management experts, AI application developers, and experts in information security and compliance.

- **Ability to work with clients to brainstorm and rank generative AI applications.** Since clients needed to focus on the highest potential generative AI applications, winning consultants would need to provide clients with effective methodologies for analyzing and ranking opportunities based on criteria such as the application's potential to increase customer value, to boost revenues and/or reduce cost, and to limit risk of losing control of proprietary data.

- **Ability to implement high-payoff, risk-controlled generative AI applications.** Given the uncertainty about which generative AI applications would deliver results, winning consultants needed the ability to build prototypes of the high-priority applications quickly, to get user feedback on the prototypes, and to change the applications quickly and effectively in response to the feedback.

- **Ability to help clients stay ahead of rapidly evolving generative AI technology.** Finally, due to the rapid rate of change in generative AI technology and the way enterprises were using the technology in their business, winning consultants needed to anticipate these changes to keep their clients ahead of their peers. To help clients remain in the vanguard of generative AI, winning consultants needed to listen to early-adopter customers and liaise with AI industry thought leaders.

Conclusion

Within months of the November 2022 launch of ChatGPT, several established consulting firms were publicly touting enormous investment in generative AI. In 2023, those consulting firms were allocating those funds to cloud computing resources, generative AI applications tailored to the needs of their consultants, and new consulting processes for helping companies deploy generative AI. Would clients flock to these services, and if so, would they reap the competitive and economic benefits anticipated from deploying high-payoff generative AI applications? Ultimately, the success of generative AI consulting firms would depend on whether their services helped clients increase their productivity, boost operational effectiveness, and heighten revenue growth.

CHAPTER 5

Generative AI Software

In the first four chapters, we explored generative AI from the perspective of people and organizations who aim to benefit from the technology. In the next three chapters, we look at the supply side, examining how technology companies compete for their share of the generative AI ecosystem and which suppliers could potentially be profitable investments. This chapter answers questions such as:

- What are the most significant groups of generative AI software providers?

- What forces are driving the profit potential of the generative AI software industry?

- Which software companies are most successfully monetizing generative AI?

- How should investors evaluate the potential returns of investing in generative AI software companies?

- What capabilities set apart the generative AI software leaders from their peers?

Generative AI Software Industry Players

A combination of well-established companies and startups supplied software to prepare data and train and operate generative AI applications. In this chapter, we will explore the following kinds of software essential to satisfying consumer and business demand for generative AI, including the following:

- **Proprietary LLMs.** In 2023, Microsoft and Google were among publicly traded companies supplying generative AI chatbots. Startups such as OpenAI, Cohere, and Anthropic supplied proprietary LLM software.

- **Open source LLMs.** Companies seeking to build their own LLMs could avail themselves of open source LLMs such as Hugging Face and Meta Platform's Llama 2.

- **Application-specific generative AI tools.** Adobe offered Firefly, a generative AI image creation tool, and publicly traded ServiceNow supplied a generative AI-powered service to enhance the productivity of cross-functional business processes. Meanwhile, startups such as Hyro, provided a generative AI service to handle call center inquiries for health care service providers and Writer's generative AI-powered service delivered high quality content generation at scale.

In this chapter, we will see the wide variation in the investment potential of these generative AI software companies. Table 5-1 summarizes the analysis of the investment potential of these companies.

Table 5-1. *Investment Potential for Selected Generative AI Software Providers*

Company	Gen AI Upside Potential	Investment Tailwinds	Investment Headwinds
Microsoft	High	Many sources of generative AI revenue; high switching costs; high market share; access to excellent generative AI technology; a clear head start	High costs to operate generative AI service platform
Google	Moderate	Positioned to capitalize on the blurring of the lines between advertising, commerce, and media consumption	Risk of losing market share to ChatGPT-powered search engines
OpenAI	High	Acceleration in revenue and private market valuation in 2023	Uncertainty about IPO and whether company could sustain rapid growth as a public company
Cohere	Moderate	Significant market opportunity and compelling customer value proposition	Lower valuation than larger, faster-growing competitors
Anthropic	High	Positioned as safest generative AI platform, rapid revenue growth, and spiking valuation	Risk of falling short of the company's high safety standards and emergence of safer rivals

(*continued*)

Table 5-1. (*continued*)

Company	Gen AI Upside Potential	Investment Tailwinds	Investment Headwinds
Hugging Face	Low/ moderate	Well-known corporate investors sustaining valuation	Relatively low revenues and growth; many risks of enterprise adoption
Meta Llama	Moderate	Meta Platforms' significant capital resources	Open source business model raises questions of whether revenue will exceed costs
Adobe	Moderate/ high	Higher prices; expansion of total addressable market; leading market share in many customer industries; new use cases for existing products; dramatic increase in the number of users; high analyst enthusiasm for Adobe's generative AI services; modest expectations for Adobe's growth	High cost of operating generative AI services
ServiceNow	Moderate/ high	Access to a much larger market opportunity; customer adoption of its generative AI-powered services.	Challenge of exceeding high investor expectations

(*continued*)

Table 5-1. (*continued*)

Company	Gen AI Upside Potential	Investment Tailwinds	Investment Headwinds
Hyro	Moderate	Solving the right problem, strong management team, compelling value proposition	Competing indirectly with Microsoft and limited market potential
Writer	Moderate/ high	Solving the right problem, strong management team, compelling value proposition compared to rivals	Competing with OpenAI

Generative AI Software Industry Attractiveness

In 2023, the most significant generative AI software companies were among the largest publicly traded technology companies. This stood in sharp contrast to the leaders in the dot-com era – startups that grew quickly to win market share from incumbents. In May 2023, analysts from investment firm NEA wrote, "Unlike with the prior shifts, incumbents do not need to re-architect their entire products to adopt this new platform shift. In addition, this shift favors companies with bigger, proprietary data sets which can give an edge to more established companies." Unlike during the dot-com era, with LLMs Google and Microsoft had "huge head starts" in developing the technology and winning over consumers. While LLM startups such as OpenAI and Anthropic performed R&D, they could only gain access to the capital required to train their models through "Faustian 'partnerships' with tech giants."[1]

These companies were competing for a share of a very large opportunity. In 2023, there were numerous estimates of the size and growth rate of the generative AI software industry. In March 2023, Goldman Sachs estimated generative AI would add $150 billion – or 22% – to the $685 billion global enterprise software total addressable market because of the technology's ability to "streamline business workflows, automate routine tasks and give rise to a new generation of business applications."[2] S&P Global Market Intelligence forecast a 58% compound annual growth in revenues – from $3.7 billion in 2023 to $36 billion by 2028 – generated by 263 generative AI providers of text, images, audio, video, code, and structured data generators.[3]

Overall, the profit potential of the US software industry was high, thanks to the strong pricing power and customer loyalty of the largest companies such as Microsoft and low supplier power and threat of substitute products. Nevertheless, forces such as high rivalry, moderate entry barriers, and moderate customer bargaining power put downward pressure on industry profitability. The five forces underlying the US software industry's moderate to high profit potential included the following:

---

[1] Yiren Lu, "A Week With the Wild Children of the A.I. Boom," *New York Times*, May 31, 2023, www.nytimes.com/2023/05/31/magazine/ai-start-up-accelerator-san-francisco.html

[2] Kash Rangan, et al., "Generative AI - Part I: Laying Out the Investment," *Goldman Sachs Equity Research*, March 26, 2023.

[3] "Generative AI Software Market Forecast to Expand Near 10 Times by 2028 to $36 Billion, S&P Global Market Intelligence Says," *PR Newswire*, June 8, 2023, www.prnewswire.com/news-releases/generative-ai-software-market-forecast-to-expand-near-10-times-by-2028-to-36-billion-sp-global-market-intelligence-says-301844631.html

- **Threat of entry: Moderate.** Entry barriers – including copyrights, product differentiation, labor intensity, and startup costs – were low for a new entrant but increased significantly when a company sought to scale enough to compete with industry leaders.

- **Rivalry among existing competitors: Moderate.** While low barriers enabled startups to enter the software industry, industry giants such as Microsoft can cross-sell to customers from a broad product portfolio, can use their patents to prevent new entrants from copying their revenue-generating features, and can use customer familiarity with their software to raise switching costs.

- **Bargaining power of buyers: Low to moderate.** Large business software providers, including Microsoft, Salesforce, Adobe, and IBM, controlled significant market share, had useful product features and very good scalability, and tightly integrated the elements of their product suite, all of which raised switching costs and limited buyer power.

- **Bargaining power of suppliers: Low.** Computer equipment and other suppliers to software developers faced significant rivalry and represented a small proportion of software industry costs.

- **Threat of substitutes: Low.** While "AI-leveraged software development tools and easy-to-use programming interfaces" gave existing client employees easy access to the tools for creating their own software and many enterprises hired their own software developers, existing software suppliers locked in most customers by imposing high switching costs.[4]

Generative AI Software Industry Participants

Generative AI software enables developers to build and operate AI-powered chatbots. As noted above, such software takes many forms, including privately owned and publicly traded providers of software for training and operating LLMs, open source software (meaning it is available to anyone for free) to build and operate chatbots, and application-specific software for building AI-powered tools for more specific uses. Below we explore companies in each of these categories, aiming to assess their ability to tap profitably the growth of generative AI and to provide investors with high returns.

Publicly Traded Proprietary LLM Providers

Microsoft and Google are among the leading publicly traded providers of company-specific generative AI software. Below, we examine each company's history in generative AI, describe the firm's related products or services, and assess the company's investment potential.

---

[4] Terry Faber, "Software Publishing in the US," *IBISWorld*, Ibid.

Microsoft

Microsoft's history with generative AI has featured amazing successes and reputation-endangering perils. In 2016, Microsoft founder and former CEO Bill Gates first met with OpenAI and was impressed with what the company was doing.[5] That same year, Microsoft unveiled Tay, a chatbot that promptly began spewing anti-Semitic and anti-feminist responses to user prompts. OpenAI's 2020 predecessor to ChatGPT "exhibited similar levels of racism and misogyny."[6] In mid-2022, Gates challenged OpenAI to train an AI to pass an Advanced Placcmcnt biology exam. That September, OpenAI amazed Gates when its GPT scored the equivalent of an A or A+ on the AP Bio exam. In 2016, Microsoft's Tay chatbot produced disastrous results.[7] This setback did not deter the software Goliath. In June 2022, Microsoft released GitHub's Copilot, enabling users to turn simple instructions into computer code. Within a month of the launch, GitHub's Copilot – which wrote "up to 35% or 40% of a file's code" – attracted 400,000 users.[8] Microsoft also announced plans to invest $10 billion in OpenAI and to integrate generative AI into its Office software and search engine, Bing.[9]

In 2023, Microsoft's dominance of the software industry put the company in a strong position to add an estimated $35 billion to its revenue from generative AI-powered services. In addition, in October 2023, a

---

[5] Bill Gates, "The Age of AI has begun," *GatesNotes*, March 21, 2023, www.gatesnotes.com/The-Age-of-AI-Has-Begun

[6] Andrew Chow and Billy Perrigo, "The AI Arms Race Is Changing Everything," *Time*, February 16, 2023, https://time.com/6255952/ai-impact-chatgpt-microsoft-google/

[7] Bill Gates, "The Age of AI has begun," *GatesNotes*, March 21, 2023, Ibid.

[8] Jeffrey Dastin, "Microsoft attracting users to its code-writing, generative AI software," *Reuters*, January 24, 2023, www.reuters.com/technology/microsoft-attracting-users-its-code-writing-generative-ai-software-2023-01-25/

[9] Andrew Chow and Billy Perrigo, "The AI Arms Race Is Changing Everything," *Time*, Ibid.

Wall Street analyst estimated Microsoft's 49% stake in OpenAI, the LLM provider on which ChatGPT operates, could be worth $100 billion. Below are more details of each observation:

- **Microsoft dominates a highly profitable industry with an average net profit margin of 31%.** Microsoft is the largest software company in a huge, profitable industry. Specifically, in 2023, the software industry's 48,422 companies generated $482 billion in revenue – having grown at a 5.9% average rate since 2018 – and earned a net profit margin of 31%. Overall, the profit potential of the US software industry was high, thanks to the strong pricing power and customer loyalty to the largest companies such as Microsoft, which had 19.2% market share, nearly four times the share of No. 2, IBM.[10]

- **Microsoft's software industry dominance could enable its ChatGPT-powered Copilot service to boost the company's revenue by $35 billion**. In contrast to the dot-com era when startups like Amazon ended up becoming dominant players, the most significant corporations in generative AI were among the largest publicly traded technology companies. As analysts from investment firm NEA wrote, "Unlike with the prior shifts, incumbents do not need to re-architect their entire products to adopt this new platform shift. In addition, this shift favors companies with bigger, proprietary data sets which can give an edge

---

[10] Peter Cohan, "Microsoft Stock Has Major Upside, Could Hit $410 On OpenAI Investment Payoff," *Forbes*, October 10, 2023, www.forbes.com/sites/petercohan/2023/10/10/24-upside-microsoft-stock-could-hit-410-on-openai-investment-payoff/

to more established companies." Microsoft planned
to offer Copilot to Word, PowerPoint, and Excel users.
Powered by ChatGPT, Copilot was intended to enable
Word users to "highlight a paragraph and the AI can
offer different options for a rewritten version of it."
PowerPoint users would be able to use Copilot to create
presentations based on text from a document and add
in images. Excel users could deploy Copilot to analyze
sales data, determine trends, and create charts. Copilot
could add $35 billion to Microsoft's revenue assuming
10% of the company's 482 million customers would pay
$60 a month for the service.[11]

- **Microsoft's 49% stake in OpenAI could be worth $100
billion.** In October 2023, Oppenheimer & Co. analyst
Timothy Horan estimated Microsoft's 49% stake in
OpenAI could be worth $100 billion. Horan applied
OpenAI rival Anthropic's valuation of 250 times its
$100 million in revenue for a private fundraising round
expected to produce $2 billion and value the AI startup
at $25 billion. With OpenAI generating an estimated $1
billion in revenue, Horan applied Anthropic's 250 times
revenue to value OpenAI at $250 billion, which he
discounted slightly to estimate Microsoft's 49% would
be worth $100 billion.[12]

---

[11] Peter Cohan, "Microsoft Stock Has Major Upside, Could Hit $410 On OpenAI
Investment Payoff," *Forbes*, Ibid.
[12] Peter Cohan, "Microsoft Stock Has Major Upside, Could Hit $410 On OpenAI
Investment Payoff," *Forbes*, Ibid.

Investors profit from buying shares in companies that exceed analysts' expectations every quarter. For example, Microsoft set modest growth guidance for its first quarter of the 2024 fiscal year ending September 2023. However, in October 2023, Wedbush analyst Daniel Ives expressed optimism that the software giant would do better than expected when its financials were to be reported in November 2023. Ives expected Microsoft to exceed guidance. "We believe while management has talked about a 'gradual ramp' for AI monetization in FY24," Ives said. We believe so far the adoption curve is happening quicker than expected based on our recent checks. Our latest Azure checks also show a clear uptick in activity sequentially (AI driven) which gives us further confidence in Microsoft exceeding its 25% to 26% Azure growth guidance in FY1Q," he added.[13]

In 2023, the high computing cost required to operate its generative AI services had the potential to limit the investment potential of Microsoft's stock. However, since investors put more of a premium on faster-than-expected growth, Microsoft may have been in a position to accept some losses to bring in large numbers of customers. For example, Microsoft used AI from OpenAI to launch GitHub Copilot, a service that helps programmers create, fix, and translate code. More than 1.5 million people used GitHub Copilot because it reduced the time and effort needed to write code. The service was unprofitable because it was so expensive to run. One of the reasons the services were costly was that some customers used the most potent AI models available, which required "more power and put more strain on computer processors to operate than standard software or cloud services." Microsoft explored using "less powerful and cheaper AI tools for its Bing search engine, including some built with Meta Platforms' open-source AI software."[14] In 2023, Microsoft stock was most

---

[13] Peter Cohan, "Microsoft Stock Has Major Upside, Could Hit $410 On OpenAI Investment Payoff," *Forbes*, Ibid.

[14] Tom Dotan and Deepa Seetharaman, "Big Tech Struggles to Turn AI Hype Into Profits," *Wall Street Journal*, October 9, 2023, www.wsj.com/tech/ai/ais-costly-buildup-could-make-early-products-a-hard-sell-bdd29b9f

likely to rise, if the company could bring in new generative AI users, lower its costs through more efficient technologies, and keep new users buying over time.

In March 2023, Goldman Sachs analysts viewed Microsoft as an early leader in generative AI. The bank expressed enthusiasm for the software giant's ability to produce a "steady flow of impressive product releases across its portfolio." These products included "Microsoft 365 Copilot, Business Chat, Dynamics 365 Copilot, GitHub Copilot, Teams Premium, Azure OpenAI Services, and Viva Sales," which Goldman anticipated would enable Microsoft to raise its average selling prices and grow steadily. The bank highlighted how quickly ChatGPT gained 100 million daily users and the company's "prioritization of R&D expenses over the last five years and continued investment in OpenAI" as evidence Microsoft has "accumulated to best position itself as a leader in this next chapter of innovation."[15]

By October 2023, Microsoft took the software industry lead by being the first participant to monetize its generative AI investments. Specifically, in the third quarter of 2023, OpenAI – in which Microsoft invested – experienced a 64% increase in its customer count. In addition, Microsoft's Azure cloud service generated 3% of its revenue from generative AI. The software giant reported its Azure OpenAI Service customer count grew 65% to 18,000 since July 2023 because Azure added graphics-processing units that boosted the service's computing capacity. Chief Financial Officer Amy Hood said about three percentage points of the Azure unit's growth was attributable to AI – more than the 2% she forecast in July 2023. Microsoft's capital expenditures increased 70% from a year earlier to a record $11.2 billion. This increase reflected the company's investment in AI. While still a small business for Microsoft, analysts and investors expect it to contribute more significantly to the company's profitability. Nevertheless, Microsoft's 365 Copilot AI add-on for existing productivity software subscriptions had

---

[15] Kash Rangan, et al., "Generative AI - Part I: Laying Out the Investment," *Goldman Sachs Equity Research*, Ibid.

not added noticeable revenue. Hood said revenue from Copilot – for which Microsoft would charge $30 per person per month – would "grow gradually over time."[16]

By October 2023, chief information officers were eagerly assessing whether the premium price Microsoft intended to charge for Copilot would generate a significant return on investment. In general, Jared Spataro, corporate vice president of Modern Work and Business Applications at Microsoft, said Copilot could perform many of a business assistant's tasks such as "summarizing video calls, writing draft responses to emails and transforming Word documents into PowerPoint presentations." CIOs felt compelled to assess whether these functions were worth paying Copilot's price, which added 60% to the standard $30 per month price for the Microsoft 365 Office suite. Northwestern Mutual's CIO Jeff Sippel said the $9,000 investment for 300 licenses was tiny compared to the millions of dollars needed to build the same function internally. While Sippel guessed Copilot would change how people work, it would be difficult to quantify the tool's financial benefits. Brian Klochkoff, executive vice president of innovation and emerging technologies at marketing and advertising agency network Dentsu, said the company bought 300 licenses and found that Copilot saved its users about five to ten hours per month. Klochkoff estimated Copilot's return on investment might not be sufficient if employees spend "more time in meetings and less time producing spreadsheets and presentations."[17] One thing seemed clear: CIOs' slow motion assessment of its return on investment seemed likely to cap a rapid acceleration in Copilot's revenue.

---

[16] Peter Cohan, "Microsoft Leads Alphabet In The Race To Monetize generative AI," *Forbes*, October 25, 2023, www.forbes.com/sites/petercohan/2023/10/25/microsoft-leads-alphabet-in-the-race-to-monetize-generative-ai/

[17] Isabelle Bousquette, "CIOs Assess Whether Microsoft's AI Copilot Justifies Premium Price," *Wall Street Journal*, October 31, 2023, www.wsj.com/articles/microsofts-hotly-anticipated-generative-ai-work-assistant-set-to-debut-aa263a18

By November 2023, the investment potential of Microsoft's stock hinged in part on the company's ability to win market share in the generative AI ecosystem. Microsoft appeared to enjoy four critical advantages:

- **Many sources of generative AI revenue.** Generative AI increased demand for Microsoft's Azure cloud services and its Copilot service had the potential to increase the prices Microsoft charged for the Microsoft Office 365 suite.

- **High switching costs with a large customer base.** Microsoft's high share of the market raised the costs for customers seeking to switch to another supplier. This made it easier for Microsoft to introduce generative AI services to its existing customers.

- **Access to excellent generative AI technology through partnerships.** Microsoft's significant stake in OpenAI gave the software giant access to ChatGPT, the most popular generative AI chatbot, and Microsoft's partnerships with consulting firms provided access to corporate decision makers.

- **A clear head start versus rivals in monetizing generative AI.** Microsoft benefited from the perception among investors that it was ahead of rivals in the race to monetize generative AI.

There were two significant risks to Microsoft's stock related to revenue from generative AI: too little demand and too much. How so? First, companies might conclude the benefits of its Copilot service did not justify the added cost. Second, given the high price of GPU chips needed to train and operate generative AI models, if demand for Copilot and other AI services was too high, Microsoft might be unable to add sufficient computing resources to satisfy the growth in demand.

Google

While Google scientists published the technical breakthrough that led to generative AI, the company did not commercialize the innovation as effectively as rivals did. In 2017, Google scientists published work on transformers, a neural network architecture that led to a deeper understanding of natural language. In 2021, Google Research released LaMDA, a conversational LLM that paved the way for the March 2023 launch of Bard, its generative AI-powered Chatbot.[18] The company, renamed Alphabet in October 2015, had grown to a $282 billion (2022 revenue) giant with $61 billion in net income, 181,798 employees, and a stock price that had increased at a 21.5% average annual rate from a split-adjusted $3.23 a share at its IPO to $137 – yielding a stock market capitalization of $1.7 trillion on October 20, 2023.[19]

Prior to its March 2023 launch, a Bard error slammed Alphabet stock. However, by July 2023 the search giant had improved the chatbot considerably. In February 2023, Bard erroneously said the James Webb telescope took the first pictures of exoplanets in response to the prompt: "What new discoveries from the James Webb Space Telescope can I tell my 9 year old about?" Bard's error? NASA confirmed the European Southern Observatory's very large telescope "took the first pictures of those special celestial bodies in 2004." That error prompted a 9% decline in Alphabet's stock price, wiping out $100 billion worth of market capitalization. The error occurred hours after Google executives had touted Bard in a Paris

---

[18] Rachel Hespell, "Our 10 biggest AI moments so far," *The Keyword*, September 26, 2023, `https://blog.google/technology/ai/google-ai-ml-timeline/`
[19] "Alphabet Inc.", *Yahoo! Finance*, accessed October 21, 2023, `https://finance.yahoo.com/quote/GOOG?p=GOOG`

marketing event. Days prior to Bard's blunder, Alphabet CEO Sundar Pichai said Bard would be available exclusively to "trusted testers" before releasing the engine publicly in the coming weeks.[20]

By September 2023, Alphabet was making improvements to Bard so it could catch up with ChatGPT. In July 2023, Alphabet was making improvements to Bard – adding 43 new languages, improving privacy to satisfy European Union regulators, and making the chatbot available to hundreds of millions more users in Europe and Brazil – to help increase Bard's market share. After expanding into more than 180 countries in May 2023 – allowing Bard to converse in Korean and Japanese – its website received about 140 million visits a month, "less than a 10th of the number of visits of ChatGPT's website." Google's efforts to minimize offensive responses delayed Bard's rollout to new countries.[21] In September 2023, Google announced Bard updates giving the chatbot access to YouTube, Google Drive, Google Flights, and others. These links aimed to help users to "plan an upcoming trip with real flight options or to summarize meeting notes made in a recent Google Drive document." Sissie Hsiao, general manager for Google Assistant and Bard, said the updates to Bard would enable people to save time, doing "in 20 seconds, in minutes, something that would have taken maybe an hour or more." Bard also launched a "double check" button to enable users to compare parts of the chatbot's response to a prompt to what a Google search would return.[22]

---

[20] Emily Olson, "Google shares drop $100 billion after its new AI chatbot makes a mistake," *NPR*, February 9, 2023, www.npr.org/2023/02/09/1155650909/google-chatbot--error-bard-shares

[21] Sam Schechner, "Google's Bard AI Chatbot Adds More Languages to Take On ChatGPT," *Wall Street Journal*, July 13, 2023, www.wsj.com/articles/googles-bard-ai-chatbot-adds-more-languages-to-take-on-chatgpt-a2acfc5b

[22] Clare Duffy, "Google rolls out a major expansion of its Bard AI chatbot," *CNN*, September 19, 2023, www.cnn.com/2023/09/19/tech/google-bard-updates/index.html

In July 2023, Alphabet was not requiring users to pay directly for its generative AI-powered services. Yet its second quarter financial report suggested the company's generative AI capabilities had contributed to its 7% revenue growth by driving more demand for the company's cloud computing services. "Despite macroeconomic uncertainty affecting customers' cloud expenditure," Google Cloud reported a 28% increase in revenue. Alphabet CEO Sundar Pichai told investors Alphabet's new AI-based services and offerings "were the biggest contributors to Google Cloud's growth momentum." The company's generative AI services – including its more than 70 foundational models – increased their customer count 15-fold during the June 2023-ending quarter, according to Pichai. Moreover, he said, "more than 70% of generative AI unicorns are Google Cloud customers, including Cohere, Jasper, and Typeface." Finally, Google Workspace customers – including "seats" and "average revenue per seat" – increased in response to new generative AI capabilities.[23]

By October 2023, Google lagged in the race to monetize generative AI. In response to investor questions about monetizing generative AI, Pichai said, "it's still early days." He continued, "We'll do everything that is needed to make sure we have the leading AI models and infrastructure in the world, bar none, and will continue driving efficiencies from there." In addition to releasing Bard, Google was experimenting with Search generative Experience, "which lets users see what a generative AI experience would look like when searching for products." Lloyd Walmsley of Deutsche Bank asked Pichai, "As we just think about the rollout of SGE across a user base. Like, how far along is that? And how do you balance the product rollout and consumer uptake versus monetization in that transition?" Pichai's response was vague. "On the first part of our SG, we are still very early days in terms of how much we have rolled it out. But we

---

[23] "Alphabet bets on generative AI as cloud boosts Q2 revenue," *CIO*, July 26, 2023, www.cio.com/article/647314/alphabet-bets-on-generative-ai-as-cloud-boosts-q2-revenue.html

have definitely gotten it out to enough people and both geographically across user segments and enough to know that the product is working well," he told Walmsley.[24]

Along with the vague responses, Google indicated AI was boosting the value to advertisers of two services. For YouTube advertisers, AI helped businesses find "their ideal audience for the lowest possible price," according to Alphabet's Chief Business Officer Philipp Schindler. "Early tests are delivering 54% more reach at 42% lower cost," helping "brands like Samsung and Toyota," Schindler added. Meanwhile, Google's Performance Max – the service enables advertisers to access all of their Google Ads inventory from a single campaign – enabled users to "achieve like an average over 18% more conversions at a similar cost per action," according to Pichai, who added that 80% of Alphabet advertisers already used at least one AI-powered search feature.[25] Since AI was helping the search giant's customers to boost their return on advertising, there was a good possibility Google would begin to monetize its generative AI investments, thus giving investors a pleasant surprise.

In 2023, Goldman Sachs offered an optimistic five-year investment outlook for Alphabet stock. Goldman wrote, "Within our Internet coverage universe, we see Alphabet as the leading collection of AI/machine learning-driven businesses that is uniquely positioned to capitalize on the blurring of the lines between advertising, commerce and media consumption in the years ahead and rising utility across a number of computing platforms including consumer desktop, consumer mobile & enterprise cloud computing." The investment bank noted that Performance Max would accelerate revenue growth by 2028 in its core advertising business, as would Google's Cloud. Goldman anticipated a rise in the company's operating

---

[24] Peter Cohan, "Microsoft Leads Alphabet In The Race To Monetize Generative AI," *Forbes*, Ibid.

[25] Peter Cohan, "Microsoft Leads Alphabet In The Race To Monetize Generative AI," *Forbes*, Ibid.

margin beyond 2024 and saw Alphabet's long-term investments in growth and its share buybacks as strengthening the company's longer-term investment potential.[26]

Despite these optimistic perspectives on Alphabet, many questions remained unresolved regarding how generative AI would alter the trajectory of the search giant's stock. Would ChatGPT's greater popularity lead more search traffic and advertising revenue to Microsoft's Bing? Would Alphabet's fear of cannibalizing its core search advertising business limit its willingness to incorporate generative AI into its business? Might other rivals – such as LLM startups or open source LLM model purveyors – take market share away from Google as the search giant did from Alta Vista and Inktomi decades ago? In 2023, my crystal ball did not reveal answers to these questions.

Privately Held Proprietary LLM Providers

Privately held providers of proprietary LLMs, such as OpenAI, Cohere, and Anthropic, are at the vanguard of generative AI innovation. What they lack in capital and access to distribution they make up for in world-class entrepreneurial and technical talent. These startups depend on partnerships with the likes of Microsoft and Google to make up for the critical capabilities they lack. Strikingly, many leaders of the LLM startups began their careers at Google, which was unable to contain their ambitions. Below, we examine each company's history in generative AI, describe the firm's related products or services, and assess the company's investment potential. To be sure, only a select few can invest in these companies before they go public.

---

[26] Kash Rangan, et al., "Generative AI - Part I: Laying Out the Investment," *Goldman Sachs Equity Research*, Ibid.

OpenAI

In 2015 Elon Musk, Sam Altman, and others founded San Francisco-based OpenAI, a private research laboratory aiming to develop and direct AI for the benefit of humanity. With a $1 billion endowment, OpenAI sought to create fundamental advances in AI in partnership with other organizations. In February 2024, having raised significant capital from Microsoft, OpenAI completed a transaction valuing the company at $80 billion or more – tripling its April 2023 valuation.[27] While OpenAI initially aimed to develop AI tools for video games, it shifted from a nonprofit to a for-profit company in March 2019 and introduced several key generative AI innovations, including the following:

- **Reinforcement learning algorithms (December 2015).** Less than a year after its official founding, OpenAI released OpenAI Gym – an open source toolkit for developing reinforcement learning algorithms.

- **Generative Pre-trained Transformer (2018).** In 2018, OpenAI published a report to explain the GPT concept: "a neural network, or a machine learning model, created to function like a human brain and trained on large data sets, to produce answers to users' questions."

- **Dall-E (January 2021).** OpenAI introduced Dall-E, a generative AI model that produced images based on natural language text from human users.

---

[27] Cade Metz and Tripp Mickle, "OpenAI Completes Deal That Values the Company at $80 Billion," *New York Times*, February 16, 2024, www.nytimes.com/2024/02/16/technology/openai-artificial-intelligence-deal-valuation.html

- **ChatGPT (November 2022).** OpenAI introduced "the world's most advanced chatbot for its ability to provide answers to users on a seemingly unlimited range of topics."[28]

Although Elon Musk left OpenAI in 2018 to avoid potential conflicts of interest with Tesla, co-founder Sam Altman – who previously led Y Combinator, a Silicon Valley startup incubator, remained CEO in 2024. OpenAI's president and chairman Greg Brockman was formerly the chief technology officer of financial services and SaaS company Stripe, and OpenAI's chief scientist was Ilya Sutskever, formerly of Google.[29] In November 2023, the media was ablaze recounting the four-day drama of Altman's surprise November 17 firing by OpenAI's board followed by his reinstatement as CEO due to pressure from Microsoft and a change in OpenAI's board on November 21.[30]

In August 2023, OpenAI was growing rapidly – reportedly approaching $1 billion in revenue by August 2024 – while losing significant amounts of money. Although OpenAI offered many services, the most significant one was ChatGPT, an LLM accepting image and text inputs to generate text and code trained on publicly available data such as public web pages and data that OpenAI licensed.[31] OpenAI made money in two ways: licensing its technology to corporate clients and via individual subscriptions. As of March 2023, between one and two million subscribers paid $20 per month

---

[28] Cameron Hashemi-Pour, "OpenAI," *TechTarget*, accessed October 21, 2023, www.techtarget.com/searchenterpriseai/definition/OpenAI.

[29] Cameron Hashemi-Pour, "OpenAI," *TechTarget*, Ibid.

[30] "A timeline of Sam Altman's firing and dramatic return to OpenAI," *Reuters*, November 22, 2023, www.reuters.com/technology/openai-ouster-microsoft-ai-research-ceo-sam-altmans-tumultuous-weekend-2023-11-20/

[31] Kyle Wiggers, "OpenAI makes GPT-4 generally available," *TechCrunch*, July 6, 2023, https://techcrunch.com/2023/07/06/openai-makes-gpt-4-generally-available/

to access ChatGPT. OpenAI's business clients included Microsoft, which used the technology for Bing, as well as companies such as Block, Canva, Carlyle, The Estée Lauder Companies, PwC, and Zapier.[32]

OpenAI faced years of losses. OpenAI lost $540 million in 2022 as it developed GPT-4. In December 2022, OpenAI CEO Sam Altman described GPT's computing costs as "eye-watering." Moreover, OpenAI was unlikely to become profitable for years because Microsoft, which had invested $13 billion in the startup, had the right to 75% of OpenAI's profits until the company repaid the software giant's investment. One big positive: ChatGPT remained way ahead of rivals as the most visited site providing an AI-powered chatbot. In June 2023, OpenAI received 1.8 billion visits, Bing attracted 1.25 billion visits, and Google's Bard chatbot was not yet in the top three, according to SimilarWeb.[33]

OpenAI's other services included

- **Dall-E and Dall-E 2.** These generative AI platforms analyzed text-based descriptions of images that users wanted them to produce and then generated those images as described.[34] In September 2023, OpenAI announced Dell-E 3 that enabled users to deploy ChatGPT to create prompts and included more safety options.[35]

---

[32] Chris Morris, "OpenAI reportedly nears $1 billion in annual sales," *Fast Company*, August 30, 2023, www.fastcompany.com/90946849/openai-chatgpt-reportedly-nears-1-billion-annual-sales#

[33] Chris Morris, "OpenAI reportedly nears $1 billion in annual sales," *Fast Company*, August 30, 2023, Ibid.

[34] Cameron Hashemi-Pour, "OpenAI," *TechTarget,* Ibid.

[35] Emilia David, "OpenAI releases third version of DALL-E," *The Verge*, September 20, 2023, www.theverge.com/2023/9/20/23881241/openai-dalle-third-version-generative-ai

- **Clip.** Clip was a neural network that synthesized visuals and the relevant text to predict captions that most accurately described the visuals.[36]

- **Codex.** Trained on billions of lines of code using GPT-3 technology, Codex helped software developers simplify coding processes.[37]

- **Whisper.** An automatic speech recognition (ASR) tool, Whisper was trained with audio data "to recognize, transcribe and translate speech in about 100 different languages, including technical language and different accents."[38]

Although OpenAI was unprofitable, in November 2023 its valuation was soaring as its revenues accelerated. Indeed, between August 2023 and October 2023, OpenAI's revenue growth continued to rise rapidly. More specifically, OpenAI's annualized revenue increased 30% in three months from $1 billion to $1.3 billion.[39] As OpenAI's revenues accelerated, so did its private market valuation – from $23 billion in April 2023 to $80 billion in February 2024 – enabling employees to sell their existing shares. Although "thousands of companies" were exploring generative AI, few had the "unusual blend of experienced researchers, enormous ambition and large amounts of money" required to build such systems from scratch.[40]

---

[36] Cameron Hashemi-Pour, "OpenAI," *TechTarget,* Ibid.

[37] Cameron Hashemi-Pour, "OpenAI," *TechTarget,* Ibid.

[38] Cameron Hashemi-Pour, "OpenAI," *TechTarget,* Ibid.

[39] Amir Efrati, "OpenAI's Revenue Crossed $1.3 Billion Annualized Rate, CEO Tells Staff," *The Information*, October 12, 2023, www.theinformation.com/articles/openais-revenue-crossed-1-3-billion-annualized-rate-ceo-tells-staff

[40] Cade Metz, "OpenAI in Talks for Deal That Would Value Company at $80 Billion," *New York Times*, October 20, 2023, www.nytimes.com/2023/10/20/technology/openai-artifical-intelligence-value.html

In 2024, OpenAI was a privately held company with tremendous potential value. Sadly, for the average investor, that value was not accessible because the startup invited only huge companies and venture capital firms to finance OpenAI's large losses. For the average investor, access to OpenAI's stock would only come if its executives decided to take the company public. Were that to occur, the company's stock price would only keep rising if its revenue could exceed investor expectations in most quarterly financial reports.

Cohere

Aidan Gomez (CEO), Nick Frosst, and Ivan Zhang founded Cohere, a provider of independent natural language processing (NLP) systems for business, in 2019. In August 2023, Cohere had raised $445 million in capital and analysts valued the company at $3 billion. Gomez completed a PhD in Computer Science at the University of Oxford and became an AI researcher at Google Brain in Toronto. In June 2017, Gomez co-authored a paper titled "Attention Is All You Need," which introduced the transformer model, a neural network architecture that enabled users to perform NLP tasks more efficiently and effectively. Cohere aimed at companies that could not afford the high prices that hyperscalers, such as Amazon and Microsoft, charged to build LLMs (over $10 million to train and even more to use). The startup launched its general-purpose language models, available to customers via application programming interface, in November 2021. The number of users increased 800% by February 2022 when Cohere announced its Series B financing round. In September 2023, the company's customers included Oracle, Notion, Jasper, Spotify, HyperWrite, and Glean[41]

---

[41] Rohan Gupta and Jason Wong, "Cohere," *Contrary Research*, September 9, 2023, https://research.contrary.com/reports/cohere

Cohere provides NLP models for businesses without requiring them to build their own models themselves, saving companies money and time. Cohere trains LLMs for three primary use cases:

- **Retrieving text**. Retrieving text enables companies to uncover trends, compare languages, and build their own text analysis applications; to search for text, documents, and articles based on meaning; and to rank searches based on a deeper understanding of the meaning of a user prompt.

- **Generating text**. Generating text helps users to extract summarized insights from long documents; to produce content for specific purposes such as emails, landing pages, and product descriptions; and to write emails or answer questions about a document.

- **Classifying text**. Cohere's text classification enables users to moderate content and analyze sentiment in product reviews.[42]

In 2023, Cohere aimed at a large market with a compelling customer value proposition. Despite significant competition, Cohere investors had driven up the company's value considerably since its initial funding round. Nevertheless, by October 2023, the potential rewards for private company investors were unclear, as was the possibility of a Cohere IPO and the company's ability to grow faster than investors' expectations as a public company.

- **Market size.** Analysts forecast the NLP market in which Cohere participated would grow 45% to $41 billion in 2023 and expand at a 40.4% average annual rate to

---

[42] Rohan Gupta and Jason Wong, "Cohere," *Contrary Research*, Ibid.

$440 billion by 2030. Growth tailwinds included AI copilots to increase the speed of coding, specialized AI assistants, and new infrastructure products.[43]

- **Cohere business strategy.** Cohere's business strategy saved companies the cost of building their own LLMs. Since the company bore these upfront costs to train and operate the models, it aimed to recoup them with usage-based pricing in three different tiers. Customers had free access to Cohere APIs for learning and prototyping; they paid to train custom models – a tiny fraction of a penny per number, letter, or symbol; and an undisclosed fee for its so-called enterprise tier in which customers received a dedicated model, the highest levels of support, and options for customized deployment.[44]

- **Competitors.** Cohere faced competitors, many of which had more resources. These included Meta Platforms and Google, public companies valued in the trillions of dollars, and private companies worth more than Cohere, most notably OpenAI with an estimated $1 billion in revenue and an estimated valuation of $80 billion in October 2023 and Anthropic ($4.1 billion in May 2023). Cohere also competed with private companies worth less, such as Stability AI ($1.1 billion in October 2022).[45]

---

[43] Rohan Gupta and Jason Wong, "Cohere," *Contrary Research*, Ibid.

[44] Rohan Gupta and Jason Wong, "Cohere," *Contrary Research*, Ibid.

[45] Rohan Gupta and Jason Wong, "Cohere," *Contrary Research*, Ibid.

- **Valuation.** In 2023, Cohere's valuation increased considerably. In May 2023, the company raised $270 million in a Series C round valuing the NLP provider at $2.1 billion. By August 2023, Cohere's valuation had grown to $3 billion after Tiger Global sold 2.1% of Cohere for $63 million while retaining its remaining 5%.[46]

In 2024, Cohere's investment trajectory appeared to depend on the extent to which hyperscalers would use their market dominance to lock in customers to their generative AI services. If many large companies bet on Cohere's services to lower the investment and shorten the time required to build generative AI applications, the startup would grow rapidly in value. Otherwise, Cohere might suffer a capping of its market share and leave investors with more modest returns, possibly following an acquisition by a larger company, such as Oracle.

Anthropic

Daniela Amodei and Dario Amodei worked for OpenAI before departing due to concerns the ChatGPT developer cared more about commercialization than safety. The siblings co-founded Anthropic in 2021. To address safety concerns, Anthropic conducted research on Constitutional AI, a process by which generative AI improves itself while following principles set by humans. Anthropic raised $500 million in capital from FTX's former CEO Sam Bankman Fried through his hedge fund, Alameda Research. In late 2022, Google invested $300 million in Anthropic, some of which Anthropic would spend on Google Cloud services to train and operate its Claude chatbot.[47] By October 2023, the 192-employee company had raised a total of $7.2 billion valuing the

---

[46] Rohan Gupta and Jason Wong, "Cohere," *Contrary Research*, Ibid.

[47] Nick Saraev, "A Brief History of Anthropic (and Claude)," *Cerebral Valley*, accessed October 31, 2023, www.cerebralvalley.com/post/a-history-of-anthropic

company at $25 billion. That month, the company raised another $2 billion of venture funding from Alphabet a month after Amazon invested $4 billion in venture funding. Anthropic aimed to deploy the capital to "accelerate the development of the company's future foundation models and make them widely accessible to AWS customers."[48]

Companies including Slack, Notion, and Quora used Anthropic's generative AI service, Claude 2, a rival to ChatGPT. Claude 2 could summarize up to about 75,000 words, the length of a typical book. Users inputted large data sets and requested summaries in the form of a memo, letter, or story. ChatGPT could handle a much smaller input of about 3,000 words. Arthur AI, a machine learning monitoring platform, concluded Claude 2 had the most "self-awareness," meaning it accurately assessed its knowledge limits and only answered questions for which it had training data to support.[49] Anthropic's concern about safety caused the company not to release the first version of Claude, which the company developed in 2022, because employees were afraid people might misuse it. Anthropic delayed the release of Claude 2 because the company's red-teamers uncovered new ways it could become dangerous.[50]

Anthropic's co-founder Dario Amodei, a Princeton-educated physicist who led the OpenAI teams that built GPT-2 and GPT-3, became Anthropic's CEO. His younger sister, Daniela Amodei, who oversaw OpenAI's policy and safety teams, became Anthropic's president. As Daniela said, "We were the safety and policy leadership of OpenAI, and we just saw this vision for how we could train large language models and large generative models

---

[48] "Anthropic," *PitchBook*, accessed October 21, 2023, https://my.PitchBook.com/profile/466959-97/company/profile#insights

[49] Hayden Field, "Google commits to invest $2 billion in OpenAI competitor Anthropic," *CNBC*, October 27, 2023, www.cnbc.com/2023/10/27/google-commits-to-invest-2-billion-in-openai-competitor-anthropic.html

[50] Kevin Roose, "Inside the White-Hot Center of A.I. Doomerism," *New York Times*, July 11, 2023, www.nytimes.com/2023/07/11/technology/anthropic-ai-claude-chatbot.html

with safety at the forefront." Initially, the Amodeis thought Anthropic would do safety research using other companies' AI models. They soon concluded innovative research was only possible if they built their own models. To do that, they needed to raise hundreds of millions of dollars to afford the expensive computing equipment required to build the models. They decided Claude should be helpful, harmless, and honest.[51]

To that end, Anthropic used Constitutional AI, the interaction between two AI models: one operating according to a written list of principles from sources such as the UN's Universal Declaration of Human Rights and a second AI to evaluate how well the first one followed its principles, correcting it when necessary.[52] In July 2023, Daniela Amodei provided examples of Claude 2's improvements over the prior version. Claude 2 scored 76.5% on the bar exam's multiple-choice section, up from the earlier version's 73%. The newest model scored 71% on the Python coding test, up from the prior version's 56%. Amodei said Claude 2 was twice as good at giving "harmless responses."[53]

By October 2023, Anthropic's growth and valuation were accelerating quickly. PitchBook estimated the company would double its revenue by the end of 2023 to $200 million. Meanwhile, between May 2023 and October 2023, Anthropic's valuation had increased fivefold to $25 billion.[54] Underlying Anthropic's value acceleration was the company's Constitutional AI training method. Claude 2's advantage over foundational AI models from OpenAI, Google, and Meta Platforms was its stronger built-in guardrails. Analysts put a large emphasis on how well a foundational

---

[51] Kevin Roose, "Inside the White-Hot Center of A.I. Doomerism," *New York Times*, Ibid.

[52] Kevin Roose, "Inside the White-Hot Center of A.I. Doomerism," *New York Times*, Ibid.

[53] Hayden Field, "Anthropic — the $4.1 billion OpenAI rival — debuts new A.I. chatbot and opens it to public," *CNBC*, July 11, 2023, www.cnbc.com/2023/07/11/ anthropic-an-openai-rival-opens-claude-2-ai-chatbot-to-the-public.html

[54] "Anthropic," *PitchBook*, accessed October 21, 2023, Ibid.

AI model prevented hallucinations and fabrications. The consequences of AI-produced errors could have "dire consequences inside an enterprise workflow or in more sensitive sectors like healthcare."[55] By October 2023, Anthropic anticipated its revenue would grow 150% to the end of 2024 to $500 million.[56] Anthropic's value had the potential to keep growing rapidly in conjunction with its revenue acceleration. The most significant risk for Anthropic's financial backers was a significant gap between the company's lofty values and Claude 2's actual performance. Another possible risk would be the emergence of new rivals whose approach to generative AI safety was more effective than Anthropic's.

Open Source LLM Providers

Open source LLM providers, such as Hugging Face and Llama, provide generative AI code for free built by volunteers. Open source generative AI software is a mixed blessing. The good news is the code is available for free and through partnerships with large companies such as Amazon, Google, and Microsoft can be customized by developers. The challenge with Open source is the risk of the software being infected with malware and the need to check the software's quality before deploying it. Below we examine two very different open source providers – privately held Hugging Face and Llama – provided by Meta Platforms. We examine each provider's history in generative AI, describe the firm's related products, and assess the company's investment potential.

---

[55] "Google Strengthens Anthropic Ties With $2 Billion Investment," *PYMNTS*, October 29, 2023, www.pymnts.com/artificial-intelligence-2/2023/google-strengthens-anthropic-ties-with-2-billion-investment/

[56] Kate Clark, Anissa Gardizy, and Stephanie Palazzolo, "Anthropic in Talks to Raise $2 Billion From Google and Others Just Days After Amazon Investment," *The Information*, October 3, 2023, www.theinformation.com/articles/openai-rival-anthropic-in-talks-to-raise-2-billion-from-google-others-as-ai-arms-race-accelerates

Hugging Face

Hugging Face is a machine learning and data science platform and community that helps users build, deploy, and train ML models. It provides the infrastructure to demo, run, and deploy AI in live applications. In 2016, French entrepreneurs Clément Delangue, Julien Chaumond, and Thomas Wolf founded Hugging Face in Brooklyn, New York. The company originally developed a chatbot app for teenagers. After open sourcing the model behind the chatbot app, Hugging Face changed itself into an ML platform. In 2023, the company announced a partnership with Amazon Web Services to make Hugging Face products available to AWS customers for building custom applications. By November 2023, Google, Amazon, Nvidia, and Salesforce were among the startup's investors.[57]

Hugging Face's Transformers Python library reduced the time required to download and train ML models. Due to its open source nature and deployment tools, Hugging Face enabled users to share resources, models, and research and to reduce model training time and resource consumption. Hugging Face enabled users to perform the following activities:

- **Implement ML models.** Hugging Face allowed users to upload models for natural language processing, computer vision, image generation, and audio.

- **Share and discover ML models.** Through Spaces and the Hugging Face Transformers library, researchers and developers shared models with the community, which other users could download and incorporate into their own applications.

---

[57] Ben Lutkevich, "Hugging Face," *TechTarget*, accessed November 1, 2023, www.techtarget.com/whatis/definition/Hugging-Face

- **Share and discover data sets.** Researchers and developers could share data sets for training ML models or discover data sets to train their models through the Datasets library.

- **Fine-tune models.** Users could refine and train deep learning models using Hugging Face's application programming interface tools.

- **Host demos.** Hugging Face lets users create interactive, in-browser demonstrations of ML models.

- **Research.** Hugging Face participated in collaborative research projects, such as the BigScience research workshop, to advance the field of NLP.

- **Develop business applications.** Hugging Face's Enterprise Hub enabled business users to "work with transformers, data sets and open source libraries in a privately hosted environment."

- **Evaluate ML models.** Hugging Face enabled users to evaluate ML models and data sets through a code library.[58]

Hugging Face presented users with considerable risks, including the following:

- **Bias.** Models available on Hugging Face were susceptible to bias, potentially causing the model to generate "sexist, racist or homophobic content."

- **Computational requirements.** Some larger models on Hugging Face did not operate effectively with the default amount of computing resources the platform

---

[58] Ben Lutkevich, "Hugging Face," *TechTarget*, Ibid.

provided. For example, to run Bloom, a multilingual language model, users needed to purchase more computing resources.

- **Support.** Most versions of the platform lacked dedicated customer support.

- **Model search.** Searching the platform for appropriate models or libraries was sometimes difficult.

- **Security.** Enterprises using Hugging Face needed to protect themselves from potential data security risks.[59]

The 170-employee company raised an estimated $235 million of Series D venture funding in a deal led by Salesforce Ventures on August 9, 2023, putting the company's pre-money valuation at $4.27 billion. Amazon, MarketX, and eight other investors also participated in the round. Hugging Face's scale and revenue growth was relatively low. For example, PitchBook estimated Hugging Face's 2023 revenue would grow 25% to $50 million in 2023.[60] Given the risks to enterprise users of adopting Hugging Face, its potential revenue growth and potential investment value appeared relatively limited in November 2023.

Meta Platforms' Llama

Meta Platforms began researching AI in 2013 and launched Llama, its open source generative AI LLM, in 2023.[61] Meta began investing in AI research in 2013. By April 2023, Meta's research output is second only to Google in the number of published AI studies, according to a 2022 analysis by AI research analysis platform Zeta Alpha. Meta planned to monetize

---

[59] Ben Lutkevich, "Hugging Face," *TechTarget*, Ibid.

[60] "Hugging Face," *PitchBook*, accessed November 1, 2023, https://my.PitchBook.com/profile/168527-08/company/profile#insights

[61] Team TBH, "From Facebook To Meta: The Journey Of Meta Platforms," *The Brand Hopper*, March 24, 2023, https://thebrandhopper.com/2023/03/24/from-facebook-to-meta-the-journey-of-meta-platforms/

its proprietary generative AI technology by December 2023. Meta CTO Andrew Bosworth formed a generative AI team and was aiming to use AI to improve the company's advertising effectiveness and to "apply the technology across Facebook, Instagram and its other products."[62] In August 2023, Meta released Code Llama, an LLM that used text prompts to generate and discuss code. Built on top of Llama 2, Code Llama expanded the relationship between Meta and Microsoft. Meta envisioned a bright future for Code Llama: the company said it "has the potential to make workflows faster and more efficient for developers and lower the barrier to entry for people who are learning to code."[63]

Meta's decision to launch Llama as an open source LLM was popular with technologists. The social network saw Llama as akin to Linux, the open source operating system that rivaled Microsoft's Windows. While Meta continued to work on developing its metaverse technologies, its sullied reputation kept some government agencies – most notably the Government Accountability Office – from using Llama. Meta saw Llama as analogous to Linux – an open source rival to Microsoft Windows to reside on corporate servers. Similarly, Meta saw Llama as "the potential digital scaffolding supporting the next generation of AI apps."[64]

Meta built Llama, a transformer neural network, using the company's Research SuperCluster supercomputer that incorporated 16,000 Nvidia A100 GPUs. Originally developed inside Meta's Fundamental AI Research

---

[62] Nicole Farley, "Meta will debut its generative AI this year," *Search Engine Land*, April 10, 2023, https://searchengineland.com/meta-will-debut-their-generative-ai-this-year-395460

[63] Matthew Galgani, "Meta Stock Rides Llama And AI Wave Toward Breakout In Bumpy Market," *Investor's Business Daily*, September 15, 2023, www.investors.com/research/ibd-stock-analysis/meta-stock-rides-llama-ai-wave-toward-breakout-as-ai-peers-nvidia-microsoft-amazon-google-stock-all-weather-bumpy-market/

[64] Jonathan Vanian, "Meta's unique approach to developing AI puzzles Wall Street, but techies love it," *CNBC*, October 26, 2023, www.cnbc.com/2023/10/16/metas-open-source-approach-to-ai-puzzles-wall-street-techies-love-it.html

team (FAIR), by October 2023, the project had moved to the company's generative AI organization led by Ahmad Al-Dahle, who previously spent over 16 years at Apple. Meta took six months to train Llama 2 using a mix of "publicly available online data" which excluded Facebook user information.[65]

Meta sought to encourage leading AI researchers to use Llama so the company would have an easier time hiring skilled technologists who would understand Meta's approach to development. In the past, Meta's PyTorch coding framework for machine learning apps had enabled the company to hire talented engineers who wanted to work on innovative software projects. Meta anticipated third-party developers would steadily improve Llama 2 and related AI software so that it would run more efficiently, enabling the company to benefit from volunteer research help. Ironclad, a legal tech startup, did not immediately adopt Llama because its chief architect Cai GoGwilt was waiting for the open source community to make Llama 2 run faster on mobile phones.[66]

In October 2023, Meta introduced generative AI tools aimed at enabling advertisers to create image backgrounds and variations of written text. More specifically, the tools would allow advertisers to "create backgrounds, expand images and generate multiple versions of ad text based on their original copy." The product's image expansion feature enabled advertisers to "adjust their assets to fit different aspect ratios required across various products, like Feed or Reels." The product's text variations feature used AI to generate "up to six different variations of text based on the advertiser's original copy" to highlight keywords the advertiser wanted to emphasize. Meta said these AI features had saved

---

[65] Jonathan Vanian, "Meta's unique approach to developing AI puzzles Wall Street, but techies love it," *CNBC*, Ibid.

[66] Jonathan Vanian, "Meta's unique approach to developing AI puzzles Wall Street, but techies love it," *CNBC*, Ibid.

advertisers an average of a month per year. Meta planned to enable businesses to use "AI for messaging on WhatsApp and Messenger to chat with customers for e-commerce, engagement and support."[67]

In October 2023, investors questioned Meta's ability to earn a return on its investment in Llama. Although CEO Mark Zuckerberg told analysts in July 2023 that third-party unpaid Llama developers were lowering Meta's costs to operate its AI software – sending the company's capital expenditures down about $4 billion to around $28 billion in 2023 – the open source business model meant users did not pay for Llama. CFO Finance chief Susan Li forecast data center and AI-related investments would grow in 2024, possibly lowering Meta's profitability. As a result, analysts questioned whether Llama could generate sufficient revenue to offset its operating costs. Zuckerberg offered dim hope for some revenue from Llama 2. He told investors Meta earned an undisclosed sum from Microsoft and Amazon, both of which offered Llama 2 as part of their generative AI enterprise services. Moreover, Meta made Llama 2 available with a commercial license that allowed companies to integrate it into their products.[68]

During Meta's second quarter 2023 investor conference call, Zuckerberg said he did not expect Llama 2 to generate "a large amount of revenue in the near term, but over the long term, hopefully that can be something." In October 2023, Meta disclosed there had been "more than 30 million downloads of Llama-based models through Hugging Face and over 10 million downloads had occurred during the preceding 30 days." Jim Fan, a senior AI scientist at Nvidia, estimated Meta paid $20 million to train Llama 2, over nine times the estimated $2.4 million cost to train

---

[67] Sarah Perez, "Meta debuts generative AI features for advertisers," *TechCrunch*, October 4, 2023, https://techcrunch.com/2023/10/04/meta-debuts-generative-ai-features-for-advertisers/

[68] Jonathan Vanian, "Meta's unique approach to developing AI puzzles Wall Street, but techies love it," *CNBC*, Ibid.

its predecessor. While AI researchers from large companies shunned Llama-1, Fan said Llama 2's commercial license had the potential to attract users from large companies. Nevertheless, an October 2023 TC Cowen survey of 680 firms in cloud computing found 32% of respondents had used or planned to use commercially packaged LLMs such as OpenAI's GPT-4. A smaller share, 28%, planned to use open source LLMs like Llama and a mere 12% of respondents planned to use in-house LLMs.[69]

Meta was undaunted by the challenges of gaining market share in generative AI. By February 2024, Meta was making a large investment with a goal of prevailing in generative AI. The social media company planned to bet the largest portion of its capital budget on AI. Specifically, Meta planned to make 2024 capital expenditures in a range between $30 billion and $37 billion, in order to build data centers and buy servers for AI and other purposes. The company planned to spend billions of dollars on Nvidia's AI chips to train Meta's AI models. "We're playing to win here and I expect us to continue investing aggressively in this area in order to build the most advanced clusters," Zuckerberg said. "We're also designing novel data centers and designing our own custom silicon specialized for our workloads." Meta planned to conduct AI research and incorporate the technology into its products. "Our updated outlook reflects our evolving understanding of our AI capacity demands as we anticipate what we may need for the next generations of foundational research and product development," Zuckerberg said. Finally Meta intended to supply capital for building AI ad tools.[70]

By February 2024, it remained unclear whether generative AI would ever boost the value of Meta Platforms' stock. These questions included

---

[69] Jonathan Vanian, "Meta's unique approach to developing AI puzzles Wall Street, but techies love it," *CNBC*, Ibid.

[70] Peter Cohan, "Why Meta Stock Tops Amazon As A 2024 generative AI Play," *Forbes*, February 2, 2024, www.forbes.com/sites/petercohan/2024/02/02/why-meta-stock-tops-amazons-as-a-2024-generative-ai-play/

- Would Meta's Llama versions attract a widespread following among developers?

- Would a significant number of those developers pay to incorporate Llama into their products or would they use an unpaid open source version?

- Would other open source LLMs prevail over Llama?

- If a large number of users were willing to pay, would Meta's revenues exceed Llama's investments and operating costs?

- Would Meta find other ways to monetize its generative AI expertise, such as to boost its advertising revenues?

Publicly Traded Application-Specific Generative AI Application Providers

Generative AI's propulsive growth created an urgent imperative to capture the opportunity. To that end, publicly traded providers of software as a service, such as Adobe and ServiceNow, offered application-specific generative AI applications. The challenge for investors in such companies is determining whether these applications have the potential to add meaningfully to their revenue growth. Below, we examine each provider's history in generative AI, describe the firm's related products, and assess the company's investment potential.

Adobe

In March 2023, Adobe launched Firefly, a generative AI text-to-image model, for internal use. By June 2023, Firefly was Adobe's most popular beta product with the "highest number of users," who had created about

200 million AI-generated images.[71] By October, that number had grown at a 5,600% average annual rate to 3 billion images.[72] The initial response to Firefly prompted Adobe to launch Firefly for its 12,000 enterprise customers. Adobe trained Firefly on more than 100 million images including Adobe's stock photos and illustrations – the company paid image contributors 33% royalties when their images were sold or used; licensed images; and public images whose copyrights had expired. In 2023, Adobe added AI-generated images submitted by contributors, which the company accepted only if contributors had the rights to use them. Meredith Cooper, senior director of digital media business at Adobe, said, "Firefly is designed to be commercially safe and backed by Adobe via indemnification."[73]

In May 2023, Adobe announced plans to widen its generative AI footprint through the following initiatives:

- **Gemini.** Adobe aimed to enable users to create synthetic images within Bard, Google's conversational chatbot, using Firefly.

- **Enable Adobe business customers to access LLMs.** Adobe enabled its enterprise customers to access language models from Microsoft's Azure OpenAI service, Google's language model Flan-T5, and others.

---

[71] Rashi Shrivastava, "Adobe Brings Its Generative AI Tool Firefly To Businesses," *Forbes*, June 8, 2023, www.forbes.com/sites/rashishrivastava/2023/06/08/adobe-brings-its-generative-ai-tool-firefly-to-businesses/

[72] Frederic Lardinois, "Adobe Firefly can now generate more realistic images," *TechCrunch*, October 10, 2023, https://techcrunch.com/2023/10/10/adobe-firefly-can-now-generate-more-realistic-images/

[73] Rashi Shrivastava, "Adobe Brings Its Generative AI Tool Firefly To Businesses," *Forbes*, Ibid.

- **Adobe Sensei.** Adobe Sensei enabled enterprise users to automate tasks such as analyzing customer information, querying data, and adjusting advertising budgets.[74]

In October 2023, Adobe generated considerable excitement among Wall Street analysts about the revenue potential of its generative AI-powered services during its Adobe Max customer conference. At the conference, Adobe presented services that analysts characterized as among the industry's clearest "use cases that could prove especially popular with its user base." These products included a second generation of Firefly with new versions for audio, video, and 3-D image creation. New AI features in Photoshop aimed to cut hours from the editing process. Adoption of the AI features in Photoshop has been ten times higher than an average major product launch, said Alexandru Costin, Adobe vice president of generative AI. "The way we achieved this with Firefly models – we integrated it natively into the creative workflows."[75] In addition, Adobe previewed a "conversational" version of its Acrobat software, which the company said could "read, analyze and create PDF documents." Bernstein analyst Mark Moerdler noted Adobe's AI could save users "hours of repetitive and mundane work."[76]

Here is a general principle of what makes stock prices go up or down: stock prices rise after a company reports better than expected results and raises its forecast for future revenue and profits. If a company reports results or makes a forecast, either or both of which disappoint investors,

---

[74] Rashi Shrivastava, "Adobe Brings Its Generative AI Tool Firefly To Businesses," *Forbes*, Ibid.

[75] Brody Ford, "Adobe Releases New AI Models Aimed at Improved Graphic Design," *Bloomberg*, October 10, 2023, https://finance.yahoo.com/news/adobe-releases-ai-models-aimed-160000461.html

[76] Dan Gallagher, "Adobe May Be Tech's Biggest AI Bet Yet," *Wall Street Journal*, October 13, 2023, www.wsj.com/tech/ai/adobe-may-be-techs-biggest-ai-bet-yet-429f640f

the company's stock price will fall. This comes to mind in considering how to assess the potential for Adobe's stock price to rise further. In 2023, Adobe had not quantified how much revenue the company's generative AI-powered services would add. While anecdotal evidence suggested these services would make a significant contribution, in the absence of specific forecasts, investors would struggle to assess whether revenues from generative AI would enable Adobe to report better than expected future results and raise its forecasts above investor expectations. In 2023, Adobe shares had risen 66% for the year as of October 13. Moreover, its stock rose 5% in the days following the first day of its Adobe Max customer conference where the company announced its new generative AI services.[77]

In the absence of concrete evidence of expectations-beating revenue growth from Adobe's generative AI products, here are seven qualitative indicators suggesting its stock price would rise:

- **Higher prices.** In November 2023, Adobe planned to raise prices for its Creative Cloud "by about 9% to 10%," *CNET* reported.[78] Adobe said its average usage fee "can vary depending on the organization's size and expected usage," a spokesperson told me.[79] Without this information, it was difficult to estimate how much this price increase would boost Adobe's total revenue. Nevertheless, in the third quarter of 2023, Creative

[77] Peter Cohan, "Adobe Shares Rising On New Generative AI Services," *Forbes*, October 14, 2023, www.forbes.com/sites/petercohan/2023/10/14/adobe-shares-rising-on-new-generative-ai-services/

[78] Stephen Shankland, "Adobe Retrained Its generative AI, and I'm Impressed With the Upgrade," *CNET*, October 11, 2023, www.cnet.com/tech/computing/adobe-retrained-its-generative-ai-and-im-impressed-with-the-upgrade/

[79] Peter Cohan, "Adobe Shares Rising On New Generative AI Services," *Forbes*, October 14, 2023, Ibid.

Cloud accounted for 59% of Adobe's revenue.[80] Hence, a 10% price increase for Creative Cloud subscribers could have added 6% to Adobe's total revenue in the quarter.

- **Expansion of total addressable market.** Adobe plans to share with analysts how much generative AI will expand its total addressable market (TAM) at its next analyst meeting, Anil Chakravarthy, President of Adobe's Digital Experience Business and Worldwide Field Operations, told me in October 2023. "As Adobe Chief Strategy Officer Scott Belsky said, 'generative AI raises the ceiling and lowers the bar.' You can produce a lot more electronic content and it opens new use cases. We charge on a per-user basis. Our new products will increase the number of users and their frequency of use," Chakravarthy said.[81]

- **Leading market share in many customer industries.** In October 2023, Adobe Analytics (AA) had a significant number of customers and leading market share among the largest companies in many industries. That month, "over 12,000 customers – including 87% of Fortune 100 companies and 74% of Fortune 500 companies," used AA. "In the retail sector, nine of the top 10 U.S. brands

[80] "Adobe Reports Record Revenue in Q3 Fiscal 2023," *News.Adobe*, September 14, 2023, https://news.adobe.com/news/news-details/2023/Adobe-Reports-Record-Revenue-in-Q3-Fiscal-2023/default.aspx#:~:text=Third%20Quarter%20Fiscal%20Year%202023%20Business%20Segment%20Highlights&text=Creative%20revenue%20grew%20to%20%242.91,15%20percent%20in%20constant%20currency

[81] Peter Cohan, "Adobe Shares Rising On New Generative AI Services," *Forbes*, October 14, 2023, Ibid.

relied on AA to understand shopper journeys that moved from online to in-store." Adobe enjoyed similar market share leadership in the hotel, airline, financial services, media, and healthcare industries.[82] Such market leadership had the potential to help Adobe exceed investor expectations.

- **New use cases for existing products.** Chakravarthy predicted a surge in the need for marketers to produce content to satisfy the demand of social media. He envisioned generative AI helping companies tailor their marketing messages to specific customer segments and sharing content to relevant social media such as Instagram and TikTok.[83] Similarly, these new use cases also had the potential to send Adobe revenues ahead of expectations.

- **Dramatic increase in the number of users.** Adobe expected generative AI to make Adobe Analytics – a tool for tracking the effectiveness of marketing campaigns – and Experience Manager (EM) – a content and digital asset management service – easy to use for more people. "We think it will increase by five to 10-fold the number of people who can use these tools," Chakravarthy said.[84] While Adobe declined to provide

---

[82] Peter Cohan, "Adobe Shares Rising On New Generative AI Services," *Forbes*, October 14, 2023, Ibid.

[83] Peter Cohan, "Adobe Shares Rising On New Generative AI Services," *Forbes*, October 14, 2023, Ibid.

[84] Peter Cohan, "Adobe Shares Rising On New Generative AI Services," *Forbes*, October 14, 2023, Ibid.

an estimate of the number of AA and EM users, such a dramatic increase in the user base of these services was likely to accelerate Adobe's revenues.

- **High analyst enthusiasm for Adobe's generative AI services.** Morgan Stanley's Keith Weiss wrote that Adobe's analyst day was "light on numbers [and] big on vision." Brent Thill of Jefferies called the day "the fastest pace of innovation we've seen in 2 decades," while Wolfe Research's Alex Zukin wrote in a client note that Adobe is "truly remaking the entire product suite to be AI native."[85] If analyst enthusiasm for Adobe's new products caused them to increase their targets for the company's stock price, the higher target could raise the risk of a disappointing quarterly report and a drop in the stock.

- **Modest expectations for Adobe's growth.** Despite expectations of 10% revenue growth in its November-ending fiscal year 2023, the slowest in nearly a decade, Adobe planned to provide fiscal year 2024 revenue projections in December 2023, which analysts expected to translate into 12% growth.[86] If Adobe's Creative Cloud price increase boosted Adobe's growth by six percentage points, its FY 2024 revenue growth would exceed analysts' expectation of 12% growth, possibly contributing to a rise in its stock price.

---

[85] Dan Gallagher, "Adobe May Be Tech's Biggest AI Bet Yet," *Wall Street Journal*, October 13, 2023, Ibid.

[86] Dan Gallagher, "Adobe May Be Tech's Biggest AI Bet Yet," *Wall Street Journal*, October 13, 2023, Ibid.

The biggest risk to betting on Adobe's generative AI strategy was the high cost of operating the computing network required to respond to user prompts. Chakravarthy told me Adobe's prices were less than the value its products delivered to customers and the "high operating cost is offset by the pricing increase."[87] Perhaps this helped explain why analysts "expected Adobe's adjusted operating margins to remain above 45% despite the high cost of powering AI services."[88]

Over the long run, Adobe investors faced the general problem of owning stock in a company trying to exceed investor expectations. If a company does better than investors expect, they will raise their expectations in order to avoid being surprised in the future. The longer the company continues to exceed rising expectations, the more difficult it becomes to hurdle them. As soon as the company falls short, its stock price falls. In October 2023, with its stock up so much, investors ran the risk of receiving a nasty shock if their expectations got ahead of the growth Adobe actually delivered.[89]

ServiceNow

ServiceNow announced its first generative AI service in May 2023. Specifically, the company added generative AI capabilities – ServiceNow generative AI Controller and Now Assist for Search – to its Now Platform workflow management service that ran on Microsoft's Azure OpenAI platform. ServiceNow envisioned the generative AI capabilities would

---

[87] Peter Cohan, "Adobe Shares Rising On New Generative AI Services," *Forbes*, October 14, 2023, Ibid.

[88] Dan Gallagher, "Adobe May Be Tech's Biggest AI Bet Yet," *Wall Street Journal*, October 13, 2023, Ibid.

[89] Peter Cohan, "Adobe Shares Rising On New Generative AI Services," *Forbes*, October 14, 2023, Ibid.

"deliver faster, more intelligent workflow automation" and help companies to "reduce costs while driving higher productivity, smarter experiences, and faster time to value."[90]

By October 2023, ServiceNow's investments in generative AI were showing signs of paying off. After reporting 25% revenue growth for its third quarter, ServiceNow cited itself as "an outlier for profitable growth," ServiceNow CEO Bill McDermott told me in an October 2023 interview. "We are the only large capitalization enterprise software company that is higher than rule of 50," McDermott added (for context, an industry rule of thumb is the sum of revenue growth rate plus free cash flow margin should be equal to or greater than 50). "We beat on subscription revenue, free cash flow, CRPO and operating margin." ServiceNow was proud of its ability to grow through internally generated new services. "The big message: Of five software companies with more than $10 billion in sales, ServiceNow is growing fastest and we are doing it organically," McDermott said. "Innovation leads to growth. We have 5,000 innovations. We are getting high value from generative AI across all industries."[91]

Generative AI was a source of new growth for ServiceNow. The company said Now Assist "embeds the power of generative AI across all workflows on the platform." Now Assist opened up a significant growth opportunity for ServiceNow, potentially adding $1 trillion to the company's total addressable market (TAM). "Gartner says $3 trillion will be invested in IT between 2023 and 2027. $1 trillion of that will go into generative AI. This adds to ServiceNow's current TAM of $200 billion," McDermott said. Now Assist aimed to boost the productivity of companies

---

[90] "ServiceNow announces new generative AI capabilities for the Now Platform for faster, more intelligent workflow automation," *ServiceNow*, May 16, 2023, www.servicenow.com/company/media/press-room/gen-ai-now-platform.html

[91] Peter Cohan, "ServiceNow Beats, Raises, And Aims At $1 Trillion generative AI Opportunity," *Forbes*, October 30, 2023, www.forbes.com/sites/petercohan/2023/10/30/servicenow-beats-raises-and-aims-at-1-trillion-gen-ai-opportunity/

by tailoring applications to their specific industries. ServiceNow used generative AI in its own operations and hoped to offer insights from its own. McDermott struck me as very excited about generative AI's potential to help ServiceNow's customers. "We are partnering with Nvidia's CEO Jensen Huang and Accenture to bring the best engineering talent to provide companies with high payoff generative AI applications for their customers and frictionless employee onboarding," he told me in July 2023. Industry-specific solutions included case summarization that used GAI "to read and distill case information across IT, HR, and customer service cases," according to ServiceNow. In addition, the company said it offered text to code, text to workflow, and a natural language human interface. These features could improve operations in industries including telecommunications, financial services, public sector, and manufacturing.[92]

Although ServiceNow did not quantify the revenue it achieved from its generative AI services, customers were biting in the third quarter of 2023. If a sufficient number of customers signed up for Now Assist, there was potential for generative AI to drive an increase in ServiceNow's stock price. In the third quarter, ServiceNow won customers including CBRE, Nvidia, and Deloitte as well as Phillips, FedEx, Mars, Bank of California, the US Department of Defense, and Ashahi Mutual, McDermott told me. ServiceNow said its services met an important customer need: to boost productivity "in the face of macroeconomic crosswinds," he said. "We deliver 30% employee productivity by replacing 13 application platforms with one ServiceNow platform. We replace bad customer service with

---

[92] Peter Cohan, "ServiceNow Beats, Raises, And Aims At $1 Trillion generative AI Opportunity," *Forbes*, October 30, 2023, www.forbes.com/sites/petercohan/2023/10/30/servicenow-beats-raises-and-aims-at-1-trillion-gen-ai-opportunity/

customer self-service. We enable text to code. It's all happening with ServiceNow. [Our clients] are achieving operational excellence, their costs are going down, and productivity and revenue are rising."[93]

In October 2023, one analyst suggested the company's stock (then trading around $530 per share) was undervalued – with a price target of $730 – as its fundamentals were improving in the face of macroeconomic headwinds. In a *SeekingAlpha* column, Analyst Dair Sansyzbayev used a discounted cash flow analysis to estimate ServiceNow's fair value at about $150 billion – representing 35% upside potential. He saw considerable strength in the company, while remaining concerned about how macroeconomic headwinds could hurt the stock. The company's fundamentals are improving even in the current unfavorable environment with several macro headwinds. The management continues successfully delivering stellar revenue growth, profitability improvement, and massive reinvestments in innovation. "The valuation also looks very attractive," Sansyzbayev wrote.[94]

By November 2023, ServiceNow appeared poised to monetize its investments in generative AI, thus creating opportunities for investors. Propelling the company's stock price were forces such as:

- **Access to a much larger market opportunity.** As McDermott noted, ServiceNow's total addressable market could expand by $1 trillion due to corporate demand for generative AI-powered services.

---

[93] Peter Cohan, "ServiceNow Beats, Raises, And Aims At $1 Trillion generative AI Opportunity," *Forbes*, October 30, 2023, www.forbes.com/sites/petercohan/2023/10/30/servicenow-beats-raises-and-aims-at-1-trillion-gen-ai-opportunity/

[94] Peter Cohan, "ServiceNow Beats, Raises, And Aims At $1 Trillion generative AI Opportunity," *Forbes*, October 30, 2023, www.forbes.com/sites/petercohan/2023/10/30/servicenow-beats-raises-and-aims-at-1-trillion-gen-ai-opportunity/

- **Access to a much larger market opportunity.**
  ServiceNow delivered significant increases in employee
  productivity, in part by replacing so many different
  platforms with ServiceNow.

- **Customer adoption of its generative AI-powered
  services.** Well-known companies were adopting
  Now Assist, creating a greater likelihood that other
  customers would join them.

One of the key risks to investors was rising investor expectations for
ServiceNow's growth and profitability. If the company missed investors'
quarterly expectations or lowered its forecasts for growth, the stock price
would be likely to decline sharply.

Privately Held Application-Specific Generative AI Application Provider

In 2023, many startups were applying generative AI to solve specific
business problems. Since so little information about startups is publicly
available, it is helpful to have a framework for evaluating them based on
limited information. As I wrote in *Scaling Your Startup*[95], when a company
is trying to win its first customers, investors should assess whether the
company can answer four questions in the affirmative:

- Is the company solving the right problem?

- Is the startup avoiding direct competition with a well-
  established rival?

---

[95] Peter Cohan, "Scaling Your Startup," (Apress, 2019), `https://link.springer.com/book/10.1007/978-1-4842-4312-1`

- Is the company fielding an outstanding leadership team?

- Is the startup delivering customers a big leap in benefits for the price that I call a quantum value leap?

Here is my assessment of two startups applying generative AI to solve specific business problems using this framework.

Hyro

New York City-based Hyro, an AI-powered health care conversational assistant valued at $68 million in July 2023, solved a big problem well. Although it faced competition from Microsoft, it fielded a team with excellent technical and business skills and delivered customers a compelling return on investment. Here is my more detailed assessment:

- **Solve the right problem: Pass.** Hyro solved a big pain point in health care, improving digital patient engagement and the patient's journey from making an appointment to completing treatment.

- **Avoid big rivals: Possible pass.** Hyro did compete with Microsoft. A Hyro customer, Contra Costa County Health Services, saw Hyro as more responsive than Microsoft to its needs.

- **Field the best team. Pass.** Hyro had a strong leadership team, including co-founder and CEO Israel Krush and CIO Rom Cohen, which enabled the company to win customers and adapt quickly and effectively to their changing needs.

- **Deliver a quantum value leap. Pass**. Hyro's value proposition was compelling to its customers, which included health care systems and providers like Intermountain Healthcare and Baptist Health. As Krush told me in a July 2023 interview, "If a company pays $120,000 for Hyro, five customer service people making $50,000 apiece can be freed up – saving a total of $250,000 – or $3 saved on every $1 invested in our app." In an August 2023 interview, Matt White, Contra Costa's data and innovation officer, told me, "Hyro enabled us to deflect 80% of the calls to our portal from patients who forgot their passwords or wanted to schedule appointments. This saved us from outsourcing call center workers at $20 per call – generating a positive return on investment."[96]

Writer

San Francisco-based Writer, a provider of a generative AI platform to produce consistent on-brand business writing, was valued at $500 million in September 2023.[97] Writer solved a big problem well. Although it faced competition from OpenAI and other larger rivals, it fielded a team with excellent technical and business skills and delivered customers a better-quality solution. Here is my more detailed assessment:

- **Solve the right problem: Pass.** Writer enabled companies to produce high-quality marketing content at scale, fixing a problem for customers that rival products left unsolved. As CEO May Habib said, "We are seeing a lot of folks reach out as they're kind of stuck in proof-of-concept purgatory. We've seen a few

---

[96] Peter Cohan, "Should You Start a Company? Use 4 Tests to Decide," *Inc.*, August 16, 2023, www.inc.com/peter-cohan/should-you-start-a-company-use-4-tests-to-decide.html

[97] "Writer," *PitchBook*, accessed November 4, 2023, https://my.PitchBook.com/profile/439866-01/company/profile#insights

customers where they haven't been able to take use cases to production because the generations weren't high quality enough."[98]

- **Avoid big rivals: Possible pass.** Writer did face competition from ChatGPT; however, Habib said Writer's ability to produce high-quality content at scale gave it an edge.[99]

- **Field the best team. Pass.** Writer had a strong leadership team, including Habib, a Harvard graduate with prior startup experience as CEO of Qordoba, a provider of software localization services founded in 2011,[100] and CTO Waseem Alshikh, previously in the same role at Qordoba.[101] Qordoba raised $21 million in capital before shutting down in October 2020. The company used machine learning and offered an AI-based writing assistant, "enabling users and machines to extract information and standardize their content."[102]

---

[98] Rashi Shrivastava, "AI Startup Writer Raises $100 Million To Take On ChatGPT Enterprise," *Forbes,* September 18, 2023, www.forbes.com/sites/rashishrivastava/2023/09/18/ai-startup-writer-raises-100-million-to-take-on-chatgpt-enterprise/

[99] Rashi Shrivastava, "AI Startup Writer Raises $100 Million To Take On ChatGPT Enterprise," *Forbes,* September 18, 2023, www.forbes.com/sites/rashishrivastava/2023/09/18/ai-startup-writer-raises-100-million-to-take-on-chatgpt-enterprise/

[100] "May Habib," *LinkedIn,* accessed November 4, 2023, www.linkedin.com/in/may-habib/

[101] "Waseem Alshikh," *LinkedIn,* accessed November 4, 2023, www.linkedin.com/in/waseemalshikh/

[102] "Qordoba," *PitchBook,* accessed November 6, 2024, https://my.pitchbook.com/profile/61278-94/company/profile#general-info

- **Deliver a quantum value leap. Pass**. Writer's high-quality customer base suggests the company provided significant value. By September 2023, the company's 150 enterprise customers included Uber, Spotify, Vanguard, Samsung, Accenture, and L'Oreal. Writer trained its models on public data from sources like web pages, books, Wikipedia, GitHub and transcribed video content from YouTube. Writer filtered out copyrighted content from the public data and gave each customer "a separate fine-tuned version of the model trained on company-specific proprietary data such as financial reports and marketing copy." Habib said customers also valued Writer's integration tools employees used, such as Salesforce and Adobe, and customers' ability to embed the app into workspaces, such as Google Chrome, Figma, Google Docs, Canva, Microsoft Word, and Outlook.[103]

Generative AI Software Critical Activities

In 2023, some software companies were generating measurable revenues from generative AI. Based on the case studies, a company's ability to perform five critical activities was likely to determine its ability to gain market share in generative AI software:

- **Ability to field a team of generative AI software industry experts.** The founding teams of the most successful generative AI software startups consisted of a blend of outstanding business and technical talent.

---

[103] Rashi Shrivastava, "AI Startup Writer Raises $100 Million To Take On ChatGPT Enterprise," *Forbes,* Ibid.

Investors rewarded this talent with enormous capital investments and very high valuations.

- **Ability to collaborate with customers to build generative AI-enabled solutions to business problems.** The most successful generative AI software companies excelled at understanding the business objectives of their customers, such as saving time, increasing productivity, boosting customer retention, and empowering employees and building generative AI software that achieved those objectives more effectively than competing products did.

- **Ability to collaborate with cloud services providers to gain access to the processing power required to train generative AI applications with large data sets**. The most successful generative AI software startups lacked sufficient computing power to train their LLMs on the largest data sets. Therefore, the most successful generative AI software companies excelled at collaborating with leading cloud services providers, including Amazon, Microsoft, and Google.

- **Ability to filter out risks from generative AI to avoid damaging customer reputations.** Corporations were eager to capture the productivity benefits of generative AI while sidestepping its reputational and legal risks. The leading generative AI software providers excelled at articulating clear principles for protecting their customers' brands, implemented processes for screening out reputation-endangering content, and aimed to prevent violations of intellectual property rights.

- **Ability to help clients stay ahead of rapidly evolving generative AI technology.** Finally, leading generative AI software providers recognized the need to stay ahead of rapidly changing customer needs, new technologies, and evolving competitor strategies aimed at providing customers with better solutions to their business problems.

Conclusion

This chapter highlighted diverse generative AI software providers, including providers of proprietary and open source LLMs and application-specific generative AI solutions. The chapter explored the powerful forces elevating the profitability of the software industry, specifically how industry leaders such as Microsoft locked in customers to their broad product portfolios. The most successful generative AI software companies worked closely with customers to provide them software to enhance their productivity, boost customer retention, and protect their brands from the risks of hallucinations and anti-social content. In November 2023, some generative AI software companies had not yet generated significant revenue and it was unclear which of them would emerge as clear industry leaders. To evaluate such companies, readers should consider applying the four tests used to analyze Hyro and Writer.

CHAPTER 6

Generative AI Cloud Platforms

In Chapter 5, we examined how various providers of generative AI software compete for customers and assessed their investment potential. In this chapter, we investigate these topics from the perspective of generative AI cloud platform providers, comprising the largest publicly traded suppliers of cloud services including Amazon, Microsoft, and Google, known as hyperscalers. Some hyperscalers used their strengths in generative AI software to encourage customers to increase their spending on cloud services. In addition, we examine providers of software and networking services essential to preparing data, training, and operating LLMs on cloud platforms. This chapter answers questions such as:

- What are the most significant groups of generative AI cloud platforms?

- What forces are driving the profit potential of the generative AI cloud platform industry?

- Which cloud platform providers are most successfully monetizing generative AI?

© Peter Cohan 2024
P. Cohan, *Brain Rush*, https://doi.org/10.1007/979-8-8688-0318-5_6

- How should investors evaluate the potential returns of wagering capital in generative AI cloud platform providers?

- What capabilities set apart the generative AI cloud platform leaders from their peers?

Generative AI Cloud Platform Industry Players

A combination of well-established companies and startups supplied cloud-based services to prepare data and train and operate generative AI applications, including the following:

- **Hyperscalers.** In 2023, Amazon's AWS, Microsoft's Azure, and Alphabet's Google Cloud were among the leading cloud services providers hosting generative AI LLM providers.

- **Data centers.** Companies such as Equinix that owned computing networks rented by companies building Generative AI applications.

- **Networking.** Companies such as Arista Networks provided networking software and hardware to enable cloud services providers to boost the efficiency of LLM training and operation.

- **Database providers.** Companies such as MongoDB, a provider of databases enhanced to boost developer productivity, and Snowflake, a supplier of cloud-based data warehousing and analytical platforms, were adding tools to help companies deploy generative AI.

- **Application performance monitoring.** Companies such as Datadog, a provider of services to monitor the real-time performance of applications companies used to serve their customers, were adding tools to help LLM providers such as OpenAI, Anthropic, and Cohere.

Table 6-1 summarizes the investment potential of these companies.

Table 6-1. *Investment Potential of Selected Generative AI Cloud Platform Providers*

Company	Gen AI Upside Potential	Investment Tailwinds	Investment Headwinds
Amazon's AWS	Moderate/High	New AI-related services for developers	Customers seeking to "optimize" cloud spending
Microsoft Azure	High	OpenAI partnership and market share gain over AWS	Uncertainty regarding OpenAI governance
Google Cloud	Moderate	Inventor of many key generative AI technologies	Loss of talented executives to LLM startups
Equinix	Moderate/High	Growing demand for data centers from LLM training and operation	Lack of generative AI innovation
Arista Networks	High	Exceptional leadership team, strong position in hyperscalers, product innovation	
MongoDB	High	Using generative AI to boost developer productivity at hyperscalers	

(continued)

Table 6-1. (*continued*)

Company	Gen AI Upside Potential	Investment Tailwinds	Investment Headwinds
Datadog	High	Strong market position among hyperscalers and potential generative AI growth from later adopters	Competition from well-funded rivals
Snowflake	Moderate/High	Accelerating growth abetted by generative AI products	Uncertainty about growth due to usage-based pricing
Databricks	Moderate/High	Rapidly growing thanks to generative AI demand	Waiting for market conditions to improve before going public

Generative AI Cloud Platform Industry Attractiveness

In 2023, corporate investment in generative AI was propelling demand for cloud computing, a huge, rapidly growing industry. While cloud computing's profitability varied, industry leader AWS produced 74% of the operating profit of its parent company, Amazon.[1] AWS and other cloud computing companies grabbed market share from a previous generation of computing service providers, known as data centers, that housed and rented out mainframes to corporate customers. Cloud computing providers grew by offering companies significant advantages over traditional data centers, including a greater ability to add or reduce the

---

[1] Aran Ali, "AWS: Powering the Internet and Amazon's Profits," *Visual Capitalist*, July 10, 2022, www.visualcapitalist.com/aws-powering-the-internet-and-amazons-profits/

amount of computing they consumed in response to changes in demand, access to the most up-to-date technologies and services, and often lower costs.[2] Moreover, as cloud-computing providers established their superior value, companies found it more cost effective to outsource their computing resources, in some cases selling them to hyperscalers and data centers.

The five forces underlying the US cloud computing industry's moderate to high profit potential included the following:

- **Threat of entry: Low.** Entry barriers blocking new entrants, including legal and regulatory requirements for protecting data, high labor costs, and the cost of locating data centers near clients while being accessible to redundant power supplies to maximize uptime, were very high. Another large entry barrier was hyperscalers' high capital expenditures on hardware to train and operate LLMs. In 2023, Amazon, Alphabet, and Microsoft planned to spend about $120 billion, 54% more than their 2022 spending.[3]

  In addition, training and operating LLMs was unprofitable because the energy and computing costs of such models exceeded the prices cloud computing providers charged customers.[4]

- **Rivalry among existing competitors: Moderate.** Rivals competed intensely by offering customers the lowest prices. Such competition forced rivals

---

[2] Terry Faber, "Data Processing & Hosting Services in the US," *IBISWorld*, October 2023, https://my-ibisworld-com.ezproxy.babson.edu/us/en/industry/51821/about

[3] "Nvidia is not the only firm cashing in on the AI gold rush," *Economist*, May 29, 2023, www.economist.com/business/2023/05/29/nvidia-is-not-the-only-firm-cashing-in-on-the-ai-gold-rush

[4] Terry Faber, "Data Processing & Hosting Services in the US," *IBISWorld*, Ibid.

to differentiate themselves by providing superior solutions to specific functional or industry challenges. At the same time, data centers and cloud services providers built offshore facilities to tap into lower labor costs which they passed on to customers in the form of lower prices.[5] Mitigating the competition was the rapid growth potential of the cloud market. In November 2023, Gartner forecast generative AI applications would unleash 20.4% growth in the global cloud market, to revenues of about $679 billion in 2024.[6] In 2023, IDC forecast AI cloud revenues would grow at a 49% compound annual rate to $62 billion by 2027, with AI growing from 6% to 10% of total cloud spending between 2023 and 2027.[7] Supporting the industry's growth was a significant untapped opportunity. In October 2023, 90% of global information technology spending still took place on companies' premises, according to Amazon CEO Andy Jassy.[8] Another force dampening rivalry was a wave of acquisitions. Specifically, leading data centers and cloud services providers eliminated rivals by acquiring data centers

---

[5] Terry Faber, "Data Processing & Hosting Services in the US," *IBISWorld*, Ibid.

[6] Isabelle Bousquette and Belle Lin, "Companies Tried to Spend Less on Cloud. Then AI Showed Up.," *Wall Street Journal*, November 15, 2023, www.wsj.com/articles/companies-tried-to-spend-less-on-cloud-then-ai-showed-up-1bb6344e

[7] Reinhardt Krause, "AI Stocks: Tech Giants, Cloud Titans, Chipmakers Battle For An Edge," *Investor's Business Daily*, November 18, 2023, www.investors.com/news/technology/artificial-intelligence-stocks/

[8] Stuart Lauchlan, "AWS revenue growth stabilizes as generative AI opportunities offer 'tens of billions of dollars' of new business," *Diginomica*, October 27, 2023, https://diginomica.com/aws-revenue-growth-stabilizes-generative-ai-opportunities-offer-tens-billions-dollars-new-business

formerly owned by Fortune 500 companies. In 2018,
such companies reduced their costs and improved
their operations by letting Equinix, AWS, Google,
or others acquire and manage their computing
operations.[9] Data centers and hyperscalers both
cooperated and competed with each other. As demand
for digital services soared during the pandemic,
hyperscalers added 111 new data centers between 2019
and 2020, said John Dinsdale, Chief Analyst at Synergy
Research Group. Hyperscalers only built a fraction of
their new data centers, leasing 70% of them from the
likes of Equinix and Digital Realty or the hyperscalers'
partners.[10]

- **Bargaining power of buyers: Moderate.** Buyers of
  data center services had less bargaining power than
  did cloud services customers. While cloud services
  providers normally enabled customers to increase
  or decrease their purchases each month, data center
  hosts negotiated longer-term contracts, thus locking
  in their customers contractually. Such contracts
  boosted data center cash flow predictability. However,
  the greater bargaining power implicit in subscription
  models encouraged many enterprises to shift from
  data centers to cloud services.[11] At the same time, large

---

[9] "How to Win In a World Dominated By AWS and Equinix," *Datacenters*,
June 14, 2018, www.datacenters.com/news/how-to-win-in-a-world-dominated-by-aws-and-equinix

[10] Mark Haranas, "AWS, Google, Microsoft Are Taking Over The Data Center
Market," *CRN*, January 27, 2021, www.crn.com/news/data-center/aws-google-microsoft-are-taking-over-the-data-center

[11] Terry Faber, "Data Processing & Hosting Services in the US," *IBISWorld*, Ibid.

businesses negotiated significant discounts with cloud services providers in exchange for multi-year contracts, pressuring buyers to monitor their usage to avoid paying for above-contract cloud consumption. For example, in 2019 Airbnb negotiated a contract with a cloud services provider, possibly AWS, to spend at least $1.2 billion between 2019 and 2027. By extending the contract term, Airbnb achieved nearly $64 million in 2020 savings.[12]

- **Bargaining power of suppliers: Low to Moderate.** Some suppliers had more power than others did. While server hardware suppliers compete on price, makers of GPUs for generative AI applications charge high prices for a resource in scarce supply relative to demand. Some hyperscalers began developing their own GPUs in an effort to mitigate GPUs' bargaining power.[13] Due to soaring demand for computing services resulting from generative AI, power prices for Northern Virginia data centers rose 7.7% in the first quarter of 2023, according to Pat Lynch, executive managing director of CBRE's data center business.[14]

- **Threat of substitutes: Low.** The cloud services industry offered a compelling value to companies compared to building and operating their own computing systems. Moreover, given the enormous costs of training and

---

[12] Isabelle Bousquette and Belle Lin, "Companies Tried to Spend Less on Cloud. Then AI Showed Up," *Wall Street Journal*, Ibid.

[13] Terry Faber, "Data Processing & Hosting Services in the US," *IBISWorld,* Ibid.

[14] Angus Loten, "Rising Data Center Costs Linked to AI Demands," *Wall Street Journal*, July 13, 2023, `www.wsj.com/articles/rising-data-center-costs-linked-to-ai-demands-fc6adc0e`

operating generative AI chatbots, companies were much better off outsourcing such computing tasks to cloud services providers.[15]

Generative AI Cloud Platform Industry Participants

Cloud services providers were popular places to host AI-powered chatbots. However, given the high capital costs of building LLMs, people seeking to deploy generative AI for more specific applications might ultimately seek to build and operate small language models on their laptops. In 2024, cloud services providers, including subsidiaries of public companies, data center operators, as well as networking, database, application performance management, and workflow management suppliers, were essential to delivering AI-powered chatbots to customers.

Generative AI Cloud Services Provider Subsidiaries of Public Companies

AWS, Azure, and Google Cloud are among the leading providers of generative AI cloud services. Some of these cloud services providers monetized generative AI more effectively than others did. Microsoft, thanks to its large number of loyal productivity software customers, was able to sell ChatGPT subscriptions and other generative AI software. Customers for whom the software created significant business value were willing to pay more for the cloud services required to deliver the generative AI services. AWS and Google, by contrast, lacked the relationships with companies needed to build and sell generative AI services that would

---

[15] Terry Faber, "Data Processing & Hosting Services in the US," *IBISWorld*, Ibid.

boost demand for their cloud services. Below, we examine each company's history in generative AI, describe the firm's generative AI cloud services, and assess the company's investment potential.

Amazon Web Services

Conceived in 2003, AWS created a new industry, enabling companies to rent computing resources and expand or contract their consumption in response to fluctuations in demand. By 2023, AWS's relatively late entry into generative AI raised questions about whether AWS would monetize generative AI. In 2003, a team of executives met at Amazon CEO Jeff Bezos's house to discuss possible solutions to an operational problem: when seeking to add new features to Amazon's e-commerce platform for selling goods online, information technology professionals spent 70% of their time building its most basic elements – storage and computing systems – which Amazon dubbed "muck." At that 2003 meeting, Amazon executives took steps to minimize the muck. They decided Amazon should build what Adam Selipsky, since 2021 the CEO of AWS, deemed a "shared layer of infrastructure services" to perform "general capabilities like storage, compute capabilities, [and] databases." Three years later, through a team led by Amazon CEO Andy Jassy, AWS launched its first such services: Simple Storage Service (S3) and Elastic Compute Cloud (EC2). AWS enabled companies to bypass the capital-intensive acquisition and operation of computer hardware and software by renting those resources from AWS on a monthly basis. AWS was immediately popular, yet rivals did not immediately respond.[16] By 2023, AWS, with 32% market share, continued to lead the cloud services industry the company pioneered.[17]

---

[16] Geoff Colvin, "How Amazon grew an awkward side project into AWS, a behemoth that's now 4 times bigger than its original shopping business," *Fortune*, November 30, 2022, https://fortune.com/longform/amazon-web-services-ceo-adam-selipsky-cloud-computing/

[17] John Dinsdale. "AI Helps to Stabilize Quarterly Cloud Market Growth Rate; Microsoft Market Share Nudges Up Again," *Synergy Research*, October 26, 2023, www.srgresearch.com/articles/ai-helps-to-stabilize-quarterly-cloud-market-growth-rate-microsoft-market-share-nudges-up-again

AWS, which entered the competition for Generative AI services late, saw its share of the cloud services market fall significantly between 2018 and 2023. More specifically, AWS's share of the cloud market declined from 42% to 32% during those five years as Microsoft's share increased from 15% to 22%.[18] In 2023, Amazon began announcing partnerships, investments, and products related to generative AI. In March 2023, months after Microsoft's November 2022 launch of ChatGPT, AWS announced a partnership with Nvidia in which the cloud giant would purchase Nvidia H100 GPU chips to operate an AWS EC2 service for "training LLMs and developing Generative AI applications." Companies using EC2 for generative AI included Anthropic, Cohere, Hugging Face, Pinterest, and Stability AI.[19] In June 2023, Amazon announced a $100 million fund aimed at teaching companies how to use generative AI.[20] The following month, Jassy noted AWS had developed its own AI-specific chips – called Inferentia and Trainium – to streamline the operation of AI language models in the cloud. He also said he intends to deploy AI throughout Amazon to improve "virtually every customer experience."[21] In September, AWS announced the general release of Amazon Bedrock, a set of tools

---

[18] John Dinsdale. "AI Helps to Stabilize Quarterly Cloud Market Growth Rate; Microsoft Market Share Nudges Up Again," *Synergy Research*, October 26, 2023, Ibid.

[19] "AWS and NVIDIA Collaborate on Next-Generation Infrastructure for Training Large Machine Learning Models and Building Generative AI Applications," *NvidiaNews*, March 21, 2023, https://nvidianews.nvidia.com/news/aws-and-nvidia-collaborate-on-next-generation-infrastructure-for-training-large-machine-learning-models-and-building-generative-ai-applications

[20] Jordan Novet, "AWS is investing $100 million in generative A.I. center in race to keep up with Microsoft and Google," *CNBC*, June 22, 2023, www.cnbc.com/2023/06/22/aws-invests-100-million-in-generative-ai-as-it-sees-a-long-race-ahead.html

[21] Annie Palmer, "Amazon CEO explains how the company will compete against Microsoft, Google in A.I. race," *CNBC*, July 6, 2023, www.cnbc.com/2023/07/06/amazon-ceo-explains-how-the-company-will-compete-in-ai-race-.html

aimed at helping companies develop their own chatbots and image-generation services.[22] That month, Amazon inked a deal to invest up to $4 billion in Anthropic.[23]

In 2023, AWS's Generative AI services served the same customers as AWS's original services – S3 and EC2 – did. Specifically, AWS's Generative AI services aimed to help developers train and operate LLMs. In addition to the Amazon-designed semiconductors, AWS offered two other elements of its generative AI stack: the Bedrock tools for helping companies build their own chatbots and an application layer providing services such as Code Whisperer that turned natural language prompts into code. Max Peterson, AWS VP for Worldwide Public Sector, described Code Whisperer as an AI "easy button."[24]

In 2023, AWS's generative AI tools for developers and end users included the following:

- **Amazon SageMaker**. Through a collaboration with Hugging Face, SageMaker enabled engineers to deploy and fine-tune pre-trained natural language processing models.

- **Amazon Bedrock**, a foundation model service, supported Cohere's Command model for text generation and its Embed model for text understanding and translation tasks. Bedrock also supported FMs from Anthropic, AI21 Labs, and Stability AI.

---

[22] Maria Diaz, "4 ways Amazon Bedrock can help businesses use generative AI tools," *ZDnet*, September 29, 2023, www.zdnet.com/article/4-ways-amazon-bedrock-can-help-businesses-use-generative-ai-tools/

[23] Ryan Deffenbaugh, "Is Amazon Stock A Buy As E-Commerce Giant Links-Up With Meta, Snap?," *Investor's Business Daily*, November 20, 2023, www.investors.com/news/technology/is-amazon-stock-buy-now-amzn/

[24] Ryan Heath, "Amazon Web Services CEO Adam Selipsky spreads his AI bets," *Axios*, September 15, 2023, www.axios.com/2023/09/15/aws-ceo-adam-selipsky-generative-ai-cloud

- **Amazon Titan** enabled users to summarize and generate text to extract information. Companies used Titan Text to automate the creation of customer quotes and other documentation. Titan Embeddings converted text inputs into numerical representations known as embeddings that enabled machines to understand relationships among text, images, audio, and video in an ML-friendly format, "making it possible to generate contextually relevant responses."

- **Amazon QuickSight** enabled organizations to query and display data more efficiently to provide insights for decision making through natural language prompts.

- **AWS HealthScribe** generated clinical notes for medical professionals by analyzing patient–clinician conversations. By integrating with Bedrock, AWS HealthScribe enabled medical professionals to automate transcription processes and generate clinical notes while securing patient data privacy.[25]

- **Amazon Q.** In November 2023, Amazon announced an artificial intelligence assistant of its own: Amazon Q. Unlike consumer-focused chatbots, such as ChatGPT, Amazon Q aimed to help employees with daily tasks, such as summarizing strategy documents, filling out internal support tickets, and answering questions about company policy.[26]

---

[25] "The Democratization of Generative AI on AWS," *Provectus*, October 24, 2023, https://provectus.com/blog/the-democratization-of-generative-ai-on-aws/
[26] Karen Weise, "Amazon Introduces Q, an A.I. Chatbot for Companies," *New York Times*, November 29, 2023, www.nytimes.com/2023/11/28/technology/amazon-ai-chatbot-q.html

By February 2024, Amazon executives said AI revenues were "accelerating rapidly" as customers expressed interest in developing AI tools. Jassy said that every consumer business at Amazon was developing multiple generative AI applications. One such AI tool, launched in February 2024, was Rufus, a new shopping assistant trained on Amazon's product catalog that "can answer customer questions and recommend products on the Amazon mobile app." The e-commerce giant said AWS revenues could increase by "tens of billions of dollars" as companies deployed AI in their operations. That's because companies used cloud services to train and run LLMs, prompting Amazon to boost 2024 capital expenditures, in large part due to the expansion of its AI operation.[27]

AWS's generative AI services supplied no measurable boost to Amazon's investment potential. In September 2023, AWS's revenue growth was a relatively slow 12%, after several quarters of decline. This result fell short of analysts' expectations as customers looked for ways to cut back on paying for AWS services.[28] In 2023's fourth quarter, AWS revenue increased 13%, a rate far below the "30% and 26% growth rates put up by Microsoft Azure and Google Cloud, respectively."[29] Nevertheless, Jassy was bullish. He told investors generative AI would drive "tens of billions of dollars of revenue for AWS over the next several years." Since companies wanted to train their LLMs on their own data, AWS, where their data resided, gave Amazon an advantage. Amazon claimed companies such as Adidas, Booking.com, Bridgewater, Clariant, GoDaddy, LexisNexis, Merck, Royal Philips, and United Airlines were using AWS to train and operate their

---

[27] Hamza Shaban, "Amazon stock climbs on revenue gains and ads growth," *Yahoo! Finance*, February 2, 2024, https://finance.yahoo.com/news/amazon-stock-climbs-on-revenue-gains-and-ads-growth-114419209.html

[28] Paul Kunert, "AWS CEO talks up AI to focus minds of Wall Street types," *The Register*, October 27, 2023, www.theregister.com/2023/10/27/aws_q3_ai/

[29] Larry Dignan, "AWS Q4 revenue growth 13% as Amazon's results shine," *Constellation Research*, February 1, 2024, www.constellationr.com/blog-news/insights/aws-q4-revenue-growth-13-amazons-results-shine

generative AI applications.[30] After rising 71% in 2023 through November 23, far more than the 37% increase in the NASDAQ during that period, Amazon stock had done well. However, it remained unclear whether Amazon would ultimately realize a significant increase in its revenue growth by realizing Jassy's hope for "tens of billions of dollars" in new revenue from generative AI.

Microsoft Azure

In Chapter 5, we examined Microsoft's history with generative AI. Since Microsoft Azure, the software giant's cloud service, trained and operated ChatGPT, the story behind Microsoft's entry into the cloud services industry sheds light into how Azure compares to AWS. The service's unique difference? Azure was a blend of computing services (dubbed infrastructure as a service), competing with the likes of AWS's S3 and EC2, tools for developers (platform as a service) and consumer software such as Word (software as a service). In 2006, AWS inspired Microsoft to build a cloud service. Bill Gates oversaw a nascent cloud services unit aiming to make a radical change at Microsoft from packaged to web-delivered software. Initially, a small team attempted to build tools for Microsoft engineers. Gates reviewed their work and announced the effort publicly, to deliver software to consumers under the banner of Windows Azure, which launched in 2010. In 2011, Microsoft replaced Bob Muglia, a software executive, with Nadella who helped lead the team that made Microsoft's software as a service much more consumer-friendly. Nadella launched a new version of Azure in 2013 that included infrastructure services that competed with AWS as well as delivering software as a service. A month after taking over as CEO from Steve Ballmer in 2014, Nadella changed the

---

[30] Stuart Lauchlan, "AWS revenue growth stabilizes as generative AI opportunities offer 'tens of billions of dollars' of new business," *Diginomica*, October 27, 2023, Ibid.

name of the service from Windows Azure to Microsoft Azure, signaling the end of Microsoft's focus on pushing its own Windows products and a shift to collaboration with others to win and keep customers.[31]

Microsoft's first entry into supplying AI software through Azure began in 2018, years before ChatGPT's late 2022 launch. Microsoft began offering so-called intelligent cloud services in 2018 based in machine learning and AI, albeit not the generative sort. The software giant added language understanding, speech, vision, search, and translation to Azure's AI services. Microsoft also provided Azure ML Studio, a cloud platform for training and deploying ML models. Microsoft's Azure ML Services supported deep learning models, NVIDIA GPUs, and "a drag and drop designer for training neural networks," among other AI services.[32] As we described in Chapter 5, Gates first met OpenAI in 2016. After recovering from significant missteps, the software giant launched its ChatGPT, the chatbot trained on and operated from Microsoft Azure. Key questions eluded an answer: How much revenue did Microsoft Azure generate? How much of that revenue came from infrastructure services, which accounted for the bulk of AWS's business? In 2023, Nadella revealed the answer: Microsoft's 2022 infrastructure revenue totaled $34 billion.[33] Microsoft Azure revenue grew 26% in Microsoft's fiscal 2023 to an estimated $43 billion, applying that growth rate to the 2022 revenue amount. In July 2023,

---

[31] Matt Day, "How Microsoft emerged from the darkness to embrace the cloud," *Seattle Times*, December 12, 2016, www.seattletimes.com/business/technology/how-microsoft-emerged-from-darkness-to-embrace-the-cloud/

[32] Janakiram MSV, "A Look Back At Ten Years Of Microsoft Azure," *Forbes*, February 3, 2020, www.forbes.com/sites/janakirammsv/2020/02/03/a-look-back-at-ten-years-of-microsoft-azure/

[33] Jordan Novet, "The biggest takeaways from Microsoft's courtroom showdown with the FTC over Activision Blizzard," *CNBC*, June 30, 2023, www.cnbc.com/2023/06/30/microsoft-activision-showdown-with-ftc-biggest-takeaways.html

Nadella said Azure represented over 50% of Microsoft's cloud revenue of $110 billion in 2023, possibly making it a $56 billion business in 2023.[34]

In 2023, analysts viewed Microsoft as the leader in generative AI. After a tumultuous November weekend, OpenAI, of which Microsoft owned 49%, went from firing CEO Sam Altman, to letting him lead a new AI unit at Microsoft, to restructuring OpenAI's board and hiring Altman back as CEO. Due to the strength of its relationships with users of application software, its ability to infuse those applications with its ChatGPT technology, its cloud services, and its new AI semiconductors, analysts perceived Microsoft as the leader in the $60 billion market for cloud AI products and services, a market expected to grow at 40% annually for years. Arun Chandrasekaran, distinguished vice president analyst at Gartner, said Microsoft's OpenAI investment and its use of OpenAI models in business applications running on the Azure cloud gave Microsoft a strong market position. In addition, the software giant could "take advantage of [its] incumbency to bake AI into existing workflows and applications," Chandrasekaran said. Such AI assistants, or Copilots, would be used by seven million US knowledge workers, predicted Forrester Research. As Nadella told Ignite conference attendees in November 2023, "Everyone will have a copilot for everything you do." Microsoft also announced specialized AI chips, including Azure Maia to support LLMs and GitHub Copilot and Azure Cobalt CPUs to process common workloads more efficiently. Nadella said Microsoft had added more than 18,000 customers for its Azure OpenAI services since January 2023.[35]

---

[34] Mike Wheatley, "Microsoft's stock falls as demand for cloud services cools," *SiliconAngle*, July 25, 2023, https://siliconangle.com/2023/07/25/microsofts-stock-falls-demand-cloud-services-cools/

[35] Paul Gillin, "Who will win the battle for AI in the cloud? Maybe everyone," *SiliconAngle*, November 24, 2023, https://siliconangle.com/2023/11/24/will-win-battle-ai-cloud-maybe-everyone/

Microsoft's Ignite 2023 featured other new products and services aimed at securing Microsoft's generative AI leadership through "a comprehensive vision for its end-to-end AI stack." Here are the most significant elements of Microsoft's strategy:

- **Generative AI operating system and applications.** Windows was the PC operating system of the 1980s and 1990s and Microsoft Office its primary applications. In the generative AI era, Azure is the operating system and Copilots – for the Bing search engine, Microsoft 365, the Windows operating system, and the Edge browser – are the applications.[36]

- **New chips include Azure Maia, Azure Cobalt, and Azure Boost.** Through its acquisition of Fungible, Microsoft gained access to a new kind of chip – called a Data Processing Unit – that offloads functions such as network and storage management and security from the CPU. Thus, Azure Boost aimed to process workloads more efficiently.[37]

- **LLMs beyond OpenAI.** Microsoft invested in training its own foundation models to complement its Azure OpenAI and Azure ML models. For example, Microsoft's Phi-1-5 and Phi-2, with 1.5 billion and 2.7 billion parameters, respectively, were much smaller than Meta's Llama 2, which ranged from seven billion to 70 billion parameters. These SLMs could power

[36] Janakiram MSV, "Microsoft's AI Transformation: From Software Giant To AI Powerhouse," *Forbes*, November 19, 2023, www.forbes.com/sites/janakirammsv/2023/11/19/microsofts-ai-transformation-from-software-giant-to-ai-powerhouse/?sh=603a3dd332b1

[37] Janakiram MSV, "Microsoft's AI Transformation: From Software Giant To AI Powerhouse," *Forbes*, November 19, 2023, Ibid.

Copilots more efficiently than LLMs. Microsoft also developed Florence, a foundation model that enabled users to understand images, video, and language for building computer vision applications.[38]

- **Microsoft Graph and Fabric.** To manage data for pre-training and fine-tuning foundation models, Microsoft announced Fabric, a data lakehouse platform for enhancing Azure's machine learning data management. Microsoft also launched Graph, a tool for customizing Copilots to the needs of individual users "by aggregating data from emails, calendar events and team interactions."[39]

Analysts envisioned Microsoft's OpenAI models and Copilots would increase the company's market share and revenues. Chandrasekaran predicted OpenAI models would encourage potential companies to try Azure for the first time to take advantage of "Open AI models." Ensono Cloud Evangelist Gordon McKenna said estimates of a mere one-percentage-point increase in Azure's market share were understated. As McKenna said, "I think a lot of the net new business is coming to Microsoft and that will accelerate with copilots." Gregg Hill, co-founder of Parkway Venture Capital, said Microsoft's decades-long relationships with large enterprise IT departments would give the software giant a "significant and durable first mover advantage." Finally, Copilots could seed "hundreds of millions of desktops," create opportunities to sell more to enterprise application customers, and be popular with customers in the $250 billion global video game market.[40]

---

[38] Janakiram MSV, "Microsoft's AI Transformation: From Software Giant To AI Powerhouse," *Forbes*, November 19, 2023, Ibid.

[39] Janakiram MSV, "Microsoft's AI Transformation: From Software Giant To AI Powerhouse," *Forbes*, November 19, 2023, Ibid.

[40] Paul Gillin, "Who will win the battle for AI in the cloud? Maybe everyone," *SiliconAngle*, Ibid.

In 2023, the tight linkages between Microsoft's infrastructure, platform, and software cloud services increased the odds favoring a rise in Microsoft's stock price as the company satisfied the rapidly growing demand for generative AI products and services. With investors hungry for evidence of tech companies' ability to boost revenue growth by satisfying demand for generative AI, Microsoft took the lead over one such rival, Alphabet. After the two tech giants reported third quarter results in October 2023, Microsoft stock rose 6% while Alphabet shares eased 7% in after-hours trading. The divergence in their post-earnings stock price changes was due to investors' happiness with Azure's expectations-beating revenue growth in contrast to Alphabet's disappointing increase in its cloud revenue. Microsoft prevailed in cloud services due to a 65% increase since July 2023 in the software giant's OpenAI customer count, to 18,000 resulting from Azure's higher processing capacity resulting from more GPUs, and Generative AI's 3% contribution to the software giant's Azure revenue, a full percentage point more than Microsoft CFO Amy Hood had anticipated. Not all the news was good. Microsoft did not specify the revenue lift from the company's 365 Copilot AI add-on for existing productivity software subscriptions at a $30 per person per month Copilot fee. Hood said Copilot's revenue would "grow gradually over time."[41]

Generative AI appeared to be providing Microsoft an advantage over its cloud rivals. Third quarter results were in for most mega-cap tech companies after a big week for tech earnings. Microsoft reported growth of 29% at Azure, faster than Google Cloud's 22% growth and more than double AWS's 12% growth. Analysts guessed Microsoft was gaining market share because companies wanted to run their artificial intelligence models on Azure. In an October client note, Bernstein Research analysts led by Mark Moerdler wrote that Microsoft "has taken the AI mantle from

---

[41] Peter Cohan, "Microsoft Leads Alphabet In The Race To Monetize Generative AI," *Forbes,* October 25, 2023, www.forbes.com/sites/petercohan/2023/10/25/microsoft-leads-alphabet-in-the-race-to-monetize-generative-ai/

Google." With the company's capital expenditures rising to $11.2 billion from $10.7 billion in the prior quarter, Azure had the potential to "become a bigger and more important hyperscale provider than AWS." Meanwhile, Amazon executives mentioned the term "optimization" some 20 times during their conference call with analysts following AWS's relatively weak growth, implying many of the company's customers reduced their spending on Amazon's cloud service.[42] In 2023, Microsoft's comprehensive strategy for maintaining its leadership in the fast-growing market for generative AI products and services suggested the software giant would be able to exceed investors' expectations. Microsoft strategy was also fraught with potential risks, including the following:

- Demand for generative AI products could slow down.

- Rivals could exceed Microsoft's capabilities.

- Microsoft's dependence on OpenAI could backfire if the startup's pace of innovation slowed down.

- Investors' expectations could rise beyond Microsoft's ability to exceed them.

Google Cloud

Google took – and failed to capitalize on – an early lead in developing generative AI technology. The company's groundbreaking generative AI innovations include

---

[42] Jordan Novet, "Microsoft's AI boost helped cloud business outpace rivals Amazon and Google in latest quarter," *CNBC*, October 27, 2023, www.cnbc.com/2023/10/27/microsoft-azure-outpaced-aws-and-google-cloud-in-latest-quarter.html

- **DeepMind Technologies**, acquired in 2014, enabled Google to build innovative weather forecasting and protein folding applications.[43]

- **TensorFlow** machine learning framework was one of the leading deep learning platforms for image and speech recognition released in 2015.[44]

- **AlphaGo** program beat the world's top Go player in 2017, then considered beyond the scope of machines.[45]

- **Transformer** neural network architecture for language understanding – the foundation for generative AI – published in 2017.[46]

- **Bidirectional Encoder Representations from Transformers,** one of the first LLMs and a standard for natural language processing launched in 2018.[47]

- **Tensor Processing Units.** dedicated AI processing chips first used inside Google in 2015. By November 2023, TPUs were in their fifth generation. Philip Moyer, vice president of Google Cloud's global AI business, said 70% of AI unicorns are running on Google Cloud.

---

[43] Paul Gillin, "Who will win the battle for AI in the cloud? Maybe everyone," *SiliconAngle*, Ibid.

[44] Paul Gillin, "Who will win the battle for AI in the cloud? Maybe everyone," *SiliconAngle*, Ibid.

[45] Paul Gillin, "Who will win the battle for AI in the cloud? Maybe everyone," *SiliconAngle*, Ibid.

[46] Paul Gillin, "Who will win the battle for AI in the cloud? Maybe everyone," *SiliconAngle*, Ibid.

[47] Paul Gillin, "Who will win the battle for AI in the cloud? Maybe everyone," *SiliconAngle*, Ibid.

"These are organizations that work very close to the metal and processor choice is important," Moyer concluded.[48]

- **LaMDA**. Google announced its chatbot – that generated text to engage in complex conversations – in 2021, a year ahead of ChatGPT's launch.[49]

Despite these innovations, Google did not launch its Bard technology for 16 weeks after Microsoft had integrated ChatGPT into its Bing search engine. Despite quality concerns, Google rushed its Bard chatbot to market, resulting in an embarrassing demo that briefly slashed $100 billion from Alphabet's market capitalization.[50] How did Google fail to capitalize on its generative AI innovations? Management failures – between 2016, when Google CEO Sundar Pichai proclaimed the company would be "AI-first," and 2023 – resulted in the search giant's failure to capitalize on its AI innovations. These failures included "scandals around Google's AI ethics research, a major backlash after the launch of a freakishly human-sounding AI called Duplex, and a persistent brain drain of AI talent."[51]

The details of these management failures suggest Google's culture makes it difficult for its talented people to collaborate with customers in a way that results in industry-leading solutions to their most significant unsolved problems.

---

[48] Paul Gillin, "Who will win the battle for AI in the cloud? Maybe everyone," *SiliconAngle*, Ibid.

[49] Richard Nieva, Alex Konrad and Kenrick Cai, "'AI First' To Last: How Google Fell Behind In The AI Boom," *Forbes*, February 8, 2023, www.forbes.com/sites/richardnieva/2023/02/08/google-openai-chatgpt-microsoft-bing-ai/

[50] Paul Gillin, "Who will win the battle for AI in the cloud? Maybe everyone," *SiliconAngle*, Ibid.

[51] Richard Nieva, Alex Konrad and Kenrick Cai, "'AI First' To Last: How Google Fell Behind In The AI Boom," *Forbes*, February 8, 2023, Ibid.

- **AI ethics scandals.** Controversies in Google's AI division made the company more reluctant to take risks. In 2018, Google drew employee anger by signing on to help the Pentagon use AI to improve drone strikes, to which the company reacted by not renewing the contract. In 2019, Google received criticism when the public learned the contractors trained the company's facial recognition software on unhoused people with "darker" skin. In 2020, Google took a "reputational hit" after "infuriating the research community" by firing "Timnit Gebru and Margaret Mitchell, the company's Ethical AI leads, after they had co-authored a paper criticizing biases in AI technology the company used in its search engine."[52]

- **Duplex backlash.** In 2018, Pichai unveiled Duplex, a human-sounding AI service that booked restaurant reservations for its users. Duplex mimicked human verbal ticks, took long pauses, and modulated its voice. Google failed to disclose Duplex was a robot, prompting *The New York Times* to call it "somewhat creepy" and sociologist Zeynep Tufecki to dub Duplex "horrifying." Two anonymous former Google managers "cited the Duplex episode as one of many factors that contributed to an environment in which Google was slow to ship AI products."[53]

---

[52] Richard Nieva, Alex Konrad and Kenrick Cai, "'AI First' To Last: How Google Fell Behind In The AI Boom," *Forbes*, February 8, 2023, Ibid.

[53] Richard Nieva, Alex Konrad and Kenrick Cai, "'AI First' To Last: How Google Fell Behind In The AI Boom," *Forbes*, February 8, 2023, Ibid.

- **AI talent drain.** All but one of the eight co-authors of Google's seminal paper on Transformers have left. Six started their own companies, and one joined OpenAI. As we discussed in Chapter 5, one co-author, Aidan Gomez, left to become CEO of AI rival Cohere. Gomez said Google's "structure does not support [product innovation]. And so you have to go build it yourself." Wesley Chan, who founded Google Analytics and left to co-found FPV Ventures, said Google's "code red," which Pichai issued after ChatGPT's success, meant "Our guys got too lazy." Emad Mostaque, CEO of Stability AI, said of ChatGPT's success, "It was [Google's] institutional inertia and the fear of cannibalizing their core business that stopped them [from competing in Generative AI]. Now this [inertia] is being shaken up a bit."[54]

In 2023, Google had the potential to learn from its management mistakes and win generative AI share. Its success would depend on how much customers valued its strategy of integrating AI across compute, storage, and applications and of providing a broad choice of foundation models. Moyer said Google, with "100 foundation models" on its platform, believes "in using the right model for the right job." These models included voice, coding, medicine, cybersecurity, and most commercial and open source LLMs. Google supplied customers with a variety of GPU and TPU chips, management tools, and an adapter layer to prevent customer data from inadvertently training LLMs. Through Duet AI, Google infused generative AI into its productivity applications. As Moyer said, "If you're

---

[54] Richard Nieva, Alex Konrad and Kenrick Cai, "'AI First' To Last: How Google Fell Behind In The AI Boom," *Forbes*, February 8, 2023, Ibid.

a software developer, we can make recommendations for how to detect security vulnerabilities in your code." Moreover, the company had access to consumers through its Chrome browser and Android mobile platform.[55]

Following a September 2023 developer conference, two Google Cloud generative AI services stood out from the rest:

- **Google Cloud positioned itself to help developers train, deploy, and fine-tune generative AI models.** Google built on its internally developed LLMs to tailor modes to the specific customer requirements. For example, Google adjusted its PaLM 2 model to deliver LLMs for medical and security domains through, respectively, Med-PaLM 2 and Sec-PaLM 2. Similarly, Codey, Google's foundation model for code completion, provided quality improvements of as much as 25% in major coding languages. Moreover, Google Cloud's Vertex AI Model Garden hosted popular open source models, such as Meta's Llama 2, Code Llama, and TII's Falcon. Google Cloud also supported third-party models such as Anthropic's Claude2 and Databricks's Dolly V2. Finally, Google Cloud enabled developers to build Google Search-quality applications (through Vertex AI Search) and natural language chatbots and voicebots (through Vertex AI Conversation). Through these tools, developers could "tell AI agents to book appointments or make purchases."[56]

---

[55] Paul Gillin, "Who will win the battle for AI in the cloud? Maybe everyone," *SiliconAngle*, Ibid.

[56] Janakiram MSV, "How Google Cloud Is Leveraging Generative AI To Outsmart Competition," *Forbes*, September 4, 2023, www.forbes.com/sites/janakirammsv/2023/09/04/how-google-cloud-is-leveraging-generative-ai-to-outsmart-competition/

- **Duet AI, Google's AI assistant, was enhancing IT professionals' productivity.** For example, Duet AI enabled developers to use natural language prompts to design, create, and publish application-programming interfaces. Duet AI helped cloud operations professionals to automate operational deployments, correct application configurations, understand and debug errors, and create more secure applications. Finally, Duet AI made security professionals more productive by analyzing threat information, enabling natural language search queries, suggesting next steps, and solving problems.[57]

In 2023, Google Cloud contributed a modest amount to the company's revenue and in response to analyst questions during the company's third quarter 2023 earnings, Pichai responded, "It's still early days" in reply to those questions about when the search giant would generate significant revenue from its investment in generative AI. To be fair, Google's third quarter revenue increased 22% to $8.41 billion, $230 million short of Wall Street estimates. While Google's clients were "reeling in their spending," CFO Ruth Porat told investors cloud growth "remained strong across geographies, industries and products." One analyst expressed hopes that Alphabet's cloud unit would grow faster and more profitably. Portfolio Wealth Advisors Chief Investment Officer Lee Munson said, "If you want this stock to keep going higher, you've got to have cloud become more profitable. It's a third-rate cloud platform. We need to see it make money."[58]

---

[57] Janakiram MSV, "How Google Cloud Is Leveraging Generative AI To Outsmart Competition," *Forbes*, September 4, 2023, Ibid.

[58] Peter Cohan, "Microsoft Leads Alphabet In The Race To Monetize Generative AI," *Forbes*, October 25, 2023, Ibid.

Alphabet, whose shares fell 7% following its third quarter report, responded to investor pressure by saying the company would supply the best generative AI technology. As Pichai told investors, "We'll do everything that is needed to make sure we have the leading AI models and infrastructure in the world, bar none, and will continue driving efficiencies from there." A significant Google AI experiment was Search Generative Experience (SGE), "which lets users see what a generative AI experience would look like when searching for products." Analysts asked Pichai about SGE. Lloyd Walmsley of Deutsche Bank said, "As we just think about the rollout of SGE across a user base. Like, how far along is that? How do you balance the product rollout and consumer uptake versus monetization in that transition?" *CNBC* wrote. Alphabet's response was relatively vague. "On the first part of our SG, we are still very early days in terms of how much we have rolled it out. But we have definitely gotten it out to enough people and both geographically across user segments and enough to know that the product is working well," Pichai responded.[59]

Despite the vagueness, Alphabet revealed some room for hope of monetization in two areas:

- **YouTube.** For YouTube advertisers, AI helped businesses find "their ideal audience for the lowest possible price," according to Alphabet's Chief Business Officer Philipp Schindler. "Early tests are delivering 54% more reach at 42% lower cost," helping "brands like Samsung and Toyota," Schindler added.[60]

---

[59] Peter Cohan, "Microsoft Leads Alphabet In The Race To Monetize Generative AI," *Forbes*, October 25, 2023, Ibid.

[60] Peter Cohan, "Microsoft Leads Alphabet In The Race To Monetize Generative AI," *Forbes*, October 25, 2023, Ibid.

- **Performance Max.** This service enabled advertisers to access their Google Ads inventory from a single campaign. "Those using it achieve like an average over 18% more conversions at a similar cost per action," according to Pichai, who added that 80% of Alphabet advertisers already use at least one AI-powered search feature.[61]

If Alphabet, which downplayed hopes for near-term generative AI revenue, exceeded those lower expectations, the company's investment value could increase in the medium term. Ultimately, a significant rise in Alphabet's value would depend on accelerating the company's revenue growth through a cultural shift along the lines of what Nadella achieved at Microsoft after taking over from Ballmer in 2014.

Publicly Traded Generative AI Data Centers

Data centers – buildings full of computing equipment rented out to businesses – had been around far longer than hyperscalers. Data centers both competed and cooperated with hyperscalers. Hyperscalers cooperated by leasing some data center space, yet they also competed by building their own data centers. Several data centers were publicly traded companies, including CyrusOne, Digital Realty Trust, Equinix, and Iron Mountain.[62] Many of these companies were real estate investment trusts (REITs), investment trusts that acquired buildings housing computing equipment and leased them back. REITs delivered "beneficial tax status

---

[61] Peter Cohan, "Microsoft Leads Alphabet In The Race To Monetize Generative AI," *Forbes*, October 25, 2023, Ibid.

[62] "Colocation Providers: Equinix Alternatives," *Gartner Peer Insights*, accessed December 2, 2023, www.gartner.com/reviews/market/colocation-providers/vendor/equinix/alternatives

and greater access to capital for growth."[63] By 2023, demand for generative AI was accelerating data center growth – Equinix was a leader in satisfying this demand. Below, we examine Equnix's history in generative AI, describe the firm's generative AI data center services, and assess the company's investment potential.

Equinix

Between 1998 and 2023, Equinix created the data center industry and sustained its industry leadership, which included serving the growing demand for generative AI. Two facilities managers from Digital Equipment Corp., Jay Adelson and Al Avery, co-founded Equinix by developing some of the first data centers in the United States. Equinix initially served the telecommunications industry, satisfying demand for "central connection points to exchange traffic. All those carriers fibered into these very first data centers, and that's what got the game started. They exchanged traffic [in these centers], and that's what helped to scale the internet in the United States," explained former Equinix CEO, Steve Smith.[64] By November 2023, abetted by 14 acquisitions totaling $10.5 billion,[65] Equinix operated data center facilities in 70 metropolitan areas across 32 countries, and collaborated with "more than 2,000 networks and over 3,000 cloud and

---

[63] Dan Swinhoe, "What is a data center REIT?," *Data Center Dynamics*, February 5, 2021, www.datacenterdynamics.com/en/analysis/what-data-center-reit/#:~:text=A%20number%20of%20companies%20in,hopefully%20reduce%20their%20overall%20Capex

[64] Anna Robaton, "Equinix: A Giant Behind the Scenes of the Digital Age," *REIT Magazine*, July 24, 2017, www.reit.com/news/reit-magazine/july-august-2017/equinix-giant-behind-scenes-digital-age

[65] "Acquisitions by Equinix," *Tracxn*, October 18, 2023, https://tracxn.com/d/acquisitions/acquisitions-by-equinix/__P5P-ARZm7UJx-gPcs1jxZdDELwz cAWzzCWWcCU1Qe-E#:~:text=Equinix%20has%20made%2014%20acquisitions, Enterprise%20Tech%20%2D%20US%20and%20others

IT companies."[66] Equinix, with nearly $7.3 billion in 2022 revenue and a November 2023 market capitalization of $75 billion,[67] generated revenue by renting server space to "the world's largest networks, cloud computing platforms and business enterprises." The company also operated co-location centers with several tenants who leased space for their equipment in "flexible increments" which lowered the costs associated with companies building and maintaining their own data centers. Tenants paid for space, power, and "interconnections – either one-to-one or one-to-many connections."[68]

Equinix began using AI in 2018 to increase sales productivity, and by 2023, the company was adapting its data center architecture to help clients improve their operations through generative AI. Equinix began using AI in 2018 to estimate prospective customers' likelihood of buying from the company, which added millions of dollars to the data center provider's revenue. In 2021, Equinix used AI to pick the partners most likely to increase sales globally and within specific regions. Equinix's partner prospecting platform used natural language processing to extract relevant excerpts from request for proposal documents and joined them with relevance scores for each sales opportunity, according to Ted Dangson, senior director of applied AI strategy and analytics at Equinix. "This allows Equinix to focus its investments and resources on the partners best suited for joint sales and resell activities," Dangson said.[69] By November 2023, Equinix

[66] "Equinix Named a Leader in 2023 IDC MarketScape Report for Worldwide Datacenter Services," *PR Newswire*, November 1, 2023, www.equinix.com/newsroom/press-releases/2023/11/equinix-named-a-leader-in-2023-idc-marketscape-report-for-worldwide-datacenter-services

[67] "Equinix," *Wall Street Journal*, accessed November 28, 2023, www.wsj.com/market-data/quotes/EQIX/financials/annual/income-statement

[68] Anna Robaton, "Equinix: A Giant Behind the Scenes of the Digital Age," *REIT Magazine*, July 24, 2017, Ibid.

[69] "Equinix goes partner prospecting with AI," *CIO*, August 24, 2023, www.cio.com/article/650140/equinix-goes-partner-prospecting-with-ai.html

was responding quickly to satisfy the specific computing requirements of companies building generative AI applications. Generative AI required unique computing workloads that demanded different technology architectures. More specifically, Equinix wanted to satisfy the high power density requirements of AI GPU chipsets. While enterprises needed the high-density equipment found in hyperscale data centers, located in lower-cost regions, to train generative AI models, they also needed data centers to be physically close to where people would use the trained models in order to minimize latency – the time lag for responding to a user prompt. For such applications, Equinix saw so-called edge data centers located near users as the right solution.[70]

Equinix generated meaningful revenue from enterprises deploying generative AI in the third quarter of 2023. As CEO Charles Meyers told investors, "On the AI front, we continue to cultivate and win significant opportunities across our existing customer base and with AI-specific prospects along three key vectors."[71]

These include the following:

- **Retail business.** Meyers told investors Equinix had nearly 40% market share of "the on-ramps to the major cloud service providers, key players in the AI ecosystem." Specifically, Meyers said in the third quarter Equinix signed up Core Wheat, a CPU cloud provider of network connectivity across multiple metropolitan areas. Moreover, Meyers said, "Lambda selected Platform Equinix to offer expanded regional connectivity, higher

---

[70] Johan Arts, "How Is Generative AI Changing Data Center Requirements?," *Equinix Blog*, November 8, 2023, https://blog.equinix.com/blog/2023/11/08/how-is-generative-ai-changing-data-center-requirements/

[71] "Equinix, Inc. (NASDAQ:EQIX) Q3 2023 Earnings Call Transcript," *Insider Monkey Transcripts*, October 25, 2023, https://finance.yahoo.com/news/equinix-inc-nasdaq-eqix-q3-141128572.html

networking performance, security and scale for an enterprise-grade GPU cloud, dedicated to large language models and generative AI workloads."[72]

- **xScale portfolio.** This portfolio enabled Equinix to "pursue strategic large-scale AI training deployments with the top hyperscalers and other key AI ecosystem players," Meyers said.[73]

- **Private AI.** Finally, Equinix won new customers in specific industries, including transportation, education, the public sector, and health care, to apply generative AI to solve specific challenges. Meyers said these included "Harrison.ai, a clinician-led healthcare artificial intelligence company that is dedicated to addressing the inequality and capacity limitations in our healthcare system, by developing AI-powered tools in radiology and pathology."[74]

Partnerships with technology providers helped Equinix support client efforts to build generative AI applications. For example, in November 2023, Equinix and Nvidia announced "instant AI infrastructure for enterprise customers," a service to train and empower LLMs to respond to user prompts, according to Lisa Miller, Equinix senior vice president of platform alliances and global channel. Equinix was also exploring ways to enable

---

[72] "Equinix, Inc. (NASDAQ:EQIX) Q3 2023 Earnings Call Transcript," *Insider Monkey Transcripts*, October 25, 2023, Ibid.

[73] "Equinix, Inc. (NASDAQ:EQIX) Q3 2023 Earnings Call Transcript," *Insider Monkey Transcripts*, October 25, 2023, Ibid.

[74] "Equinix, Inc. (NASDAQ:EQIX) Q3 2023 Earnings Call Transcript," *Insider Monkey Transcripts*, October 25, 2023, Ibid.

their data centers to manage the energy-intensive nature of generative AI workloads, through the evaluation of potentially applying liquid cooling to diffuse heat from data centers, Miller explained.[75]

In 2023, generative AI was propelling demand for Equinix's services to a level that exceeded investors' expectations. As long as such rapid growth continued, Equinix's stock had the potential to rise further. In October 2023, Forrester Research Senior Analyst Abhijit Sunil told me Equinix had the potential to benefit from generative AI demand; Equinix's third quarter 2023 growth was strong, driven by "integration of AI into enterprise business strategies" along with profit increases and winning new customers. Meyers said, "While we continue to operate in an environment characterized by customer caution, this caution is balanced by a clear commitment to digital transformation and accelerating interest in AI and a growing reliance on Equinix as a critical partner in designing and implementing hybrid, multi-cloud and data-centric architectures." Equinix was adding to its global data center network, with 56 major projects underway across 39 markets in 23 countries in November 2023. New projects added in the third quarter include "new builds in Madrid, Osaka, Sao Paulo, and Silicon Valley [and a] $42 million investment in its fourth International Business Exchange (IBX) data center in Mumbai."[76]

One analyst expressed optimism about Equinix's potential to benefit from generative AI. As Ben Forster, a Schroders portfolio manager, wrote, "Equinix owns a portfolio of 248 multi-tenant data centres across 32 countries that host 10,000+ companies, with 450,000+ inter-connections

---

[75] O'Ryan Johnson, "Equinix Exec Talks Generative AI, Storage And The Future Of The Data Center, *CRN*, November 13, 2023, www.crn.com/news/data-center/equinix-exec-talks-generative-ai-storage-and-the-future-of-the-data-center/.

[76] Peter Cohan, "2 Stocks That Could Benefit From Generative AI's Energy Demand Growth," *Forbes*, November 10, 2023, www.forbes.com/sites/petercohan/2023/11/10/2-stocks-that-could-benefit-from-generative-ais-energy-demand-growth/

between them. Their services have grown beyond offering physical space, power, cooling, and connectivity to increasingly focusing on network services, growing their competitive advantages. In 2023, Equinix identified a $21 billion addressable market for data centres services to support AI by 2026, based on their current operations and capacity. Whilst they will likely only take a percentage share of this opportunity, it could significantly grow their current revenue of around $8 billion per annum."[77]

Publicly Traded Generative AI Networking Technology Providers

Networking technology companies provided hardware, such as switches and routers, and software to accelerate the flow of data between servers, data storage hardware, and other devices. Many publicly traded companies, including Arista Networks, Cisco Systems, Extreme Networks, and Juniper Networks, competed to supply such networking technology.[78] While many of these providers satisfied the growing demand for generative AI networking technology, Arista was a clear leader. Below, we examine Arista Network's history in generative AI, describe the firm's generative AI networking services, and assess the company's investment potential.

---

[77] Ben Forster, "How AI is set to accelerate demand for data centres," *Schroders*, July 3, 2023, www.schroders.com/en-be/be/professional/insights/how-ai-is-set-to-accelerate-demand-for-data-centres/

[78] "Data Center and Cloud Networking Technology: Arista Networks Alternatives," *Gartner Peer Insights*, accessed December 2, 2023, www.gartner.com/reviews/market/data-center-and-cloud-networking/vendor/arista-center/alternatives

Arista Networks

In 2004, industry luminaries Andy Bechtolsheim, Ken Duda, and David Cheriton co-founded Arista Networks, a Santa Clara, California-based provider of computer networking technology.[79] A decade later, the company went public, and by 2023, Arista had developed networking products to boost the efficiency of hyperscaler and other customers that were training and operating generative AI applications. When Jayshree Ullal joined as CEO in September 2008, Arista had 30 engineers and no revenue. Lehman Brothers, which went bankrupt the month she became CEO, was Arista's client. Arista adapted effectively to that challenge. As Ullal told me in May 2021, "We had built a system for the finance vertical and it helped our other finance customers to survive because we had lower latency—nanoseconds versus milliseconds and a software and stack that was programmable. The economy crashed and the customers loved it." At Arista, Ullal built a culture that encouraged people to work together to make customers successful. "Our focus is on creating disruptive innovation and creating a happy customer experience. When I was at Cisco, I led a $15 billion business and joked that it was running me. Here we are growing a platform. We architect how we are leading it. We have nurturing founders and our ongoing leadership works well long term," she told me in May 2023.[80]

Arista earned much of its revenue from hyperscalers before ChatGPT launched in November 2022. Therefore, the company benefited from the rapid increase in corporate demand for generative AI. In 2022, Arista earned roughly 40% of its revenue from hyperscalers, with 26% of revenue coming from Meta and about 17% from Microsoft. Arista sold switches

---

[79] "About Arista," *Arista.com*, accessed November 29, 2023, www.arista.com/en/company/company-overview

[80] Peter Cohan, "Generative AI Could Sustain Arista Networks' 31% Annual Stock Growth," *Forbes*, June 1, 2023, www.forbes.com/sites/petercohan/2023/06/01/generative-ai-could-sustain-arista-networks-31-annual-stock-growth/

to these hyperscalers aimed at speeding up communications among racks of servers.[81] In October 2023, Arista acknowledged the importance of AI to its growth by renaming its cloud customers, from "cloud titans" to "cloud and AI titans." As a result, Arista added Oracle, which achieved significant growth from its LLM training service running on Nvidia GPUs, to this major vertical. Ullal told investors not to "read too much into" the new classification, yet she told them, "AI is going to become such an important component of all our cloud types that it's now a combined vertical."[82] By November 29, 2023, Arista generated $4.4 billion in 2022 revenue, employed about 3,600 people, and its stock price had risen at a 34% average annual rate since its June 2014 IPO to a record high market capitalization of $69.1 billion.[83]

Arista's generative AI products help speed up the flow of traffic between servers and storage devices to enable customers to build and operate LLMs more efficiently. Arista aims to "maximize the performance of the application while optimizing network operations by providing an IP/Ethernet architecture with high-performance Arista switches."[84] Two key system components enabled Arista to meet these goals:

- **Network platforms.** Arista supplied network platforms through its 7060X5 series and 7388X5 series that enabled fast data transmission at speeds ranging from 800 billion bits per second to 25.6 trillion bits per

---

[81] Peter Cohan, "Generative AI Could Sustain Arista Networks' 31% Annual Stock Growth," *Forbes*, Ibid.

[82] Mary Jander, "Arista sees Ethernet and AI in the future," *Futuriom*, October 31, 2023, www.futuriom.com/articles/news/arista-sees-ethernet-and-ai-in-the-future/2023/10

[83] "Arista Networks," *CNBC*, accessed November 29, 2023, www.cnbc.com/quotes/ANET?tab=profile

[84] "AI Networking," *Arista.com*, accessed November 29, 2023, www.arista.com/en/solutions/ai-networking

second. Such network platforms enabled customers to "build a high performing AI network in a simple and scalable manner."[85]

- **Network operating software.** Arista's Extensible Operating System provided the tools needed to operate a "premium lossless, high bandwidth and low latency network."[86]

In May 2023, Arista identified minimizing system idle time as a key requirement for operating large AI clusters at high speed. Ullal said Arista could achieve this with "networking that runs at a high-speed of 400 to 800 gigabits per second." To that end, Arista supported AI clusters with a unique blend of technologies: Ethernet, using a combination of Remote Direct Memory Access and RDMA over Converged Ethernet. Ullal said Arista's engineering teams optimized "the platform for dealing with different types of AI workloads. We do expect AI to be meaningful this year as opposed to not material the last couple of years, and we believe the Arista 7800 series will be the flagship product for that."[87]

In 2023, demand for generative AI had the potential to accelerate Arista's growth. For example, in October 2023 Arista reported expectations-trouncing quarterly results. With help from the generative AI tailwind, Arista stock soared 14% to a record high north of $200 a share after that third quarter 2023 earnings report.[88] At the time, Arista had positioned itself to ride the generative AI tidal wave in the following ways:

---

[85] "AI Networking," *Arista.com*, accessed November 29, 2023, Ibid.

[86] "AI Networking," *Arista.com*, accessed November 29, 2023, Ibid.

[87] Sean Michael Kerner, "Arista sees AI as 'killer application' for high-speed networking," *sdxcentral*, May 2, 2023, www.sdxcentral.com/articles/news/arista-sees-ai-as-killer-application-for-high-speed-networking/2023/05/

[88] Peter Cohan, "Arista Networks Stock Gains 14% To Hit Record High," *Forbes*, November 1, 2023, www.forbes.com/sites/petercohan/2023/11/01/arista-networks-stock-gains-14-to-hit-record-high/

- **Aimed at the large market for AI networking.** Morgan Stanley analyst Meta Marshall estimated AI networking would be an $8 billion opportunity by 2028 "with Arista being one of the biggest beneficiaries."[89]

- **Provided customers a compelling value proposition.** While not alone in developing technology for speeding up generative AI, Arista offered a uniquely valuable product. Cisco Systems and Juniper Networks supplied proprietary technology. Other vendors offer so-called white box solutions that save customers money by running bespoke software on commodity hardware rather than expensive, proprietary switches. Arista provided customers a hybrid approach depending on the type of application. "We are comfortable with the idea of a white box since that is how we started as software running on everyone else's hardware. We want to provide customers what they need. For less mission-critical applications, they can use white boxes. For specialized applications—such as turnkey healthcare or financial solutions—they need Arista," Ullal told me in May 2023.[90]

- **Developed new products with customers in mind.** Arista innovated to keep its customers buying. "We look at our talent, the market potential, and we listen to the customer," Ullal told me. "They ask us to do more. High performance data switching was number one.

---

[89] Peter Cohan, "Arista Networks Stock Gains 14% To Hit Record High," *Forbes*, November 1, 2023, Ibid.

[90] Peter Cohan, "Arista Networks Stock Gains 14% To Hit Record High," *Forbes*, November 1, 2023, Ibid.

Next year, 70% said 'You should be in the campus.' We went from routing, to campus, to wide area (Ethernet)." Arista builds or acquires to add "natural adjacencies" to its product portfolio. An example is security for which the company built "a security network telemetry." When Arista saw it was missing wireless, it made an acquisition. Arista wanted to retain the services of the entrepreneur who founded the companies it acquired. "They should fit with our culture, share our cloud vision, and one plus one should be greater than two. We want to get the entrepreneur to integrate with us and deliver customer solutions," Ullal said.[91]

- **Fielded an outstanding leadership team.** During her tenure as CEO, Ullal evolved from being very hands-on to setting strategic direction and empowering experts. Her leadership style changed as the company scaled through three phases. "In the first phase, I was jumping into everything. I worked with Bechtolsheim, Duda and the leadership team as we grew from $1 billion to $5 billion in revenue. I looked at the strategic direction of the company and to empowered experts. In the third phase, as we aim to achieve revenue in the multi billions, I am thinking about Arista's purpose and its platform as we diversify to security and availability," Ullal said.[92]

---

[91] Peter Cohan, "Arista Networks Stock Gains 14% To Hit Record High," *Forbes*, November 1, 2023, Ibid.

[92] Peter Cohan, "Arista Networks Stock Gains 14% To Hit Record High," *Forbes*, November 1, 2023, Ibid.

- **Acted in accordance with a culture of customer-focused collaboration.** At Arista, Ullal built a culture that encouraged people to work together to make customers successful, she told me in May 2023. "When a startup is trying to get off the ground, the CEO often feels compelled to get involved in everything. Such centralized control limits a company's ability to reach escape velocity. At that limit, the company faces a choice. Either the CEO learns how to delegate and empower people or the board replaces the current CEO with a new one who can," she said.[93]

- **Learned to let go.** When a startup is trying to get off the ground, the CEO often feels compelled to get involved in everything. Such centralized control limits a company's ability to reach escape velocity. At that limit, the company faces a choice. Either the CEO learns how to delegate and empower people or the board replaces the current CEO with a new one who can. As Ullal said, "I start to see people achieving more and ask them questions. Their answers get me comfortable that they have command. If I poke and they still need help, I continue to coach them. I move away from playing the role of being a mentor and coach." People who carry Arista's culture are role models. "When it comes to software, our co-founder Ken Duda is passionate about quality. If there is downtime, it costs a customer millions of dollars. We have to make sure the network works. He worries about it and he's the one empowered

---

[93] Peter Cohan, "Arista Networks Stock Gains 14% To Hit Record High," *Forbes*, November 1, 2023, Ibid.

to make it happen. He would rather apologize for
lateness than quality. The field demands merit
and excellence. We know our stuff and contribute,"
Ullal said.[94]

- **Deepened management bench strength.** Ullal felt a
  fiduciary responsibility to build the next generation of
  Arista's leaders. "For succession planning, I have one or
  two candidates internally or externally. It starts with me
  and others to build bench strength. There are people
  in their 40s, 50s, and 60s who might want to retire.
  For the next CEO, we need an operator, someone who
  can embrace our vision and fit it with their style," she
  explained.[95]

In November 2023, Goldman Sachs expressed optimism about
Arista's prospects. Goldman analyst Michael Ng wrote, "As the leading
branded provider of switches to US hyperscalers, ANET is well positioned
to capitalize on the ongoing growth in data, the continued digital
transformation driving workloads from on-premise to public and hybrid-
cloud, and the growing demand for higher bandwidth, faster speed, and
lower latency."[96]

Goldman was optimistic Arista would achieve its forecast of more
than $750 million in revenue from AI networking. Ng estimated Arista
would achieve about a 30% share of the $2.5 billion AI Ethernet market in
2025. He noted the company's strong presence among the so-called Cloud

---

[94] Peter Cohan, "Generative AI Could Sustain Arista Networks' 31% Annual Stock
Growth," *Forbes*, June 1, 2023, www.forbes.com/sites/petercohan/2023/06/01/
generative-ai-could-sustain-arista-networks-31-annual-stock-growth/

[95] Peter Cohan, "Arista Networks Stock Gains 14% To Hit Record High," *Forbes*,
November 1, 2023, Ibid.

[96] Michael Ng, "Arista Networks, Inc. Analyst Day: 2024 outlook in-line; long-term
AI networking beneficiary," *Goldman Sachs*, November 9, 2023.

Titans, such as Meta Networks and Microsoft, as well as from "tier 2 cloud and service providers." He expected Arista to "deliver strong double-digit revenue and EPS growth over the several years."[97]

In 2023, Arista stock's potential investment value hinged on many factors outside of the company's control such as slowing demand for generative AI, more intense competition for AI networking technology, a global economic contraction, or the emergence of new technology that took market share from Arista. Yet Ullal's rare longevity as a leader from 2008 to its 2014 IPO and nine years beyond, gave reason to believe her leadership would sustain Arista's rapid stock price appreciation.

Generative AI Database Providers

Databases – software for storage and retrieval of data – were essential for operating computing systems. While databases initially consisted of tables of words and numbers, the proliferation of unstructured data, such as social media posts, videos, animations, photographs, and others, created a need for new technologies to manage this data. Many publicly traded companies, including Couchbase, Google, Oracle, Microsoft, MongoDB, and Snowflake, competed to supply cloud database software.[98] By 2023, generative AI was boosting the productivity of software developers. While many of these providers satisfied the growing demand for generative AI database technology, MongoDB and Snowflake were clear leaders. In March 2024, Databricks was a rapidly growing rival to Snowflake waiting for the IPO market to open up before going public. Below, we examine each company's history in generative AI, describe their generative AI products, and assess their investment potential.

---

[97] Michael Ng, "Arista Networks, Inc. Analyst Day: 2024 outlook in-line; long-term AI networking beneficiary," *Goldman Sachs*, November 9, 2023.

[98] "Cloud Database Management Systems: MongoDB Alternatives," *Gartner Peer Insights*, accessed December 2, 2023, www.gartner.com/reviews/market/cloud-database-management-systems/vendor/mongodb/alternatives

MongoDB

Between 2007 and 2023, MongoDB transformed itself from a database company adapting to the demands of ecommerce into a beneficiary of the growing business demand for generative AI. Underlying MongoDB's successful evolution was the principle of delivering customers a Quantum Value Leap (QVL),[99] namely, much more value for customers for the price than competing products deliver. The team behind DoubleClick, the Internet advertising company acquired by Google in 2004 – Dwight Merriman, Eliot Horowitz, and Kevin Ryan – co-founded MongoDB in 2007. The co-founders aimed to solve a problem they encountered at DoubleClick: while serving 400,000 ads per second, they "struggled with scalability and agility."[100] As founder Eliot Horowitz said, "MongoDB was born out of our frustration using tabular databases in large, complex production deployments. We set out to build a database that we would want to use, so that whenever developers wanted to build an application, they could focus on the application, not on working around the database."[101]

Six years later, a new CEO was in charge and MongoDB was winning market share from database incumbents on the strength of its QVL. In October 2013, MongoDB raised $150 million in pre-IPO capital and took market share from Oracle and IBM. According to my October 8 interview with MongoDB CEO, between February 2011 and December 2014, Max Schireson, a self-proclaimed math, computer science, and physics nerd from Berkeley who spent nine years at Oracle, "Relational databases were designed in the 1970s during the time that computers were going from punch cards to

---

[99] Peter Cohan, "Hungry Start-Up Strategy: Creating New Ventures with Limited Resources and Unlimited Vision," *Berrett-Koehler Publishers* (2012).

[100] "Our story," *MongoDB*, accessed November 30, 2023, www.mongodb.com/company#:~:text=MongoDB%20was%20founded%20in%202007,the%20shortcomings%20of%20existing%20databases

[101] Pete DeJoy, "A Short History of MongoDB," *PeterDejoy.com*, July 31, 2020, https://petedejoy.com/writing/mongodb

terminals. They are well designed for data that is stored in rows and columns. And Oracle and IBM now dominate the industry that enjoys 50% margins." MongoDB drilled a big gash in the moat surrounding those incumbents' customers, in the form of delivering big companies more bang for the database buck. As Schireson explained, "We deliver enterprises a 10 to 1 improvement – we charge tens of thousands of dollars to complete projects in a few months that they charge millions of dollars to finish in years." When you take into account the full cost to a company, MongoDB offers an irresistible bargain. "We believe that the cost of the software should equal that of the hardware. We typically charge $5,000 per server per year for the software to run on a server that costs about $5,000. Our competition charges hundreds of thousands of dollars per server-year plus $50,000 a year in maintenance and their software runs on $10,000 servers," Schireson concluded.[102]

By 2017, a new CEO rewarded the company's investors by taking MongoDB public. Dev Ittycheria, MongoDB's CEO since Schireson's departure, told me in May 2017 the company, which had raised another $80 million in capital in 2015, was not planning an IPO. "We are optimizing for growth not profitability and we are fortunate that our investors are patient as we target an enormous opportunity – a $36 billion to $40 billion market growing at 8% to 9% annually – that is ripe for disruption," Ittycheria explained. "We are taking a new approach and are the best, biggest, and growing faster than the industry. We now have over 3,000 customers and are approaching 800 employees. We are winning market share because we increase developer productivity (at $250,000 a year they are very expensive), we offer high performance at scale, our product is fault-tolerant, it runs anywhere, and it costs less."[103] That October,

[102] Peter Cohan, "Fidelity, T. Rowe Price In $150 Million Bet That MongoDB Will Beat Oracle, IBM," *Forbes*, October 9, 2013, www.forbes.com/sites/petercohan/2013/10/09/fidelity-t-rowe-price-in-150-million-bet-that-mongodb-will-beat-oracle-ibm/

[103] Peter Cohan, "Don't Invest After MongoDB's Successful IPO," *Forbes*, October 20, 2017, www.forbes.com/sites/petercohan/2017/10/20/dont-invest-after-mongodbs-successful-ipo/

MongoDB went public at $33 a share, and by December 2023, its shares had appreciated at a 50% average annual rate to $412 a share, representing a market capitalization of nearly $30 billion.[104]

In 2023, MongoDB aimed to create a data platform for developers that incorporated open source and proprietary AI models into the development experience. More specifically, Sahir Azam, chief product officer of MongoDB, said the company sought to incorporate "operational data, metadata, search data, vector data, all in a single platform." To that end, MongoDB's Atlas Vector Search allows developers to access unstructured data, such as images or words, by creating numerical representations, called "vectors," which an AI model could interpret. MongoDB collaborated with Amazon Bedrock to enable developers to embed AI technologies in an application programming interface.

MongoDB was also adding other capabilities aimed at helping its customers deploy generative AI. The company's strategic initiatives included

- **Google Cloud partnership** to enable MongoDB's customers to build generative AI applications using Google's foundation models.[105]

- **AI Innovators Program** to give customers access to technology and partnerships to help them "build with Generative AI."[106]

[104] "MongoDB," *CNBC*, accessed December 1, 2023, www.cnbc.com/quotes/MDB?qsearchterm=mongo

[105] "MongoDB (MDB) to Report Q3 Earnings: What's in the Offing?," *Zacks Equity Research,* December 1, 2023, www.zacks.com/stock/news/2192101/mongodb-mdb-to-report-q3-earnings-whats-in-the-offing

[106] "MongoDB (MDB) to Report Q3 Earnings: What's in the Offing?," *Zacks Equity Research*, December 1, 2023, Ibid.

- **Intelligent developer experiences** incorporating generative AI to help developers build applications on MongoDB more effectively.[107]

- **Relational Migrator** service enabled companies to save millions of dollars by automating the conversion of legacy applications into "modern day architecture," Azam said. Through this technology, MongoDB expected development teams to satisfy the demand that they become "competent" in applying generative AI "to the software experiences that they're building every day."[108]

- **New generative AI features** in MongoDB Compass, MongoDB Atlas Charts, and MongoDB Documentation performed easy tasks so developers can "instead focus on hard-to-solve problems and building modern applications."[109]

- **Plans to integrate MongoDB Atlas Vector Search with Amazon Bedrock** to enable companies to build generative AI applications on AWS's cloud infrastructure.[110]

---

[107] "MongoDB (MDB) to Report Q3 Earnings: What's in the Offing?," *Zacks Equity Research*, December 1, 2023, Ibid.

[108] Davony Hof, "How MongoDB's data solutions are powering generative AI applications," *SiliconAngle*, November 29, 2023, https://siliconangle.com/2023/11/29/mongodbs-data-solutions-powering-generative-ai-applications-supercloud5/

[109] "MongoDB (MDB) to Report Q3 Earnings: What's in the Offing?," *Zacks Equity Research*, December 1, 2023, Ibid.

[110] MongoDB Announces Integration of MongoDB Atlas Vector Search with Amazon Bedrock to Power Next-Generation Applications on AWS," *PR Newswire*, November 29, 2023, www.prnewswire.com/news-releases/mongodb-announces-integration-of-mongodb-atlas-vector-search-with-amazon-bedrock-to-power-next-generation-applications-on-aws-302000917.html

In 2023, MongoDB stock soared 126% between January 1 and December 1 and analysts expected generative AI to provide a strong growth tailwind. "MongoDB is a best-of-breed next generation database vendor that is well-positioned in the rapidly growing NoSQL unstructured database market," BofA Securities analyst Brad Sills wrote in an October 2023 client note. Sills added that generative AI would increase the volume and sophistication of data applications. He wrote, "This should serve as a tailwind for MongoDB, given the platform's flexible document model to handle complex data structures and evolving data models." For MongoDB's October 2023-ending quarter, analysts expected the company to report 22% revenue growth to $406 million and a 121% boost in earnings per share to 51 cents. In August, MongoDB saw more growth potential from enterprise demand for generative AI: "We are at the early stages of AI powering the next wave of application development," Ittycheria said. He added, "We believe MongoDB provides developers a unified platform that supports both the foundational requirements necessary for any application and the exceptionally demanding needs of AI-specific applications."[111]

In 2023, MongoDB faced considerable competition. While Sills wrote that MongoDB had the potential to win market share from Amazon and Microsoft, the company had only 2% of the $108 billion database market. Sills also noted that Oracle controlled significant market share. Nevertheless, he saw the potential for MongoDB to capture a larger share. The reasons? The company had "a huge developer community, a proprietary document storage model and supported 13 programming

---

[111] Ryan Deffenbaugh, "Database Player MongoDB Surged 98% Amid AI Boom," *Investor's Business Daily*, November 17, 2023, www.investors.com/research/ibd-stock-of-the-day/mdb-stock-ai-potential-powers-mongodb-to-98-gains-this-year/

languages," noted Sills' report. Moreover, feedback from buyers suggested MongoDB's Atlas increasingly was "the database of choice to support growing AI applications."[112]

Despite the competition, in September 2023, analysts were optimistic about demand for generative AI contributing to MongoDB's growth prospects. Needham viewed MongoDB as a "key beneficiary of generative AI, especially as organizations continue to iterate and discover new use cases." RBC Capital said MongoDB was "well-positioned to be a long-term beneficiary of the generative AI platform shift." Goldman Sachs expected generative AI to add new customers and sell more services, boosting the company's revenue by $6 billion over the long term.[113] From 2015 to 2022, MongoDB's revenue increased at a 53.4% average annual rate from $65 million to $1.3 billion, sporting a Price/Sales ratio of 19.9 on December 1, 2023 (more than three times Oracle's 6.4).[114] With revenue growing more slowly than its long-term rate, MongoDB's stock price trajectory would slow unless it kept exceeding investor expectations.

Snowflake

Founded in 2012 by three data scientists, Snowflake took on the challenge of building a data warehouse for the cloud. Microsoft's Muglia took over as CEO in 2014 and in 2019 Frank Slootman, who had previously taken Data Domain and ServiceNow public, took over from Muglia. In 2020, Snowflake enjoyed a very successful IPO of its own, and in 2023, Snowflake

---

[112] Ryan Deffenbaugh, "MongoDB Stock Nabs Buy Rating As Analyst Sees Boost From 'Explosive Data Growth'," *Investor's Business Daily*, October 12, 2023, www.investors.com/news/technology/mdb-stock-explosive-data-growth-makes-mongodb-a-buy-analyst-says/

[113] Robert DeFrancesco, "Investors Eye MongoDB As A Promising AI Play," *Forbes*, September 11, 2023, www.forbes.com/sites/robertdefrancesco/2023/09/11/investors-eye-mongodb-as-a-promising-ai-play/

[114] "MongoDB, Inc. (MDB)," *Stock Analysis*, accessed December 1, 2023, https://stockanalysis.com/stocks/mdb/revenue/

was introducing new services to tap into market demand for generative AI. Snowflake's initial success resulted from decisions by the company co-founders, three data warehousing experts: Benoit Dageville, Thierry Cruanes, and Marcin Zukowski. In 2014, the board appointed Muglia CEO. During his tenure, he made strategic decisions – to separate data storage from computing and to make Snowflake much easier for data analysts and scientists to use in performing data analytics – that drove rapid market adoption of the company's product following its 2015 launch.[115] In June 2018, Muglia explained that Snowflake's product did more of what customers wanted at a small fraction of the price of competing products from Oracle and SAP. For the year ending January 2018, Snowflake's customer count soared 300%, and investors had plowed $473 million into the company since its founding.[116] In October 2018, Snowflake raised another $450 million, valuing the company at $3.95 billion.[117]

In May 2019, the board decided to replace Muglia with Slootman, who led Snowflake's successful 2020 IPO. Snowflake's board emphasized Slootman's IPO experience. He took ServiceNow public in 2012 and its shares had risen 925% since, as of August 2019 when I spoke with Slootman. He also led Data Domain's 2007 IPO; EMC acquired the company in 2009. Slootman, who left as ServiceNow's CEO in March 2017, credited Muglia with building Snowflake into a company that had "crossed the chasm" with a strong customer base. Snowflake continued

---

[115] Liz Elfman, "A brief history of Snowflake," *Bigeye*, August 15, 2023, `www.bigeye.com/blog/a-brief-history-of-snowflake`

[116] Peter Cohan, "$1.5B Snowflake Computing Is Beating Oracle In $15B Data Warehousing Market," *Forbes*, June 15, 2018, `www.forbes.com/sites/petercohan/2018/06/15/1-5b-snowflake-computing-is-beating-oracle-in-15b-data-warehousing-market/`

[117] Peter Cohan, "Growing At 237%, Snowflake Says It's Taking Business From Teradata and IBM," *Forbes*, August 16, 2019, `www.forbes.com/sites/petercohan/2019/08/16/growing-at-237-snowflake-says-its-taking-business-from-teradata-and-ibm/`

growing in 2019. About a year later, in September 2020, Snowflake enjoyed the "biggest software IPO ever" with its stock rising 112% on its first day of trading.[118]

By May 2023, Snowflake was benefiting from corporate demand for generative AI.

Slootman said generative AI's need to consolidate "massive amounts of data into a single cloud-enabled platform from which customers can derive insights and build applications" would boost demand for the company's products. He said, "Data science, machine learning, and AI use cases on Snowflake are growing every day. In Q1, more than 1,500 customers leverage Snowflake for one of these workloads, up 91% year over year." One happy customer was State Street, a provider of financial services to institutional investors. State Street used Snowflake as a building block for its Alpha platform, "one of the industry's first front- to-back asset servicing platforms." As Executive Vice President, John Plansky told me in a June 2023 interview, "Snowflake is a great partner. We started working with them in 2018. Their data management-as-a-platform works better in the cloud than other databases do. Snowflake also has the ability to see interesting new opportunities in the asset management and other industries. They meet with us every three months and will keep investing in solving problems in our industry. Snowflake enables things we want to do faster."[119]

---

[118] Paul R. La Monica, "Snowflake shares more than double. It's the biggest software IPO ever," *CNN Business*, September 17, 2020, www.cnn.com/2020/09/16/investing/snowflake-ipo/index.html

[119] Peter Cohan, "Partnering With Nvidia, Snowflake Aims At $100 Billion + Generative AI Market," *Forbes*, June 27, 2023, www.forbes.com/sites/petercohan/2023/06/27/partnering-with-nvidia-snowflake-aims-at-100-billion--generative-ai-market/

Snowflake's generative AI strategy hinged on partnerships and new services, including the following:

- **Generative AI partnership with Nvidia.** During its Snowflake Summit 2023, which began that June, the company announced a partnership with Nvidia to help companies build LLMs that solve company-specific problems using their own data. Snowflake and Nvidia's partnership enabled companies to use Nvidia NeMo to train LLMs by accessing proprietary data they fed into the Snowflake Data Cloud. Jensen Huang, Nvidia founder and CEO, expressed enthusiasm for the partnership. "Together, Nvidia and Snowflake will create an AI factory that helps enterprises turn their own valuable data into custom generative AI models to power groundbreaking new applications—right from the cloud platform that they use to run their businesses."[120]

- **Iceberg for Generative AI.** As Slootman told me in a June 2023 interview, "We will offer full support for Iceberg which will expand the amount of data companies can bring into the cloud."[121]

- **Document AI**, based on AI technology Snowflake obtained when it acquired Applica in September 2022. Christian Kleinerman, Snowflake SVP of products, said, "This allows you to take unstructured documents and

---

[120] Peter Cohan, "Partnering With Nvidia, Snowflake Aims At $100 Billion + Generative AI Market," *Forbes*, June 27, 2023, Ibid.

[121] Peter Cohan, "Partnering With Nvidia, Snowflake Aims At $100 Billion + Generative AI Market," *Forbes*, June 27, 2023, Ibid.

unstructured files and convert them into structured data that can be moved into traditional analytics or AI or even other machine learning processes."[122]

- **Snowflake Native App Network**, an App Store-like service for developers to build native Snowflake applications. "It will be an efficient, safe, and compliant way to build enterprise grade applications. We will send developers the check and make the apps available to small and medium enterprises in specific vertical markets without requiring them to build a complete enterprise stack," Slootman told me.[123]

- **Snowpark Container Services**, a way to make legacy systems more easily accessible. "Container Services enable companies to wrap their legacy systems in Snowflake so they do not need to rebuild everything. It streamlines their access. One of our customers is Blue Yonder, a $1.5 billion revenue partner with 15 to 20 years of supply chain expertise," Slootman said.[124]

- **Snowflake Cortex.** Cortex's application varied by user. For business analysts, Cortex provided access to AI tools built on Snowflake's own custom LLMs to speed interaction with data stored on Snowflake. Cortex helped developers build generative AI applications on top of the data stored in Snowflake. Cortex included three specific applications:

[122] Peter Cohan, "Partnering With Nvidia, Snowflake Aims At $100 Billion + Generative AI Market," *Forbes*, June 27, 2023, Ibid.

[123] Peter Cohan, "Partnering With Nvidia, Snowflake Aims At $100 Billion + Generative AI Market," *Forbes*, June 27, 2023, Ibid.

[124] Peter Cohan, "Partnering With Nvidia, Snowflake Aims At $100 Billion + Generative AI Market," *Forbes*, June 27, 2023, Ibid.

- *Document AI*, a way of extracting data from unstructured documents like PDFs and analyst reports and querying that information. "What Document AI does is make it easy for an analyst without any specialized knowledge of programming or large language models to be able to extract these structured values from these documents and put them into a table," Slootman said.

- *Universal Search*, the capability that came to Snowflake when it acquired Neeva in May. "Search, as many people realize, is the basis for doing interesting things with language models, and we are exposing the core of search on top of Snowflake objects," he said. This enables users to search across all of their Snowflake data and the Snowflake marketplace to locate data or apps they have built.

- *Snowflake Copilot*, which takes plain language questions about data stored in Snowflake, and turns them into SQL queries. If done correctly, this could potentially save a lot of time analysts spend familiarizing themselves with the data and column structure to build meaningful queries.[125]

One Snowflake customer, Freddie Mac, told me Snowflake was delivering faster answers to important questions. In December 2023, Aravind Jagannathan, vice president and chief data officer at the company, told me, "In 2019 we wanted to move our data from on-premises to the

---

[125] Ron Miller, "Snowflake brings together developer and analyst needs in new GenAI tool," *TechCrunch*, November 1, 2023, https://techcrunch.com/2023/11/01/snowflake-brings-together-neeva-and-streamlit-acquisitions-in-new-genai-tool/

cloud. We wanted to be quicker in providing insights from the data while reducing the risk of having multiple copies of our data moving back and forth." Freddie Mac picked Snowflake for its faster speed to market and better query performance. "A report that used to take until 3 pm to deliver arrived at 8 am," Jagannathan said. He added, "Processing that used to take 12 hours is now done in 35 minutes. A capital report that used to take many hours can be done in 10 minutes." Freddie Mac said it would take its time before deploying Generative AI. "We are being thoughtful about regulators and senior management," he said. "Snowflake can support Generative AI. We are going to make sure we have the right data governance and have identified the right use cases."[126]

Slootman declined to quantify how much additional revenue these services would generate. He said, "It is bigger than a bread box. It will take a large total addressable market and make it larger. Our Container Service will put us in a good position to help companies train LLMs." He anticipated LLMs would enable companies to ask and answer more important business questions. "For example, an insurance company might want to know 'Why do we have a disproportionate number of injury claims in Florida and what should we do about it?' To answer the questions, businesses would add more of their own data into the cloud and use it to train their LLM. Enrichment of data will drive demand from industries such as pharmaceuticals, healthcare, and retail," Slootman concluded.[127]

By November 2023, generative AI appeared to be contributing to a revival in Snowflake's growth. For example, the company's third quarter 2023 revenue increased 32% to $734.2 million, more than $20 million higher than analysts had projected. Snowflake's outlook for the January

---

[126] Peter Cohan, "Snowflake Stock Rises On Growth From Generative AI," *Forbes*, December 6, 2023, www.forbes.com/sites/petercohan/2023/12/06/snowflake-stock-rises-on-growth-from-generative-ai/

[127] Peter Cohan, "Partnering With Nvidia, Snowflake Aims At $100 Billion + Generative AI Market," *Forbes*, June 27, 2023, Ibid.

2024 quarter of about $719 million exceeded analysts' expectations by $25 million. Snowflake said, "[Snowflake] now has 436 customers with trailing 12-month product revenue greater than $1 million and 647 Forbes Global 2000 customers, representing 52% and 10% year-over-year growth, respectively."[128] Slootman, speaking on a conference call after the results, said AI was spurring demand for the company's software. "Generative AI is at the forefront of customer conversations, which in turn drives renewed emphasis on data strategy in preparation of these new technologies," Slootman said on the call. "We've said it many times—there's no AI strategy without a data strategy. The intelligence we're all aiming for resides in the data and the quality of that underpinning is critical." Jeffries Analyst Brent Thill noted usage of Snowflake's product, and thus revenue "should increase next year with a boost in artificial intelligence workflows."[129]

Goldman Sachs expressed optimism about Snowflake's investment potential. As Goldman Sachs managing director Kash Rangan told me in a November 2023 interview, "Snowflake provides data analytics at scale. It is easy to get one right but not both. The previous generation ran on prem. Snowflake runs in the cloud that demands greater capacity to crunch through data. Snowflake is like a Ferrari—it is bigger, faster, and has more power. These days we are talking about analyzing so much more data— exabytes. Creating an architecture that runs in the cloud is essential for providing accurate analysis at scale."[130]

---

[128] Reinhardt Krause, "Snowflake Earnings, Revenue Top Estimates As Cloud Spending Rebounds," *Investor's Business Daily*, November 30, 2023, www.investors.com/news/technology/snow-stock-snowflake-earnings-news-q32023/

[129] Brody Ford, "Snowflake Outlook Tops Estimates on Stable Sales Growth," *Bloomberg*, November 29, 2023, https://finance.yahoo.com/news/snowflake-gives-outlook-topping-estimates-210921120.html

[130] Peter Cohan, "Snowflake Stock Rises On Growth From Generative AI," *Forbes*, December 6, 2023, Ibid.

Goldman saw Snowflake as providing significant business value. "Snowflake can help you compare three suppliers and identify which one delivers on time and at the lowest price. An investment bank can run daily analysis to find out which customer is the most profitable, which equity and fixed income trades made the most money. It is really hard to get those answers fast. If you have to wait a week, the information is not actionable," Rangan said. He continued, "Generative AI is an opportunity for Snowflake in two areas: data and training LLMs. Snowflake has so much data that companies can use to train LLMs. And once the LLM is trained you can do inference. You can ask a question in plain English that enables you to get access to all that data. For example, you can ask, 'My supply chain is gnarled up. How can I configure it so I can deliver what customers ordered in three days rather than seven?' Snowflake uses SQL so before LLMs, only experts in SQL coding could tap into that valuable business data. Now anyone can access it."[131]

Goldman viewed Snowflake's product strategy and management team as strong. "Snowflake acquired Neeva to get access to that technology a couple of quarters back. In the process, they brought on an executive who had grown that business from $1 billion to $25 billion. The technology enables you to run inference on top of Snowflake. The data is a mixture of structured (90%) and unstructured (10%). Databricks finds the kernels of value in unstructured data—such as Tweets or your Facebook activity. Snowflake is developing its own services—Snowpark to handle unstructured data," Rangan said. He added, "Snowflake's opportunity is large but it will attract well capitalized competition. Snowflake has a bright future. It has core technology, a great business model, an outstanding management team, and the ability to execute."[132]

---

[131] Peter Cohan, "Snowflake Stock Rises On Growth From Generative AI," *Forbes*, December 6, 2023, Ibid.

[132] Peter Cohan, "Snowflake Stock Rises On Growth From Generative AI," *Forbes*, December 6, 2023, Ibid.

By February 2024, a shadow was cast on Snowflake's bright future. In a February 28 earnings call, Slootman announced he was retiring, which came as a surprise since in June 2023 he had denied a report he was planning to retire, along with issuing a disappointing product revenue forecast for the new fiscal year. Snowflake stock promptly shed 20% of its value.[133] Slootman's successor was Sridhar Ramaswamy, a former Google executive who joined in 2023 after Snowflake acquired Neeva, his AI-focused startup. "2023 is the year of AI," Ramaswamy told me in December 2023. "First we have the ability to synthesize information in a fluid conversation through ChatGPT using Neeva." Snowflake was developing this vision in stages. First, search can be done through frequently asked questions. Next, the company is offering CoPilot to make it easier for people to write SQL code to provide faster access to the data. "We are building out the capability to query data in real time," he concluded.[134] Sadly for Snowflake investors, Ramaswamy had no prior experience running a publicly traded company. Slootman told investors Ramaswamy was chosen due to his strong technical skills which would be essential for navigating the challenges of the new world of generative AI.[135] With Slootman's retirement, investors needed to consider whether Ramaswamy could lead Snowflake to faster than expected growth.

Databricks

Founded in 2013, by March 2024, San Francisco-based Databricks was a multibillion-dollar data-warehousing service provider long expected to

---

[133] Dan Gallagher, "Heard on the Street: Snowflake's CEO Surprise Triggers a Needed Cold Plunge for Its Stock," *Wall Street Journal*, February 29, 2024, www.wsj.com/livecoverage/stock-market-today-dow-jones-02-29-2024/card/heard-on-the-street-snowflake-s-ceo-surprise-triggers-a-needed-cold-plunge-for-its-stock-99t77DiUuQ77FcIOnGPw

[134] Peter Cohan, "Snowflake Stock Rises On Growth From Generative AI," *Forbes*, December 6, 2023, Ibid.

[135] Dan Gallagher, "Heard on the Street: Snowflake's CEO Surprise Triggers a Needed Cold Plunge for Its Stock," *Wall Street Journal*, February 29, 2024, Ibid.

go public. Given the weak condition of the IPO market, Ali Ghodsi, the company's co-founder and CEO, decided to report its financial results to the public while remaining privately held: "We're certainly ready as a company: The way we're operating, the way we're doing our audits, the way our financials are, the CFO, the board structure," Ghodsi said. "So we'll make a strategic decision whenever that time comes."[136]

In March 2024, Databricks reported very rapid growth for its fiscal-year ending January 2024. Boasting a status as the fourth largest privately held company based on valuation, Databricks revenue for 2023 rose 40% to $1.6 billion. Databricks generated revenue by renting out analytics, AI, and other cloud-based software to deploy "AI-ready data for building enterprise tech systems." The company's data-warehousing product, launched to the public in December 2021, exceeded $250 million in annual run-rate in 2023. Databricks SQL helped businesses store and collect their data inside "Databricks' data-management 'lakehouse' platform – accounting for more than 10% of the company's business," Ghodsi said.[137]

Since 2024 is an election year, "the window for IPOs is likely to close by August," said Conor Moore, global head of KPMG Private Enterprise. Companies with $100 million to $200 million in revenue with "strong balance sheets won't be rushing to make that window this year, and can wait out the election," he added. The startup investments enable Databricks to build its product line while waiting for the IPO market to reopen. "It feels like having your cake and eating it, too," Ghodsi concluded.[138]

---

[136] Belle Lin, "AI is Driving Record Sales at Multibillion-Dollar Databricks. An IPO Can Wait," *Wall Street Journal*, March 6, 2024, www.wsj.com/articles/ai-is-driving-record-sales-at-multibillion-dollar-databricks-an-ipo-can-wait-f8a55bd4

[137] Belle Lin, "AI is Driving Record Sales at Multibillion-Dollar Databricks. An IPO Can Wait," *Wall Street Journal*, March 6, 2024, Ibid.

[138] Belle Lin, "AI is Driving Record Sales at Multibillion-Dollar Databricks. An IPO Can Wait," *Wall Street Journal*, March 6, 2024, www.wsj.com/articles/ai-is-driving-record-sales-at-multibillion-dollar-databricks-an-ipo-can-wait-f8a55bd4

Publicly Traded Generative AI Application Performance Monitoring Service Providers

Application performance monitoring (APM), software dashboards to provide companies with real-time information about the performance of their cloud-based applications, was essential for sustaining relationships between a company and its employees, customers, and suppliers in the virtual world. Many publicly traded companies, including Datadog, Dynatrace, and New Relic, competed to supply APM software.[139] By 2023, corporate adoption of generative AI created considerable demand for APM services. While many of these providers satisfied the growing demand for generative AI database technology, Datadog was a clear leader with measurable revenue from generative AI. Below, we examine Datadog's history in generative AI, describe the firm's generative AI services, and assess the company's investment potential.

Datadog

Olivier Pomel, a native of France, came to the United States in 1999 and co-founded Datadog in 2010 to satisfy an unmet need: monitoring the performance of their cloud-based applications. Pomel took Datadog public in 2019, and by 2023, the company told investors 2.5% of its revenues were coming from AI. In November 2023, Pomel told me "I came to the US to work at IBM Research in upstate New York for six months in 1999. In 2000, I moved to startups. I saw the dot-com bust and what went wrong." In 2002, he joined Wireless Generation, a Brooklyn, New York-

---

[139] "Application Monitoring and Observability: Datadog Alternatives," *Gartner Peer Insights*, accessed December 2, 2023, `www.gartner.com/reviews/market/application-performance-monitoring-and-observability/vendor/datadog/product/datadog/alternatives`

based provider of technology to track public school student progress and provide individualized lesson plans based on the results. In 2010, News Corp. paid $360 million in cash for 90% of the company.[140]

Pomel co-founded Datadog to solve a problem causing pain for many companies. At Wireless Generation, Pomel worked with Alexis Lê-Quôc, Datadog's co-founder and chief technology officer. "When Alexis and I worked together [at Wireless Generation] engineering development was separate from technology operations. We asked 'How do we get teams to work together?' That was the problem Datadog was trying to solve," Pomel said. They started Datadog at a time when the cloud was new and did not envision how fortunate they would be to have chosen to build a cloud services. "Our goal was to bring operations close to cut cycle time and reduce barriers."[141]

Datadog noticed companies running 50 to 100 applications so their customers could shop and purchase items. Companies were piloting 1,000 applications at the same time, creating challenges of "complexity and understanding what was going on," Pomel said. Datadog's application performance monitoring and log management services saved companies money and time. "Companies were using 50 different APMs. We saved them money by bringing everything under one roof and breaking down silos," he said. "The majority of customers who adopted us did not have a lot of products in the cloud. They started small with us and three to five years down the road they eliminated 10 to 15 other products—they used Datadog," Pomel told me.[142]

---

[140] Peter Cohan, "Up 205% Since IPO, Why Generative AI Could Boost Datadog Stock," *Forbes*, November 18, 2023, www.forbes.com/sites/petercohan/2023/11/18/up-205-since-ipo-why-generative-ai-could-boost-datadog-stock/

[141] Peter Cohan, "Up 205% Since IPO, Why Generative AI Could Boost Datadog Stock," *Forbes*, November 18, 2023, Ibid.

[142] Peter Cohan, "Up 205% Since IPO, Why Generative AI Could Boost Datadog Stock," *Forbes*, November 18, 2023, Ibid.

By November 2023, Datadog had monetized the wave of demand from generative AI. "Our customers include producers of LLMs for video models and development tools," he said. Pomel added, "They are getting a lot of traction. Companies are using and trying to use AI much earlier—it is not in production yet. In our latest investor earnings call, we said we got 2.5% of our revenue from AI."[143]

In 2023, Datadog envisioned generative AI as a growth tailwind of uncertain significance to its future. "We continue to be excited about the opportunity in generative AI and large language models," Pomel told investors in November 2023. He added, "We believe adopting next-gen AI will require the use of cloud and other modern technologies and drive additional growth in cloud workloads. So we are continuing to invest by integrating with more components at every layer of the new AI stack and by developing our own LLM observability products." Datadog satisfied demand for AI monitoring from "next-gen AI-native customers" and expected customers of all industries and sizes to keep adding value to their products using AI over the medium and long term, Pomel noted. While Datadog expected AI to generate significant future growth, Pomel said, "we're only seeing a tiny, tiny bit of it, which is early adoption by mobile providers and a lot of companies that are trying to scale up and experiment and figure out how it applies to their businesses and what they can ship to use the technology." Finally, Datadog expected to incorporate AI into its own operations, generating significant amounts of "deep and precise observability data" that would provide valuable insights for customers. Pomel said Datadog would turn that value into products such as "Bits AI assistant, AI generated synthetic tests, and AI-led error analysis and resolution."[144]

---

[143] Peter Cohan, "Up 205% Since IPO, Why Generative AI Could Boost Datadog Stock," *Forbes*, November 18, 2023, Ibid.

[144] Ambhini Aishwarya, "Earnings call: Datadog Reports 25% Revenue Growth, Eyes DevSecOps and AI Investments," *Investing.com*, November 8, 2023, https://au.investing.com/news/stock-market-news/earnings-call-datadog-reports-25-revenue-growth-eyes-devsecops-and-ai-investments-93CH-3031139

To broaden its AI monitoring services, Datadog also expanded a partnership with Google Cloud to help monitor the health and performance of generative AI models. In November 2023, Datadog provided AI observability services to Google Cloud's Vertex AI platform that built machine learning models. The collaboration between the companies enabled AI operations teams and developers to "monitor, analyze and optimize the performance of AI and machine learning models." Datadog's AI observability services expanded the company's relationship with Google Cloud. Datadog President Amit Agarwal said, "The new Vertex AI integration gives AI and ML developers full observability into their production applications." Agarwal added, "With out-of-the-box dashboards and real-time monitors, customers can get started quickly and ensure their models are performing at an optimal level while delivering predictions responsively at scale and without errors."[145]

In 2023, generative AI had the potential to add significantly to Datadog's investment value, depending on the accuracy of Pomel's prediction that companies would widely adopt the technology. Like any company, Datadog's stock market value rose or fell with its ability to exceed investor expectations each quarter. In November 2023, Datadog reported faster than expected growth – revenue increased 25% to $548 million in the third quarter of 2023 – and its stock price soared 28%. Investors may also have rewarded Datadog for being one of the few companies to quantify how much Generative AI contributed to growth. The surge in its shares following Datadog's third quarter report came as a relief to one analyst. "Into the print there was a lot of anxiety about whether Datadog would follow AWS to improving QoQ growth and stable

---

[145] Mike Wheatley, "Datadog integrates with Google Cloud's Vertex AI to monitor health and performance of generative AI models," *SiliconAngle*, November 8, 2023, https://siliconangle.com/2023/11/08/datadog-integrates-google-clouds-vertex-ai-monitor-health-performance-generative-ai-models/

YoY, or demonstrate a worried disconnect and continue to decelerate on a YoY basis," Bernstein Research analysts led by Peter Weed wrote in a November 2023 investor note. Weed added, "Datadog emphatically dispelled these worries.[146]

Growing faster than the market was a longer-run accomplishment for Datadog. Since going public on September 20, 2019, Datadog stock had risen 205%, outpacing the NASDAQ index's 74% rise between September 20, 2019, and November 17, 2023. That month, Pomel saw a bright future for the adoption of generative AI to boost demand for its products. "Generative AI is now very expensive to train and operate. We think open source models will be used more widely for copy generation, image generation, and coding. These applications are creating real productivity gains," he told me. Yet he saw high expectations as a risk. "Most companies are not in production," he said. Pomel added, "It might take longer than people expect but it will be massive. Training models is a game of scale and that will persist depending on how quickly open source models are more widely adopted."[147]

Like Arista's Ullal, Pomel is among the 0.4% of public company CEO-founders who remained in their post and in control of the company at least three years after taking their company public. Pomel's leadership also appeared likely to contribute to Datadog's bright prospects. Here is how he infused cognitive hunger into five key business processes:

- **Solve the right problem well.** To turn an idea into a public company you must start by building the best solution to a painful problem that rivals, especially very

---

[146] Peter Cohan, "Up 205% Since IPO, Why Generative AI Could Boost Datadog Stock," *Forbes*, November 18, 2023, Ibid.

[147] Peter Cohan, "Up 205% Since IPO, Why Generative AI Could Boost Datadog Stock," *Forbes*, November 18, 2023, Ibid.

large ones, are ignoring. Pomel and his co-founder Lê-Quôc correctly identified the right problem: the pain of interdepartmental conflict slowing down a company's response time.[148]

- **Win and keep customers**. To demonstrate they have solved the right problem well, leaders must win and keep customers. In 2010, investors doubted Datadog would succeed, so rather than rushing to raise capital, the company met with potential customers and built a product they would love. As Pomel said, "We were obsessed with solving the real problem. We spent time with financial customers; we went to conferences and gave demos. We met a lot of potential early customers. When we built the product for the first paying customer, we knew them from our previous company." Datadog discovered an unmet need and collaborated with customers to develop new products. "People said, 'Heh, I need that'. We developed products in collaboration with customers," he told me. Those collaborations boosted Datadog's revenues. Most Datadog customers used many different products to monitor their operations. Ultimately, Datadog created loyal customers by saving them time and money. "They started small with us and three to five years down the road they eliminated 10 to 15 other products – they used Datadog," Pomel told me.[149]

---

[148] Peter Cohan, "5 Lessons From This Founder's 13-Year Journey From Idea to $36 Billion." *Inc.*, November 23, 2023, www.inc.com/peter-cohan/5-lessons-from-this-founders-13-year-journey-from-idea-to-36-billion.html

[149] Peter Cohan, "5 Lessons From This Founder's 13-Year Journey From Idea to $36 Billion." *Inc.*, November 23, 2023, Ibid.

- **Surf industry tailwinds.** Business leaders must adapt quickly to rapidly changing growth headwinds and tailwinds. Datadog monetized the expanding wave of demand from generative AI. "Our customers include producers of large language models for video and software development tools," he said.[150]

- **Invest in growth opportunities.** If a company rests on its laurels, it will ultimately lose ground to rivals that invest in growth opportunities. In 2023, Datadog was operating efficiently so the company could invest in new products for its customers. "We want to make room to spend 30% of revenue on investing in new products for our customers," he said.[151]

- **Develop the next generation of leaders.** Business leaders who want their companies to make a difference in the world must invest in the next generation of leaders. Datadog did that by building a low-ego culture and encouraging its talented people to keep growing professionally. Datadog aimed to minimize internal conflict and build products customers were eager to buy. "Our culture is to be low on drama. We are here to learn. We want to help people build good products for customers. They should love our products," Pomel said. Datadog also aimed to keep smart people from

---

[150] Peter Cohan, "5 Lessons From This Founder's 13-Year Journey From Idea to $36 Billion." *Inc.*, November 23, 2023, Ibid.

[151] Peter Cohan, "5 Lessons From This Founder's 13-Year Journey From Idea to $36 Billion." *Inc.*, November 23, 2023, Ibid.

plateauing by maintaining high standards. "If someone tells you that something isn't right, it's important to accept that feedback and do it again," he concluded.[152]

In 2023, realizing Pomel's vision of widespread generative AI adoption offered the best hope for Datadog to continue to exceed investor expectations.

Generative AI Cloud Services Critical Activities

In 2023, cloud services providers and providers of related software were beginning to earn revenue from generative AI. Based on the case studies, a company's ability to perform five critical activities was likely to determine its ability to gain market share in generative AI cloud services:

- **Ability to build and operate efficient data centers.** The most effective cloud services providers collaborated and/or built data centers to provide high-quality cloud services efficiently. In addition, industry leaders designed and built computing platforms that could train and operate LLMs efficiently on behalf of customers.

- **Ability to build, collaborate, or acquire to supply generative AI software tools.** The most successful generative AI cloud services providers offered software as a service to enterprises. Such software enabled companies to operate online, providing a platform for cloud services providers to sell new generative AI software and service to their customers.

---

[152] Peter Cohan, "5 Lessons From This Founder's 13-Year Journey From Idea to $36 Billion." *Inc.*, November 23, 2023, Ibid.

- **Ability to attract and motivate excellent generative AI talent.** The most successful cloud services providers employed outstanding AI innovators and provided them an opportunity to turn their ideas into products that customers eagerly purchased. Less successful industry participants were unable to attract such talent or did not provide the opportunities needed to retain that talent.

- **Ability to help clients stay ahead of rapidly evolving generative AI technology.** Finally, leading generative AI cloud services providers recognized the need to stay ahead of rapidly changing customer needs, new technologies, and evolving competitor strategies aimed at providing customers with better solutions to their business problems.

Conclusion

This chapter highlighted diverse generative AI cloud services providers, including hyperscalers, data centers, networking technology, database software, and application performance monitoring. The chapter explored the powerful forces elevating the profitability of the cloud services industry, specifically how industry leaders such as AWS and Microsoft locked in customers to their broad product portfolios. The most successful generative AI software cloud services and software providers worked closely with customers to deliver services and software to enhance their productivity, and boost customer retention. In November 2023, some cloud services and related software suppliers had not yet generated significant revenue and it was unclear which of them would emerge as clear industry leaders. Chapter 7 concludes this section of the book by investigating the generative AI strategies and assessing the investment prospects of hardware makers, including semiconductor designers and manufacturers, lithography machine providers, server makers, and liquid cooling system manufacturers.

Generative AI Hardware

In Chapter 6, we examined how various generative AI cloud services providers compete for customers and assessed their investment potential. In this chapter, we investigate these topics from the perspective of generative AI hardware providers – comprising diverse makers of hardware – including semiconductor designers and manufacturers, providers of machines for carving semiconductor designs into silicon wafers, servers, and liquid cooling technology – on which generative AI depends to train and operate chatbots. As we saw in earlier chapters, many of the leading generative AI hardware companies collaborate with other participants in the industry value network, including consultants, generative AI application developers, data platform providers, and cloud service providers, to create and satisfy demand for their products. This chapter answers questions such as

- What are the most significant groups of generative AI hardware providers?

- What forces are driving the profit potential of the generative AI hardware industry?

- Which generative AI hardware are most successfully monetizing generative AI?

© Peter Cohan 2024
P. Cohan, *Brain Rush*, https://doi.org/10.1007/979-8-8688-0318-5_7

- How should investors evaluate the potential returns of wagering capital on generative AI hardware providers?

- What capabilities set apart the generative AI hardware leaders from their peers?

Generative AI Hardware Industry Players

Large hardware industry incumbents have adapted their strategies to satisfy the growth in demand resulting from generative AI, including the following:

- **Semiconductor designers.** In 2023, Nvidia and AMD were among the leaders in designing GPUs and related semiconductors for training and operating LLMs. GPUs worked differently than CPUs used for personal computers. While CPUs performed one operation at a time, GPUs performed many operations at the same time, speeding up the matrix multiplication calculations required to train and operate LLMs.[1]

- **Semiconductor manufacturers.** Companies such as TSMC and Samsung were leaders in manufacturing these designs.

- **Lithography system providers.** ASML was the world's leading provider of extreme ultraviolet lithography systems used to build semiconductors.

---

[1] Brian Colello, "After Earnings, Is AMD Stock a Buy, a Sell, or Fairly Valued?," *Morningstar*, November 10, 2023, www.morningstar.com/stocks/after-earnings-is-amd-stock-buy-sell-or-fairly-valued

- **Computers server manufacturers.** Dell, Hewlett Packard Enterprise, and Super Micro Computing were leaders in the manufacturing of computer servers used by cloud services providers.

- **Liquid cooling product providers.** Companies such as Vertiv manufactured liquid cooling systems to manage the heat generated by GPUs.

Table 7-1 summarizes the investment potential of these companies.

Table 7-1. *Investment Potential of Selected Generative AI Hardware Providers*

Company	Gen AI Upside Potential	Investment Tailwinds	Investment Headwinds
AMD	Moderate to High	Nvidia's inability to make enough processors to satisfy customer demand	Lagging in providing software for developers to apply GPUs to generative AI challenges
Nvidia	High	Dominant market position in GPUs, largest software library, broad industry partnerships and investments	Inability to fulfill orders quickly
TSMC	Moderate to High	Leading position in GPU manufacturing	Dependence on declining PC industry and geopolitical risk
ASML	Moderate to High	Monopoly position in EUV lithography	Significant lag time to fulfill customer orders

(*continued*)

Table 7-1. (*continued*)

Company	Gen AI Upside Potential	Investment Tailwinds	Investment Headwinds
Dell	Moderate	Strong financial position and good products for companies who want to build LLMs on premises	Heavily dependent on declining PC industry, time lag in GPU order fulfillment, and risk companies will prefer to develop LLMs in the cloud
Super Micro Computing	High	Rapid revenue and profit growth, decades-long partnership with Nvidia, good AI server and liquid cooling products	
Vertiv	High	Leading industry position in immersive cooling and ability to satisfy the needs of data centers running generative AI workloads	

Generative AI Semiconductor Industry Attractiveness

In 2023, the explosion in demand for semiconductors to power the training and operation of LLMs set off an investment frenzy for generative AI. The signal moment occurred in May 2023 when Nvidia's reported results and expectations vastly exceeded what investors had forecast. Indeed the two most important forces driving capital into the generative AI industry were the explosive number of people who used ChatGPT following its November 2022 launch and the enormous amount of money companies were spending on Nvidia GPUs to build and operate those LLMs. While most people were not paying to use ChatGPT, the sums spent on GPUs – trumpeted to the world in Nvidia's first quarter 2023 financial report – validated the investment opportunity in generative AI.

GPUs were a fast-growing subset of the enormous, moderately profitable US semiconductor industry. Entry barriers to the semiconductor manufacturing industry – including the capital requirements, high-priced labor, intense price competition, patents, and regulatory hurdles – were so high that only a small number of corporate behemoths could operate profitability. Many leading semiconductor firms specialized in designing new semiconductors and forming partnerships to develop industry-specific solutions while outsourcing the manufacturing. While there were no substitutes available for semiconductors, price competition among incumbents gave customers some bargaining power. Nevertheless, Nvidia enjoyed high pricing power because its technology, services, and partnerships surpassed those of rivals.[2]

The semiconductor industry in the United States totaled about $65 billion, barely grew (at a 0.4% average annual rate), and generated a modest 7.1% net profit margin for the average participant. The five forces underlying the semiconductor industry's moderate profit potential included the following:

- **Threat of entry: Low.** Entry barriers blocking new entrants were very high. Large companies filled high-volume orders for semiconductors, circuit boards, and electronic components, leaving few scraps for aspiring

---

[2] Evan Jozkowski, "Global Semiconductor & Electronic Parts Manufacturing," *IBISWorld*, November 2023, https://my-ibisworld-com.ezproxy.babson.edu/gl/en/industry/c2524-gl/at-a-glance

new entrants. Major contract manufacturers enjoyed competitive advantages including strong patents and existing partnerships between manufacturers, designers, and customers. Upfront costs and continued research and development investments prevented chip buyers from easily transitioning to new products, for example from memory chips to GPUs. Large-scale manufacturing plants often had low unit costs relative to smaller plants and could spread their R&D costs over more customers. Environmental, workplace, and waste management regulations were strict. Finally, trade tensions, for example between the United States and China, presented severe legal risks for companies involved in trade between these countries.[3]

- **Rivalry among existing competitors: Moderate.**
  Rivals competed on price that was most important for widely available general-purpose chips. More generally, customers chose vendors based on "product quality, reliability, selling price, customer service, product range, innovation, and timely delivery." For GPUs, another important decision factor was the depth of the software library for enabling developers to build applications. While slow growth intensified competition among rivals, the high cost of switching to a competing product somewhat offset the intensity of industry rivalry.[4]

---

[3] Evan Jozkowski, "Global Semiconductor & Electronic Parts Manufacturing," *IBISWorld*, November 2023, Ibid.

[4] Evan Jozkowski, "Global Semiconductor & Electronic Parts Manufacturing," *IBISWorld*, November 2023, Ibid.

- **Bargaining power of buyers: Moderate.**
  Companies required semiconductors and other
  electrical components for most consumer
  electronics, computers, vehicles and tech-enabled
  products. Despite the strong customer demand for
  semiconductors, intensive rivalry and rapid product
  innovation forced companies to price competitively,
  thus limiting their ability to extract high prices from
  buyers. However, some markets, such as GPUs
  for training and operating LLMs, were effectively
  monopolies or duopolies – buyers of these products
  paid price premiums "to acquire necessary niche
  products."[5]

- **Bargaining power of suppliers: High.** Semiconductor
  manufacturers required specialized machinery, some
  of which was extremely precise. For example, a single
  company – ASML – made lithography presses used to
  make specific semiconductors. Such suppliers enjoyed
  considerable market power. Moreover, suppliers of rare
  earth metals and specific oxides had strong bargaining
  power with the semiconductor manufacturers who
  purchased these inputs.[6]

- **Threat of substitutes: Low.** There were no substitutes
  for semiconductors when it came to data storage,
  electricity transmission, and processing power.[7]

---

[5] Evan Jozkowski, "Global Semiconductor & Electronic Parts Manufacturing,"
IBISWorld, November 2023, Ibid.

[6] Evan Jozkowski, "Global Semiconductor & Electronic Parts Manufacturing,"
IBISWorld, November 2023, Ibid.

[7] Evan Jozkowski, "Global Semiconductor & Electronic Parts Manufacturing,"
IBISWorld, November 2023, Ibid.

Generative AI Hardware Industry Participants

GPUs – designed by Nvidia and AMD – performed the calculations used to build and operate LLMs. Semiconductor manufacturers invested billions of dollars – to purchase extreme ultraviolet lithography and other machines – to fabricate GPUs. Data centers purchased AI servers containing GPUs and other electronics and deployed liquid cooling systems to dissipate heat generated by the operation of these servers.

Publicly Traded Generative AI Semiconductor Companies

In 2023, publicly traded semiconductor designers dominated the market for GPUs used to train and operate LLMs. Generative AI – along with the Internet of Things and virtual reality – was among the most significant drivers of growth in GPU demand – expected to expand at a 33.8% annual rate between 2022 and 2032 from $42 billion to $733 billion in annual revenue. Leading GPU providers included AMD, Nvidia, and Samsung.[8] Below, we profile three publicly traded AI chip companies: AMD, Nvidia, and TSMC. We examine each company's history in generative AI, describe their generative AI products, and assess their investment potential.

---

[8] "Graphic Processing Unit (GPU) Market Will Grow at CAGR of 33.8% By 2032," *Precedence Research*, November 9, 2023, www.precedenceresearch.com/press-release/graphic-processing-unit-market#:~:text=33.8%25%20By%202032-,Graphic%20Processing%20Unit%20(GPU)%20Market%20Will%20Grow%20at,CAGR%20of%2033.8%25%20By%202032&text=The%20global%20graphic%20processing%20unit,33.8%25%20between%202023%20and%202032

AMD

In 1969, Jerry Sanders and seven other Fairchild Semiconductor employees started Santa Clara, California-based Advanced Micro Devices, going public in 1972.[9] By December 2023, AMD, with $23.6 billion in 2022 revenue and a stock market capitalization exceeding $220 billion, was the leading challenger to Nvidia's supremacy in the GPU market. AMD had once before come from behind to challenge an industry leader. For decades, after competing with limited success against Intel in the personal computer and server markets, AMD stock had dropped to around $2 a share after cutting 25% of the chipmaker's staff.[10] A decade later, its chip innovations for smartphones and tablets enabled AMD to become Intel's leading challenger. AMD's smart design decisions coupled with Intel's "technological stumbles" left AMD with four times its 2017 revenue in December 2023 – during the same period, Intel's business shrank by 16%.[11] In June 2023, AMD announced an AI chip to challenge Nvidia's 80% share of the GPU market. AMD said its MI300X GPU would start shipping in the third quarter of 2023 and ramp up mass production by the end of the year. AMD CEO Lisa Su called MI300X "the world's most advanced accelerator for generative AI" and claimed AI would become the company's "most significant and strategically important long-term growth opportunity."[12] By December 2023, AMD, which had lost ground to Nvidia, as its data center revenue fell 6% from the previous year, proudly announced its MI3000

---

[9] Editors of Encyclopedia Britannica, "Advanced Micro Devices," *Britannica*, December 15, 2023, www.britannica.com/topic/2023-The-Year-in-Review

[10] Connie Lin, "AMD aims to dethrone Nvidia in the AI-chip wars," June 14, 2023, *Fast Company*, www.fastcompany.com/90909537/amd-nvidia-artificial-intelligence-ai-chip-war

[11] Dan Gallagher, "AMD's Piece of the AI Pie Will Need to Prove Sticky," *Wall Street Journal*, December 7, 2023, www.wsj.com/tech/ai/amds-piece-of-the-ai-pie-will-need-to-prove-sticky-46f39e16

[12] Connie Lin, "AMD aims to dethrone Nvidia in the AI-chip wars," June 14, 2023, *Fast Company*, Ibid.

family of AI accelerator chips. Su told investors AMD would generate $2 billion in GPU revenue in 2024. While this projection represented 20% of Wall Street's $10 billion forecast for AMD's 2024 data center revenue, the $2 billion was a pittance compared to Nvidia's projected $76 billion in 2024 data center revenue.[13] Given the strong industry demand for GPUs, AMD was positioning itself well to provide the chips Nvidia could not supply. It remained to be seen whether AMD could assemble the capabilities to win over Nvidia customers and keep them buying over the long term.

In 2023, AMD's strategy for generative AI hinged on selling a better-performing GPU, expressions of interest in the chip from large customers, and a proprietary software platform. AMD claimed its AI chip – the MI300 system – would outperform Nvidia's flagship H100. Moreover, in December 2023, AWS, OpenAI, and Microsoft expressed interest in incorporating its MI300 chip into their generative AI workflows. AMD was confident in the competitiveness of its MI300, especially for LLM inference. As Su said, the MI300 "is definitely going to be competitive from training workloads, and in the AI market, there's no one-size-fits-all as it relates to chips. There are some that are going to be exceptional for training. There are some that are going to be exceptional for inference, and that depends on how you put it together. What we've done with MI300 is we've built an exceptional product for inference, especially large language model inference. So when we look going forward, much of what work is done right now is companies training and deciding what their models are going to be. But going forward, we actually think inference is going to be a larger market, and that plays well into some of what we've designed MI300 for."[14] In December 2023, AMD debuted its ROCm 6 software platform, aiming to compete

---

[13] Dan Gallagher, "Nvidia's Rivals Prepare Their AI Assault," *Wall Street Journal*, December 4, 2023, www.wsj.com/tech/ai/nvidias-rivals-prepare-their-ai-assault-0cf9ba01

[14] Nilay Patel, "AMD CEO Lisa Su on the AI revolution and competing with Nvidia," *The Verge*, September 29, 2023, www.theverge.com/23894647/amd-ceo-lisa-su-ai-chips-nvidia-supply-chain-interview-decoder

with Nvidia's proprietary platform Cuda. "Software actually is what drives adoption," Su said.[15]

AMD indicated interest in the MI300 from several large potential customers including the following:

- **AWS.** In June 2023, an AWS executive told *Reuters* that the cloud computing giant may enlist AMD as its supplier, although it has not reached a final decision.[16]

- **Microsoft and Meta.** At a December AMD conference, Microsoft chief technology officer Kevin Scott and Meta AI's senior director of engineering Ajit Mathews discussed how they were incorporating the MI300 into their AI workloads.[17]

- **OpenAI.** The ChatGPT developer said it intended to incorporate AMD's new chips in the latest version of OpenAI's Triton AI software. "We plan to support AMD's GPUs including MI300" in the latest release of Triton, OpenAI engineer Philippe Tillet said in a statement. "On raw specs, MI300X dominates H100," Dylan Patel and Daniel Nishball at semiconductor consulting firm SemiAnalysis wrote. They said OpenAI's announcement in particular was "a big deal."[18]

---

[15] Michael Acton, "AMD rolls out new rival to Nvidia's AI chip," *Financial Times*, December 6, 2023, www.ft.com/content/fa0c97af-c20f-461e-96c9-f2357496c599

[16] Connie Lin, "AMD aims to dethrone Nvidia in the AI-chip wars," June 14, 2023, *Fast Company*, Ibid.

[17] Michael Acton, "AMD rolls out new rival to Nvidia's AI chip," *Financial Times*, December 6, 2023, Ibid.

[18] Michael Acton, "AMD rolls out new rival to Nvidia's AI chip," *Financial Times*, December 6, 2023, Ibid.

Analysts disagreed on AMD's prospects for mounting a strong challenge to Nvidia. One analyst, Deutsche Bank's Ross Seymore, expressed optimism about AMD's ability to compete with Nvidia. "We believe that today's event highlighted how AMD remains extremely well positioned to take advantage of the rapidly expanding AI TAM, as they continue to stack up customer partnerships and roll out products with impressive (and extremely competitive) performance metrics," Seymore wrote in a note.[19] By contrast, *Morningstar* expressed greater skepticism about AMD's prospects. The analyst argued AMD was far behind Nvidia in its software, thus holding the challenger back even if AMD's GPU designs were "up to par (or better)." Meanwhile, *Morningstar* expected generative AI cloud services providers to continue their efforts to build their own GPUs. "Google's TPUs and Amazon's Trainium and Inferentia chips were designed with AI workloads in mind, while Microsoft and Meta Platforms META have announced semiconductor design plans."[20]

In 2023, generative AI had the potential to increase the value of AMD's stock. AMD needed to overcome two obstacles: a significant portion of its revenue came from the declining market for CPUs powering personal computers and servers and AMD needed to exceed its modest MI300 revenue forecast. Following AMD's third quarter 2023 earnings report, *Morningstar* estimated revenues in the company's client sector – which sold chips to PC makers – would fall 24% in 2023 to $4.7 billion due to a post-pandemic "pause in PC demand." *Morningstar* anticipated 2027 client revenue of $6.1 billion in 2027 resulting from a modest "rebound in PC demand and some share gains over Intel." *Morningstar* was more

---

[19] Kif Leswing, "AMD stock spikes after company launches AI chip to rival Nvidia," *CNBC*, December 7, 2023, www.cnbc.com/2023/12/07/amd-stock-spikes-after-company-launches-ai-chip-to-rival-nvidia.html

[20] Brian Colello, "After Earnings, Is AMD Stock a Buy, a Sell, or Fairly Valued?" *Morningstar*, November 10, 2023, www.morningstar.com/stocks/after-earnings-is-amd-stock-buy-sell-or-fairly-valued

optimistic about growth in AMD's data center business, the unit housing the company's AI accelerator products that AMD expected to reach $400 billion by 2027.[21] Anticipating 30% average annual growth, *Morningstar* envisioned AMD's data center revenue reaching $10 billion in 2024 and rising to $22 billion by 2027.[22]

In 2023, AMD's stock had the potential to rise if it could exceed investors' expectations for growth and profitability while raising guidance for the future. The outcome depended on whether AMD's data center revenue grew faster than investors expected it would. AMD optimists argued its stock would rise for three reasons: the company's increased share of the PC CPU market with help from Intel's manufacturing problems; its manufacturing partnership with TSMC which enabled AMD to get new designs to market faster, and the high demand for AI GPUs, some of which Nvidia left unsatisfied. By contrast, AMD bears argued Intel could solve its manufacturing woes and regain its PC market share; AMD would not be able to catch up with Nvidia's superior software; and it could take years for new gaming consoles to accelerate demand for AMD's gaming chips. By December 2023, it appeared AMD stock was overvalued. The company's median price target was $130 a share according to 46 analysts who had set 12-month price targets for the chip designer, some 7% below the company's December 19 price of about $140.[23] While many things could change, that month it appeared AMD might not be the most compelling way for investors to tap growing demand for AI chips.

---

[21] Kif Leswing, "AMD stock spikes after company launches AI chip to rival Nvidia," *CNBC*, December 7, 2023, Ibid.

[22] Brian Colello, "After Earnings, Is AMD Stock a Buy, a Sell, or Fairly Valued?" *Morningstar*, November 10, 2023, www.morningstar.com/stocks/after-earnings-is-amd-stock-buy-sell-or-fairly-valued

[23] "Advanced Micro Devices, Inc.," *CNN Business*, accessed December 20, 2023, www.cnn.com/markets/stocks/AMD

Nvidia

In 1993, Jensen Huang co-founded Nvidia at a Denny's in San Jose, California. Thirty years later the chip design giant controlled about 85% of the market for GPUs. In between, Nvidia encountered two periods of time: in 2002 following the dot-com crash and at the beginning of the 2008 financial crisis, when Huang encountered bone-crushing pressure due to a plunge in demand for its products.[24] Between 2006 and 2023, Nvidia accumulated capabilities that enabled the company to build a difficult-to-surmount lead in the market for generative AI GPUs. These competitive advantages included

- **Launching CUDA.** In 2006, Nvidia announced Compute Unified Device Architecture (CUDA) – software for programming GPUs for other fields such as physics or chemical simulation. In 2012, researchers used the chips to identify a cat with precision.[25]

- **Hiring an AI team.** Nvidia hired a team to train LLMs, gaining early insights into what AI practitioners wanted. Using that market intelligence, Nvidia built libraries, to perform tasks common to AI development, thus saving the developers' time.[26]

- **Building faster chips every few years and expanding to complete computers.** Nvidia consistently delivered faster chips every few years. In 2017, it began tailoring

---

[24] Ben Cohen, "He Built a Trillion-Dollar Company. He Wouldn't Do It Again," *Wall Street Journal*, December 9, 2023, www.wsj.com/business/nvidia-jensen-huang-ceo-ai-chips-89d305de?mod=hp_lead_pos7

[25] Peter Cohan, "Why Nvidia Stock Could Soar To $1,000 A Share," *Forbes*, August 23, 2023, www.forbes.com/sites/petercohan/2023/08/23/why-nvidia-stock-could-soar-to-1000-a-share/

[26] Peter Cohan, "Why Nvidia Stock Could Soar To $1,000 A Share," *Forbes*, August 23, 2023, Ibid.

GPUs to handle specific AI calculations, sold chips or circuit boards for other companies, and provided complete computers aimed at faster AI processing.[27]

- **Introducing H100 chips.** In September 2022, Nvidia announced production of H100 chips to enhance transformer operations, which were essential for training ChatGPT and other generative AI chatbots.[28]

- **Forming partnerships with large technology companies and investing in startups.** Nvidia collaborated with large technology companies such as ServiceNow and Snowflake and funded startups. In June 2023, Nvidia invested in a $1.3 billion financing for Inflection AI, which used the money to help pay for 22,000 H100 chips.[29]

These competitive advantages were difficult for rivals to copy. As Moor Insights semiconductor analyst Patrick Moorhead said in August 2023, "Nvidia has a double moat right now in that they have the highest performance training hardware. Then on the input side of the software, in AI, there are libraries and CUDA." Nvidia's moat was so high that customers were willing to pay more for its products and wait longer for Nvidia to fill their orders. As Futurum Group analyst Daniel Newman said, "Customers will wait 18 months to buy an Nvidia system rather than buy an available, off-the-shelf chip from either a start-up or another competitor. It's incredible." Nvidia argued the LLM training time customers

---

[27] Peter Cohan, "Why Nvidia Stock Could Soar To $1,000 A Share," *Forbes*, August 23, 2023, Ibid.

[28] Peter Cohan, "Why Nvidia Stock Could Soar To $1,000 A Share," *Forbes*, August 23, 2023, Ibid.

[29] Peter Cohan, "Why Nvidia Stock Could Soar To $1,000 A Share," *Forbes*, August 23, 2023, Ibid.

slashed by using the company's GPUs more than offset their higher price – its H100's price ranged between $15,000 and more than $40,000. As Huang explained, "If you can reduce the time of training to half on a $5 billion data center, the savings is more than the cost of all of the chips. We are the lowest-cost solution in the world." Finally, Nvidia adapted to rapidly changing market realities much faster than rivals did. Naveen Rao, an entrepreneur who sold his startup that built GPU chips for gaming and AI to Intel, saw Nvidia adapting GPUs for AI far more rapidly than did Intel. He left Intel and started a software company, MosaicML, where he compared Nvidia chips to its rivals. Rao said, "Everybody builds on Nvidia first. If you come out with a new piece of hardware, you're racing to catch up."[30] Nvidia's significant head start in AI paid off in 2023 when the company's stock soared 245%, increasing the company's market capitalization to more than $1.2 trillion.[31]

Nvidia provided GPUs and software for training and operating LLMs. Nvidia specialized in GPUs, chips originally designed for displaying video, images, and animations for PC video games, a market that quadrupled in value to more than $12 billion between 2016 and 2022. Nvidia also realized GPUs – with many small chip cores operating in parallel – were good for training and operating LLMs such as ChatGPT. Providers of cloud computing and consumer-Internet services, such as Google, Microsoft and Amazon, generated the most explosive demand for Nvidia's GPUs, generating $15 billion in 2022 revenue, at an 88% average annual growth

---

[30] Peter Cohan, "Why Nvidia Stock Could Soar To $1,000 A Share," *Forbes*, August 23, 2023, Ibid.

[31] "Nvidia," *Google*, accessed December 27, 2023, www.google.com/sea
rch?q=nvidia+stock&rlz=1C1CHBF_enUS860US893&oq=nvidia+st&gs_
lcrp=EgZjaHJvbWUqDQgAEAAYgwEYsQMYgAQyDQgAEAAYgwEYsQMYgAQyDQgBEAAYgw
EYsQMYgAQyBggCEEUYOTINCAMQABiDARixAxiABDINCAQQABiDARixAxiABDIKCAUQ
ABixAxiABDINCAYQABiDARixAxiABDINCAcQABiDARixAxiABDIKCAgQA
BixAxiABDIHCAkQABiPAqgCALACAA&sourceid=chrome&ie=UTF-8#cso=chart-
annotations-carousel:443.6363525390625

rate in the preceding five years. Nvidia also provided software to enable developers to program GPUs "to solve mathematically-intensive problems that were previously cost prohibitive." By October 2023, CUDA had grown to include 250 software libraries, the most popular ones for AI developers. Credit Suisse analysts said those libraries "provide a starting point for AI projects that aren't available on non-NVDA systems," in a 2023 report. In a July 2023 call sponsored by Bernstein Research, former Nvidia Vice President Michael Douglas called software "a key arrow in the quiver" that sets Nvidia apart from the competition. Douglas predicted that software, rather than hardware, would be the source of most of the performance improvements for Nvidia's systems by 2028.[32]

The fear Huang experienced when the company was a month away from running out of cash during its 2002 and 2008 crises permanently forged Nvidia's mindset. By 2023, Huang's fear kept the company from becoming complacent as AMD took aim at its lead in the GPU market. To keep rivals from catching up, Nvidia invested to keep the overall performance of its chips and software ahead of competing products. To that end, in November 2023, Nvidia unveiled its H200, a GPU with sufficient computer memory to generate text, images, or predictions using AI models. Compared to its predecessor, the H100, the new chip included 141GB of next-generation "HBM3" memory for enabling the chip to perform "inference," generating creative responses in the form of text, images, or predictions about twice as quickly in response to user prompts. Nvidia, which planned to launch the new chip in the second quarter of 2024, said the H200 would compete with AMD's MI300X GPU. In 2023, Nvidia was picking up the pace of its new product launches. While Nvidia based the H100 and H200 on the Hopper architecture that introduced new products every two years, in October 2023 the company

[32] Dan Gallagher, "How Nvidia Got Huge—and Almost Invincible," *Wall Street Journal*, October 6, 2023, www.wsj.com/tech/ai/how-nvidia-got-hugeand-almost-invincible-da74cae1?mod=hp_lead_pos3

announced "a one-year release pattern due to high demand for its GPUs." Nvidia's forthcoming Blackwell architecture would enable the company to announce and ship its B100 chip in 2024.[33]

By 2023, Nvidia's growth rate had accelerated so much that investors bid up its stock to a value exceeding almost any expectation for future growth. This left investors considering whether the company would continue to enjoy the same rapid growth in revenue and stock price it enjoyed in 2023 or whether the stock could rise no further because Nvidia could not surpass investors' high expectations. Nvidia bulls included TD Cowen analyst Matthew Ramsay, who chose the chip giant as his top chip stock pick for 2024. In a December 2023 note to clients, Ramsay noted Nvidia was the leader in "the most consequential growth vector of computing." Ramsay argued Nvidia's "accelerating product roadmap" would keep the company in the lead. Despite competition from AMD, he envisioned Nvidia maintaining its strong market position through 2025 due to its broad line of superior products, a history of successful innovation, a faster new product development cycle, and a product line that would expand from chips to systems. Ramsay expected Nvidia shares to appreciate 50% from its early December 2023 price of $466 to $700 a share.[34] A six-fold increase – to 35 – in the number of venture capital investments in which the company participated in 2023 bolstered the view that Nvidia stock could keep rising. These investments enabled startups to buy Nvidia chips. A case in point was Inflection AI, which in June announced a $1.3 billion fundraising round jointly led by Nvidia, Microsoft, Bill Gates, and others. Inflection AI boasted it had access to

---

[33] Kif Leswing, "Nvidia unveils H200, its newest high-end chip for training AI models," *CNBC*, November 12, 2023, www.cnbc.com/2023/11/13/nvidia-unveils-h200-its-newest-high-end-chip-for-training-ai-models.html

[34] Emily Bary, "Nvidia's stock dubbed a top pick for next year after monster 2023: 'No need to overthink this,'" *MarketWatch*, December 11, 2023, www.marketwatch.com/story/nvidias-stock-dubbed-a-top-pick-for-next-year-after-monster-2023-no-need-to-overthink-this-e0486050

22,000 H100 GPUs, thanks to its alliances with Nvidia and cloud services provider CoreWeave. Late in 2022, CoreWeave said it was among the first companies to receive H100 shipments, alongside cloud giants Amazon, Google, Microsoft, and Oracle.[35]

By February 2024, Nvidia had again vanquished those arguing the company's growth was unsustainable. Bearish analysts argued Nvidia's AI chip business was too dependent on a small number of large companies, including Microsoft, Meta Platforms, Google, and Amazon, who could decide quickly to curtail their orders if demand from their customers tapered off. Moreover, with Nvidia stock having increased 40% in the first two months of 2024, skeptics did not expect the company to continue to deliver expectations-beating growth when it reported results for the fourth quarter of 2023. On February 21, Nvidia delivered expectations-beating growth in revenue and profitability, sending its shares up 14% in after-hours trading. The AI chip maker delivered 265% growth, posted an 804% increase in earnings per share, and told investors the company expected to deliver 300% revenue growth in the first quarter of 2024, all of which were much better than investors had forecast. Nvidia CEO Jensen Huang described AI as hitting "the tipping point" as hunger for computing to build and operate generative AI remains enormous. "Demand is surging worldwide across companies, industries and nations," he said.[36] As analysts raised their expectations, Nvidia would need to keep innovating in order to keep dazzling investors every quarter. In early 2024, it was perhaps inevitable that the company would some day disappoint – but that day seemed far in the future as long as Huang remained CEO.

---

[35] "Nvidia emerges as leading investor in AI companies," *Financial Times*, December 11, 2023, www.ft.com/content/25337df3-5b98-4dd1-b7a9-035dcc130d6a

[36] Peter Cohan, "Nvidia Stock Soars After-Hours On 265% Revenue Growth," *Forbes*, February 21, 2024, www.forbes.com/sites/petercohan/2024/02/21/nvidia-stock-soars-after-hours-on-265-revenue-growth/

TSMC

Founded in 1987 by Dr. Morris Chang, with significant support from the Taiwanese government, Taiwan Semiconductor Manufacturing Company pioneered the idea of enabling chip designers to outsource chip manufacturing. By 2023, TSMC controlled about 50% of the global chip manufacturing market. TSMC made chips for smartphones and computers in cars, health care equipment, and satellites for customers including Apple, Qualcomm, and AMD. By 2023, its partnerships with Nvidia and other AI chip designers – along with its expertise at building and operating large-scale, capital-intensive semiconductor foundries – made TSMC the world's leading AI chip manufacturer.[37] In September 2022, Nvidia announced a partnership with TSMC to manufacture the designer's AI-powered video game chips. While Nvidia collaborated with Samsung to manufacture its previous generation of video game chips, TSMC built the designer's then latest Lovelace gaming chips.[38]

By December 2023, TSMC anticipated demand for AI chips would help to offset a sharp decline in demand for PC chips. TSMC CEO CC Wei anticipated a low point for the December 2023 ending quarter due in part to economic and trade challenges with China and a drop in PC demand, with IDC projecting a 16% decline in consumer shipments to 252 million units. TSMC was relying on demand for AI chips from Nvidia, AMD, which forecasted a $45 billion market for its AI data center processors in 2023, AWS, and others to pick up some of the revenue slack. At a December 2023 Supply Chain Management Forum in Taiwan, Wei discussed AI chip

---

[37] Moataz Helmy, "The story behind the most important tech company in the world: TSMC Taiwan," *LinkedIn*, August 13, 2023, www.linkedin.com/pulse/story-behind-most-important-tech-company-world-tsmc-taiwan-helmy/

[38] Stephen Nellis, "Nvidia unveils new gaming chip with AI features, taps TSMC for manufacturing, *Reuters*, September 20, 2022, www.reuters.com/technology/nvidia-unveils-new-gaming-chip-with-ai-features-taps-tsmc-manufacturing-2022-09-20/

demand from applications such as health care, remote work, and reducing energy consumption. Demand for AI chips exceeded supply. In 2023, market researchers forecast a 52-week lead-time for Nvidia's flagship H100 AI GPU while Dell told investors the company faced a 39-week lead-time for its AI servers. In part to hedge its operations from a feared invasion or blockade of Taiwan by China, TSMC was investing $40 billion in an Arizona-based factory that aimed to begin production in the first half of 2025.[39]

TSMC enjoyed overwhelming competitive advantages in the manufacturing of advanced semiconductors and GPUs used for generative AI with help from its collaboration with Nvidia. In 2023, TSMC manufactured about 90% of the world's advanced chips. Moreover, Nvidia designed 95% of the GPUs the chip giant manufactured. Meanwhile, TSMC and Nvidia earned substantial profits, with gross margins of 60% and 74%, respectively. Nvidia's high margins result from its high prices and enormous switching costs. For example, Nvidia's HGX H100 systems sell for roughly $300,000 each. Used for financial applications and analytics, the chips consisted of 35,000 parts and required the hardware and software libraries protected by thousands of patents Nvidia had developed over two decades.[40]

Meanwhile, TSMC maintained its leadership due to the following competitive advantages:

- **Time and cost to build new fabs.** The time and cost to build a new chip fabrication plant represents a significant barrier to entry for aspiring rivals. For example, TSMC's Arizona plant was expected to

---

[39] Sam Reynolds, "TSMC bets on AI chips for revival of growth in semiconductor demand," *Network World*, December 8, 2023, www.networkworld.com/article/1252992/tsmc-bets-on-ai-chips-for-revival-of-growth-in-semiconductor-demand.html

[40] June Yoon, "AI chip contenders face daunting 'moats,'" *Financial Times*, November 27, 2023, www.ft.com/content/89745f19-1968-4c46-aaf2-5c6a6a50067f

consume $40 billion in capital and take more than three years to begin producing chips, despite TSMC's more than three decades of experience building fabs.[41]

- **Skilled labor requirements.** Once built, a fab requires workers with advanced degrees in "electrical engineering, physics, or material science." By November 2023, a shortage of such workers had already delayed the start date for TSMC's Arizona plant.[42]

- **High costs and long wait times for chip-making equipment.** One of the most essential pieces of equipment for making chips is an extreme ultraviolet lithography machine, produced by a single company, ASML. Sporting a price tag of over $300 million each, in November 2023, buyers faced a two-year wait once they placed an order.[43] TSMC's wait times represented a barrier to all new entrants into advanced chip manufacturing.

- **Advanced packaging patents.** Ultimately, its huge patent portfolio, particularly for advanced packaging, gave TSMC an advantage over Samsung. With more than 52,000 patents related to chip making, 3,000 of which pertained to advanced packaging, rivals faced enormous challenges in winning over TSMC customers. Moreover, the chip giant's eight years of

---

[41] June Yoon, "AI chip contenders face daunting 'moats,'" *Financial Times*, November 27, 2023, Ibid.

[42] June Yoon, "AI chip contenders face daunting 'moats,'" *Financial Times*, November 27, 2023, Ibid.

[43] June Yoon, "AI chip contenders face daunting 'moats,'" *Financial Times*, November 27, 2023, Ibid.

investment in advanced packaging meant TSMC would likely obtain new patents to block rivals from gaining market share.[44]

In 2023, generative AI had the potential to revive TSMC's growth while the threat of a Chinese invasion of Taiwan could interrupt the flow of GPUs around the world. In the absence of a sufficient amount of chip production capacity outside of China's control, TSMC's investment potential was uncertain. Given TSMC's third quarter 2023 revenue decline, down 11% to $17.8 billion for the quarter ending in September 2023,[45] much of the company's investment potential hinged on its ability to satisfy the strong demand for GPU chips. With AI chip revenue expected to rise at a 50% average annual rate, TSMC planned to invest $2.9 billion in a plant in Western Taiwan to provide advanced packaging – dubbed Chip-on-Wafer-on-Substrate (CoWoS) – putting several chips in the same package and interlocking them to operate as a single chip. In July 2023, Wei indicated TSMC was increasing its capacity as quickly as possible to satisfy demand for AI chips from Nvidia, AMD, AWS, Microsoft, Google, and Apple. In September 2023, TSMC chair Mark Liu said the company would alleviate the CoWoS bottleneck by the end of 2024.[46] By 2028, Wei estimated TSMC's

---

[44] June Yoon, "AI chip contenders face daunting 'moats,'" *Financial Times*, November 27, 2023, Ibid.

[45] "Taiwan Semiconductor Mfg. Co. Ltd.," *Google*, accessed December 28, 2023, www.google.com/search?q=tsmc+stock&rlz=1C1CHBF_enUS860US893&oq=tsmc+s&gs_lcrp=EgZjaHJvbWUqDQgAEAAYgwEYsQMYgAQyDQgAEAAYgwEYsQMYgAQyDQgBEAAYgwEYsQMYgAQyBggCEEUYOTINCAMQLhjHARjRAxiABDIHCAQQQABiABDINCAUQABiDARixAxiABDIHCAYQABiABDIHCAcQABiABDIHCAgQABiABDIHCAkQABiABKgCALACAA&sourceid=chrome&ie=UTF-8

[46] Natalia Toczkowskain, "TSMC sees AI chip output constraints lasting 1.5 years," *Nikkei*, December 4, 2023, https://asia.nikkei.com/Business/Tech/Semiconductors/TSMC-sees-AI-chip-output-constraints-lasting-1.5-years

total sales from AI chips – including CPUs, GPU, and AI accelerators performing training and inference – as growing to 6% of total sales to "the low teens."[47]

While TMSC aimed to add sufficient CoWoS capacity to satisfy burgeoning demand for AI chips, a Chinese invasion or blockade of Taiwan risked imperiling TSMC and its ability to produce AI chips on which Nvidia depended to fulfill orders for its products. In May 2023, China was carrying out military exercises around Taiwan of unprecedented scale and intensity. Many policymakers in Washington predicted a Chinese invasion of Taiwan by 2025 or 2027. Such an invasion could idle TSMC's Taiwan-based fabs, sending the value of its stock plummeting. Moreover, given the so-called Grand Alliance between TSMC and its partners such as Nvidia, ASML, and chip design software companies such as Cadence, a Chinese invasion of Taiwan would not only paralyze TSMC, it would slash the growth potential of the Grand Alliance members as well. In October 2022, the Biden administration raised the competitive stakes with China by announcing measures to stop US-based companies from shipping the fastest-performing GPUs to China. In late 2022, TSMC announced it would invest $40 billion to build two fabs in Arizona, anticipated to come online in 2027. Sadly, for TSMC, these two fabs would not take up the slack left by the potential idling of Taiwan-based fabs following a hypothetical invasion by China. The 600,000 wafers produced in Arizona would represent 4.6% of TSMC's global output of 13 million wafers per year.[48] In 2023, there was no

---

[47] Hideaki Ryugen, "TSMC to invest $2.9bn in advanced packaging plant for AI chips," *Nikkei*, July 26, 2023, https://asia.nikkei.com/Business/Tech/Semiconductors/TSMC-to-invest-2.9bn-in-advanced-packaging-plant-for-AI-chips

[48] Rob Toews, "The Geopolitics Of AI Chips Will Define The Future Of AI," *Forbes*, May 7, 2023, www.forbes.com/sites/robtoews/2023/05/07/the-geopolitics-of-ai-chips-will-define-the-future-of-ai/

good estimate of the probability of a Chinese invasion of Taiwan. However, if it did happen, TSMC's $67.5 billion in revenue (12 months ending September 2023)[49] and its December 28, 2023, stock market capitalization of $498 billion would surely fall sharply.

Publicly Traded Semiconductor Manufacturing Equipment Suppliers

In 2023, while Canon and Nikon made lithography machines, ASML was the only publicly traded company supplying the machines used to etch circuit pathways into silicon wafers for manufacturing GPUs. Below, we examine ASML's history in generative AI, describe the firm's generative AI products, and assess the company's investment potential.

ASML

Founded in 1984, Advanced Semiconductor Materials Lithography (ASML) is the Veldhoven, Netherlands-based provider of photolithography machines that use light to etch integrated circuits onto silicon wafers. By 2023 ASML was the industry's leading beneficiary of demand for its machines due to its 1995 embrace of extreme ultraviolet (EUV) technology, an essential technology for building GPUs required for generative AI. ASML, which competes with Canon and Nikon, provides its EUV lithography machines to Intel, Samsung, and TSMC. The firm began as a joint venture between Dutch electronics giant Philips and semiconductor equipment maker ASM International. After struggling for years to build a product customers would buy, in 1995, ASML went public and bet the company on EUV. Sadly, it was not until 2018 that the company had

---

[49] "Taiwan Semiconductor Manufacturing Revenue 2010-2023," *Macrotrends*, accessed December 28, 2023, www.macrotrends.net/stocks/charts/TSM/taiwan-semiconductor-manufacturing/revenue

worked out the kinks in the product so commercial customers could start
to use it. The machines cost $300 million, weighed "180 tonnes and were
the size of a double-decker bus." ASML had 5,000 suppliers, including Carl
Zeiss, a German optics firm that provided its lenses, VDL, a Dutch maker
of robotic arms that fed wafers into the machine, and Cymer, an American
light source supplier ASML bought in 2013. ASML was so important to chip
makers that Intel, Samsung, and TSMC paid for the company's R&D in
exchange for equity.[50]

By 2023, ASML enjoyed a monopoly on the EUV lithography machines
prized by GPU manufacturers supplying the providers of computers used
to train and operate LLMs. In March 2023, Jefferies forecast demand would
grow because GPU manufacturers required ASML machines to produce
advanced process nodes, including TSMC's 5 nanometer and 3 nanometer
parts, required to build the GPUs "used to power machine learning and
AI training and inference workloads." Jeffries anticipated generative
AI would "result in a sharp increase in GPU, CPU, memory and high
speed connectivity chip demand," pushing foundries to buy ASML EUV
lithography machines. Jeffries forecast this pressure would boost ASML's
revenue growth to a 21% average annual rate between 2022 and 2025.[51]

ASML made two models of EUV lithography machines – a $200
million EUV and the $330 million High NA – both of which offered huge
advantages over incumbent deep ultraviolet (DUV) machines. Lithography
used light to create an image of the printed circuit on a semiconductor. For
about 20 years, light created these images. The shorter the wavelength, the
smaller the chips. While DUV had a wavelength of 193 nanometers, EUV
and High NA were 93% shorter at 13.5 nanometers. EUV increased the

---

[50] "How ASML became chipmaking's biggest monopoly," *The Economist*,
February 29, 2020, www.economist.com/business/2020/02/29/
how-asml-became-chipmakings-biggest-monopoly

[51] Tobias Mann, "There's one sure winner in the AI explosion, say analysts:
Dutch outfit ASML," *The Register*, www.theregister.com/2023/03/24/
asml_clear_winner_in_run/

printing precision, packing more transistors into a chip and boosting its processing power. High NA used a larger lens, enabling fabricators to build chips capable of meeting generative AI's high processing requirements. Goldman Sachs predicted the EUV and High NA machines would enable the global semiconductor market to grow from $600 billion to over $1 trillion by 2030 while facilitating the production of chips for "AI, high-powered computing, and autonomous driving." Without EUV machines, AI chips would be built using DUV, requiring multiple wafer exposures to light, thereby increasing production costs of both labor and energy required to fulfill orders. While investors initially doubted EUV technology, by July 2023, ASML expected to make more than 80 EUV machines a year by 2025. In addition, the company was building the capacity required to manufacture 20 High NA machines annually. "There's a sizable commitment for this technology – because it works and adds a lot of value," noted Goldman Sachs.[52]

Despite the advantages of its technology, by the end of 2023, ASML's investment potential was uncertain due to a disappointing 2024 revenue forecast and the expected appointment of a new CEO. In ASML's third quarter, profit declined and the company's exceeding estimates while revenue increased 15.5% to $7.1 billion. The company forecast no revenue growth for 2024 due to uncertainty about how US export restrictions on GPUs for AI might affect shipments of ASML's machines. Meanwhile, the Netherlands was imposing export restrictions on the advanced semiconductor equipment ASML made. Moreover, ASML net bookings declined 42% between the second and third quarters as its customers cut back on spending. "The semiconductor industry is currently working

---

[52] Alexander Duval, "EUV-made semiconductor chips will enable the next wave of AI," *Goldman Sachs Research*, July 13, 2023, www.goldmansachs.com/intelligence/page/euv-made-semiconductor-chips-will-enable-next-wave-of-ai.html

through the bottom of the cycle and our customers expect the inflection point to be visible by the end of this year," ASML CEO Peter Wennink said in a statement. He added, "But we also look at 2024 as an important year to prepare for significant growth that we expect for 2025."[53]

ASML stock ended 2023 about 13% below its all-time high reached in September 2021. The company began 2024 facing the question of whether Wennink's April 2024 retirement, announced in November 2023, would make the company better or worse off in the future. Meanwhile, analysts expected investors would have to wait until 2025 to see the revenue benefit from generative AI. Christophe Fouquet, ASML's chief business officer, would have big shoes to fill when he took over from Wennink as CEO after a decade at the helm. During his tenure, revenue quadrupled and ASML shares rose 1,000% as chip demand for smartphones and vehicles soared. While Wennink was able to make four acquisitions during his tenure as CEO, ASML's market power made it less likely Fouquet would be able to follow a growth-by-acquisition strategy. Moreover, the US-China trade war made it likely ASML would not be able to sell its most sophisticated machines to China.[54] Analyst Alexander Peterk of Société Générale forecast ASML would not receive a revenue boost from generative AI until 2025. Peterk, who wrote it took more than a year for the Dutch firm to fulfill EUV equipment orders, expected the machines to ship in 2025, boosting ASML's revenue that year by as much as 3%.[55]

---

[53] Arjun Kharpal, "Shares of critical chip firm ASML drop 4% after new U.S. curbs, outlook warning," *CNBC*, October 18, 2023, www.cnbc.com/2023/10/18/asml-earnings-report-q3-2023.html#:~:text=Here's%20how%20ASML%20did%20in,versus%206.71%20billion%20euros%20expected

[54] Karen Kwok, "ASML's new CEO has tricky path to a 1,000% return," *Reuters*, December 1, 2023, www.reuters.com/breakingviews/asmls-new-ceo-has-tricky-path-1000-return-2023-11-30/

[55] Deanna Walker, "Nvidia surge fails to rub off on those who need it most," *Bloomberg*, June 22, 2023, www.bloomberg.com/news/articles/2023-06-22/nvidia-surge-fails-to-rub-off-on-those-it-needs-most-tech-watch

Publicly Traded Computer Server Manufacturers

In 2023, several firms made the servers used for processing generative AI workloads in data centers. Server suppliers included Dell, Hewlett Packard Enterprise, Huawei, Lenovo, and Super Micro. Below, we examine two such companies, Dell and Super Micro, describing their history in generative AI, their generative AI server products, and their investment potential.

Dell

In 2023, Dell had been in business nearly 39 years before launching products aimed at generative AI. Michael Dell founded PC's Limited in 1984 to provide customized personal computer upgrades out of his University of Texas at Austin dorm room. In May 2023, Dell announced its intent to offer products and services to help companies tap into the benefits of generative AI. Dell dropped out of college in 1984 to build PCs. In 1985, Dell designed and built Turbo PCs and sold them directly to consumers through advertisements and mail order catalogs. By bypassing retail channels, Dell could offer high-quality PCs, excellent service, and competitive prices. In 1988, Dell Computer Corporation went public.[56]

In May 2023, Dell announced a partnership with Nvidia, dubbed Project Helix, at the Dell Technologies World conference. Project Helix supplied companies with the systems, including a Dell XE9680 server and eight Nvidia H100 Tensor Core GPUs, required to train and operate LLMs on premise rather than by outsourcing to cloud service providers. In June 2023, Michael Dell aimed to plant fear in the hearts of companies that were not reinventing their companies using AI. "The real opportunity is to reimagine your organization and what you can become given the superpowers AI unleashes," he wrote in a LinkedIn post. "If you're not applying AI across your organization and thinking deeply about

---

[56] The Editors of Encyclopedia Britannica, "Dell Inc." *Britannica*, December 26, 2023, www.britannica.com/topic/Dell-Inc

reinvention, you're already behind." Dell wrote society would find ways to manage generative AI's risks while tapping its benefits. He also outlined his vision of enterprises operating a blend of private and public LLMs.[57] By December 2023, demand for Dell's AI-enabled servers – "over $500 million" sold or 2.2% of Dell's third quarter 2023 revenue of $22.3 billion – was not yet been high enough to offset the decline in demand for PCs.[58]

In 2023, Dell's generative AI strategy included products, such as servers and enterprise storage for generative AI applications, and services for helping enterprises prepare data for LLM training.

- **Servers.** By October 2023, Dell had found customers for its Project Helix. For example, Sanjeev Arora, a computer science professor at Princeton, said the university had implemented hardware from Dell and Nvidia "within a high-performance computing cluster to develop large language models." The system enabled researchers to work in areas such as "visualization, modeling and quantum computing," Arora said.[59] Other server customers included CoreWeave and Imbue, which used Dell's XE9680 servers to "train foundational models."[60]

---

[57] O'Ryan Johnson, "Michael Dell: Use AI 'Superpowers' To 'Reimagine Your Organization,'" *CRN*, June 8, 2023, www.crn.com/news/channel-news/michael-dell-use-ai-superpowers-to-reimagine-your-organization

[58] "Dell Technologies Inc. (NYSE:DELL) Q3 2024," *Insider Monkey Transcripts*, December 1, 2023, https://finance.yahoo.com/news/dell-technologies-inc-nyse-dell-135957077.html

[59] Mike Wheatley, "Dell enhances its generative AI hardware and software portfolio to cover more extensive use cases," *SiliconAngle*, October 4, 2023, https://siliconangle.com/2023/10/04/dell-enhances-generative-ai-hardware-software-portfolio-cover-extensive-use-cases/

[60] "Dell Technologies Inc. (NYSE:DELL) Q3 2024," *Insider Monkey Transcripts*, December 1, 2023, Ibid.

- **Enterprise storage.** In December 2023, Dell announced new storage products, dubbed PowerScale, to help enterprises to process AI workloads more effectively. Martin Glynn, senior director of product management for Dell unstructured data storage solutions, said most Dell customers planned to shift to "an AI-first operating model." To that end, they would use their own data, he said. Dell expected its new storage products to double data storage and retrieval efficiency. Dell planned to ship its enterprise storage product in the first half of 2024.[61]

- **Services.** Through partnerships, Dell offered services to enable customers to build open source LLMs and analyze the resulting data. As Dell COO Jeff Clarke told investors in December 2023, "We are collaborating with Meta to make it easy for our customers to deploy Meta's Llama 2 models on-premises, with Dell AI-optimized portfolio." He also highlighted a collaboration with Hugging Face to help users build open source GenAI models. In November 2023, he said Dell introduced the ObjectScale XF960, an appliance to help users operate LLMs and perform real-time analytics.[62] Dell's generative AI professional services included helping companies prepare data to train LLMs, speeding up

---

[61] Andy Patrizio, "Dell Technologies updates storage products for AI," *Network World*, December 12, 2023, www.networkworld.com/article/1257328/dell-technologies-updates-storage-products-for-ai.html

[62] "Dell Technologies Inc. (NYSE:DELL) Q3 2024," *Insider Monkey Transcripts*, December 1, 2023, Ibid.

the implementation of a company's private LLM, and educating company employees in the latest generative AI developments.[63]

Dell took a bullish view of the growth potential of its AI strategy. However, in December 2023, that potential did not show signs of making a significant difference in Dell's revenue trajectory. Dell took a bullish view of its future. "Our AI-optimized server backlog nearly doubled versus the end of Q2 with a multibillion-dollar sales pipeline, including increasing interest, across all regions," Clarke said. He added, "We believe Dell is uniquely positioned with our broad portfolio to help customers size, characterize and build GenAI solutions that meet their performance, cost and security requirements. Our AI strategy, AI in our products, AI built on our solutions, AI for our business and AI for our ecosystem partners is the foundation for our actions, priorities, roadmaps and partnerships."[64]

While Clarke told investors Dell would return to growth in 2025, Sanford Bernstein analyst Tony Sacconaghi noted Dell had said the same thing in the previous quarter. Clarke said customers were cutting their budgets and imposing pricing pressure on Dell. AI was a source of good news, but not enough of it. Although Dell's server business suffered a 10% revenue decline, the company's high-margin AI servers grew 9%. Dell also generated positive net cash flow and ended the quarter with $9.9 billion in cash and short-term investments.[65] Many analysts expressed skepticism about Dell's growth prospects. Daniel Newman, CEO of The Futurum Group, said AI-based devices were essential to Dell's ability to grow faster

---

[63] Mike Wheatley, "Dell enhances its generative AI hardware and software portfolio to cover more extensive use cases," *SiliconAngle*, October 4, 2023, Ibid.

[64] "Dell Technologies Inc. (NYSE:DELL) Q3 2024," *Insider Monkey Transcripts*, December 1, 2023, Ibid.

[65] Paul Gillin, "Hardware sales trough sends Dell revenue down for the fifth straight quarter," *SiliconAngle*, November 30, 2023, https://siliconangle.com/2023/11/30/hardware-sales-trough-sends-dell-revenue-fifth-straight-quarter/

than investors expect. Newman argued Dell would not enjoy a significant growth boost from such devices until people upgraded to AI-based phones and PCs that enabled users to "do something new on the device," He predicted that might "not happen until the latter half of 2024."[66] Research firm Canalys projected AI-capable PCs would hit the market in 2025 and grow quickly. By 2027, such devices would account for "around 60% of all PCs shipped," Canalys noted.[67]

By March 2024, Dell shares were surging after reporting faster than expected growth in its fourth quarter, thanks in part to demand for its AI servers. Investors responded to Dell's expectations-beating results by bidding up the company's stock by 30% on March 1. For the fourth quarter of 2023, Dell reported an 11% drop in revenue to $22.32 billion, slightly exceeding analysts' expectations. The company's adjusted earnings per share for the quarter reached $2.20, 47 cents a share more than analysts' consensus estimate. Dell impressed analysts with the strong demand for its AI servers. Morgan Stanley analysts raised their price target 29% to $128. "AI server commentary stole the show," wrote the analysts. "The strength of AI server orders, backlog, pipeline, and expanding CSP/enterprise customer base show DELL's AI story is early days and gaining momentum."[68] Morgan Stanley's enthusiasm for Dell's AI server-powered growth potential, coupled with the 20% increase in its dividend for the year, strengthened the case for a bullish bet on Dell's stock.

---

[66] Shashwat Sankranti, "Dell's stock rally faces reality check as AI demand fails to keep pace," *WION*, December 7, 2023, www.wionews.com/business-economy/dells-stock-rally-faces-reality-check-as-ai-demand-fails-to-keep-pace-667085

[67] Harshita Mary Varghese, "Dell misses quarterly revenue estimates on slow PC market recovery," *Reuters*, December 1, 2023, www.reuters.com/technology/dell-misses-quarterly-revenue-estimates-slow-pc-market-recovery-2023-11-30/

[68] Alex Koller," Dell shares have best day since return to stock market in 2018," *CNBC*, March 1, 2024, www.cnbc.com/2024/03/01/dell-shares-have-best-day-since-return-to-stock-market-in-2018.html

Super Micro Computer

Super Micro Computer, the San Jose, California-based maker of generative AI servers and liquid cooling products, was founded in 1993. The company's generative AI products were launched in parallel with Nvidia, based on a business partnership extending for more than 30 years. Super Micro CEO Charles Liang immigrated to the United States from Taiwan as did Nvidia's Huang. By February 2024, Liang had been collaborating with Nvidia for more than 30 years, according to *CRN*. This long-standing partnership contributed to Super Micro's success. "Whatever Nvidia develops, we pretty much sync up with them," Liang said. "And that's another reason why, whenever they have a new product out, we have a new product available quicker than our competitors do," he added.[69]

Super Micro's generative AI products were growing in tandem with Nvidia. Nvidia's revenue grew 265% in the final quarter of 2023 while earning a 57% net margin and issuing a forecast of 300% growth in the first quarter of 2024. In February 2024, Super Micro, which collaborated with Nvidia to make AI servers and workstations supporting the chip designer's H100 GPUs, was the third-largest server provider with 5% market share. Super Micro also worked to help data centers remove the heat they generated while doing calculations to build LLMs. While air conditioners did this work in some data centers, a better way to remove the heat was liquid cooling. Like Vertiv, which we examine later in this chapter, Super Micro made liquid cooling systems for data centers. In February 2024, Rosenblatt Securities said it expected Super Micro to increase its market share from single digits to "double digits in the next few years with a special emphasis on enterprise solutions," Rosenblatt analyst Hans Mosesmann

---

[69] Peter Cohan, "Why Super Micro Stock's 20% Plunge Is An AI Investing Opportunity," *Forbes*, February 26, 2024, www.forbes.com/sites/petercohan/2024/02/26/why-super-micro-computer-stocks-20-plunge-is-a-buying-opportunity/

wrote in a note. "A pivotal factor in Supermicro's growth trajectory is the adoption of liquid cooling technology, a critical development for overcoming challenges in cloud computing at scale in AI," he added.[70]

In February 2024, Super Micro, whose stock had soared 195% in the first two months of the year, had excellent investment potential. In the quarter ending December 2023, the company reported expectations-beating results, including a 103% increase in revenue to $3.66 billion and a 71% rise in earnings per share to $5.59, and raised guidance for 2024 by 40%. At the same time Super Micro, which earned about half its revenue from generative AI-related products, was growing rapidly, some investors, who concluded the stock had risen too far too fast, were betting on a decline in the company's stock by selling its shares short. (Short sellers borrow shares from a broker, sell them in the open market, and hope to repay the stock loan by buying back the shares after they have declined in price.) Fortunately for Super Micro investors, a short seller must cover their short bets if the stock goes up in price. Given the stock's rapid increase, the buying of the stock at higher prices to repay the stock loan drives up the price further. While short sellers had lost $4.3 billion on their bets against Super Micro in the year ending February 2024, the stock did fall 20% that month after the company announced it would raise $1.5 billion to finance capital expenditures through a stock sale.[71]

Fortunately for investors betting the stock would rise, Jiang and some analysts remained optimistic about the Super Micro's prospects for growth. "Overall, I feel very confident that this AI boom will continue for another many quarters if not many years," he added. "And together with the related inferencing and other computing eco system requirements, demand can last for even many decades to come, we may call this an AI revolution."

---

[70] Peter Cohan, "Why Super Micro Stock's 20% Plunge Is An AI Investing Opportunity," *Forbes*, February 26, 2024, Ibid.

[71] Peter Cohan, "Why Super Micro Stock's 20% Plunge Is An AI Investing Opportunity," *Forbes*, February 26, 2024, Ibid.

One analyst, Barclays' George Wang, raised his price target on Super Micro. "AI demand is still outstripping supply," Wang wrote in a research note. "Once supply fully normalizes in next quarters, demand pipeline and expanded capacity support $25 billion-$30 billion in revenue over the next 2-3 years, vs. Dec Q annualized run rate of $15 billion," Wang added. He said, "a potential heat dissipation upgrade from air to liquid cooling could be another key transformation in data center design, which could benefit Supermicro."[72] Super Micro investors were only likely to enjoy a high return if the company continued its pattern of exceeding investor expectations and raising its forecasts for future growth. Accomplishing that would depend on the company's ability to continue building products that satisfied growing demand, for generative AI and other significant growth opportunities.

Publicly Traded Data Center Cooling Product Manufacturers

In 2023, several firms made the equipment used to remove heat from data centers resulting from the operation of GPUs handling generative AI workloads. While Vertiv was the leader, making immersive cooling products, suppliers, such as Eaton and Schneider, made other kinds of data center cooling products. Below, we examine Vertiv's history in generative AI, describe the firm's data center cooling products, and assess the company's investment potential.

Vertiv

Vertiv, a Westerville, Ohio-based provider of power management and cooling equipment for data centers, underwent many corporate transformations before emerging as a leading beneficiary of the generative AI boom. Vertiv was formerly the network-power business of Emerson

---

[72] Peter Cohan, "Why Super Micro Stock's 20% Plunge Is An AI Investing Opportunity," *Forbes*, February 26, 2024, Ibid.

Electric built with help from the 2010 acquisition for $1.5 billion of Chloride Group. Emerson later took a $508 million write-down on that deal, causing its former CEO Dave Farr to express his regret for getting into the industry. Emerson acquired the business in 2016 and sold it to Platinum Equity for $4 billion. In 2020, the business, called Vertiv, went public by merging with a Goldman Sachs-led special purpose acquisition company. Vertiv's Executive Chairman Dave Cote had previously served as CEO of Honeywell and as an executive at GE. In 2023, Vertiv was a major beneficiary of data centers' need to cool off the GPU-laden computing systems used to train and operate LLMs. As Bank of America analyst Andrew Obin wrote in a June 2023 report, a 10% increase in power use would require "a more than 10% increase in electrical-equipment capacity because of the need for redundant infrastructure to help guard against power failures." Higher power means more heat generated, creating demand for equipment to cool down the servers to ambient temperature. Vertiv's liquid cooling systems solved the problem of overheated data centers very effectively. In June 2023, Vertiv was struggling to satisfy demand for its products for data centers processing generative AI workloads. About a third of Vantiv's revenue came from hyperscale data center customers, considerably higher than the single-digit percentages at larger rivals such as Eaton and Schneider, noted Obin.[73]

Vertiv provided immersive cooling systems and other products for data centers hosting generative AI applications. The level of densely packed servers doing calculations all day long boosted the amount of heat that data centers needed to eliminate to keep the equipment from overheating. Liquid cooling, which circulated water or other coolants through heat exchangers to absorb the heat generated by computer components, was

---

[73] Brooke Sutherland; "The AI boom has enough room for manufacturers," *Bloomberg*, June 17, 2023, www.bloomberg.com/opinion/articles/2023-06-16/industrial-strength-the-ai-boom-has-enough-room-for-manufacturers-liyxOmhm

more efficient than fans or air conditioning, KPMG Managing Director Brian Lewis said. Liquid cooling's efficiency advantage also challenged data center operators to make sure their buildings could handle the technology's added heft. "Liquid cooling adds weight because it is sitting on the floor and is embedded into the circuit boards," Forrester Research senior analyst Abhijit Sunil told me. "It is heavier than air cooled which has big fans blowing in the data center."[74]

To satisfy the demands generative AI places on data centers, Vertiv offers products including the following:

- **Immersive cooling.** In December 2023, Vertiv announced it would provide liquid cooling to Intel's Gaudi AI accelerator. Vertiv's liquid cooling product was able to handle four times the power and much higher temperatures than air-cooled solutions. Vertiv's pumped two-phase liquid cooling product used a low-power pump to move non-toxic refrigerant through cold plates attached directly to the chip. Vertiv's P2P system transferred heat from the chips to the fluid by changing phases from liquid to gas. The system captured and cooled the gas, turning it back into a liquid, thus reducing or eliminating a data center's need for chillers. Intel's Devdatta Kulkarni, principal engineer, said Vertiv's P2P system would help Intel Gaudi AI accelerator customers to "meet critical sustainability goals."[75]

---

[74] Peter Cohan, "2 Stocks That Could Benefit From Generative AI's Energy Demand Growth," *Forbes*, November 10, 2023, www.forbes.com/sites/petercohan/2023/11/10/2-stocks-that-could-benefit-from-generative-ais-energy-demand-growth/

[75] Andy Patrizio, "Intel and Vertiv partner to liquid cool AI processors," *Network World*, December 12, 2023, www.networkworld.com/article/1257405/intel-and-vertiv-partner-to-liquid-cool-ai-processors.html

- **Microgrids.** Since generative AI required more power, data center operators needed to anticipate the capacity and availability limitations of traditional electric utilities. To address this, Vertiv collaborated with American Electric Power to implement the microgrid application. Microgrids meet the power needs of processing generative AI while reducing data centers' dependency on the electrical grid for power capacity and availability. They also presented an alternative to frequent diesel generator backups. Vertiv's microgrids reduced the risk to data centers of electric utility outages by supplementing the electrical utility with solar arrays and hydrogen fuel cells.[76]

In 2023, Vertiv's performance and prospects appeared strong. However, the trajectory of its stock price depended on whether the company continued to exceed investor expectations. However, Vertiv had two things going in its favor:

- **The liquid cooling industry was growing quickly, propelled in part by demand for generative AI.** Liquid cooling represented a fast-growing market opportunity. According to *Polaris Market Research*, the global data center liquid cooling market was valued at $1.81 billion in 2021 and expected to grow at a 24% average annual rate through 2026.[77]

---

[76] Sean Mitchell, "Vertiv Introduces Innovative Microgrid Solution for Data Centers," *Data Center News*, October 28, 2023, https://datacenternews.asia/ story/vertiv-introduces-innovative-microgrid-solution-for-data-centers

[77] Peter Cohan, "2 Stocks That Could Benefit From Generative AI's Energy Demand Growth," *Forbes*, November 10, 2023, Ibid.

- **Vertiv dominated its industry.** In its third quarter of 2023, Vertiv posted better-than-expected results and provided investors with an ambitious forecast for the year. Specifically, revenue increased about 18% to $1.74 billion and analysts expected nearly 20% growth for the company in fiscal 2023 to $6.82 billion. Moreover, Vertiv's earnings per share grew 126% in the third quarter of 2023 and analysts expected the company' EPS to rise by 203% in fiscal 2023.[78]

In 2023, Wall Street analysts were optimistic about Vertiv stock. Deutsche Bank wrote, "Vertiv clearly caught the AI wave," in a September 14 research note. The firm, which raised its price target to $48 per share, saw potential for over 50% further upside "if data center investments continue growing at a double-digit clip." Meanwhile, Evercore ISI saw Vertiv as an industry leader. In an October 1 investor note, the firm wrote that the company "has the top market share for thermal management solutions and is a powerhouse in the arena." Evercore added that the company's association with Leibert, the inventor of precision cooling, gave Vertiv an advantage over rivals such as Eaton and APC. Moreover, Evercore, which set a $50 price target on the company's shares, noted Vertiv offers contracts on energy savings "to earn higher payouts, if a higher percentage of operating expenses is saved."[79]

Vertiv was optimistic about its future. The company expected strong demand for products related to generative AI as well as products to help data centers handle more traditional processing. "If we talk about technologies that are applied to high-density GPU or compute, as for example, liquid cooling, GPUs or some rack-level power distribution

---

[78] Peter Cohan, "2 Stocks That Could Benefit From Generative AI's Energy Demand Growth," *Forbes*, November 10, 2023, Ibid.

[79] Peter Cohan, "2 Stocks That Could Benefit From Generative AI's Energy Demand Growth," *Forbes*, November 10, 2023, Ibid.

solutions, I will still say our order book is in the tens of millions of dollars," said Vertiv CEO Giordano Albertazzi.[80]

He added, "Many elements of our portfolio, chillers, direct expansion cooling, heat rejection systems, switchgear, busbars, UPS, you name them are used – regardless if GPU or CPU compute, high density or normal density. The majority of our products will support many types of compute, including AI. That is the beauty of having a comprehensive portfolio of all critical infrastructure technologies, across the entire span of the powertrain, the thermal chain and IT-wide space infrastructure, something that very few companies truly have."[81]

Generative AI Hardware Critical Activities

In 2023, chip designers, chip manufacturers, semiconductor equipment and server providers, and liquid cooling manufacturers were among the leading beneficiaries of demand for generative AI. Based on the case studies, a company's ability to perform four critical activities was likely to determine its ability to gain market share in generative AI hardware:

- **Ability to design and build the most advanced technology to satisfy customer needs.** Particularly in the fields of chip design, chip manufacturing, and immersive cooling, generative AI hardware companies needed to stay ahead of rivals by solving technology problems at the frontier of the challenges facing customers.

---

[80] "Vertiv Holdings Co (NYSE:VRT) Q3 2023 Earnings Call Transcript," *Insider Monkey Transcripts*, October 26, 2023, https://finance.yahoo.com/news/vertiv-holdings-co-nyse-vrt-140900648.html
[81] "Vertiv Holdings Co (NYSE:VRT) Q3 2023 Earnings Call Transcript," *Insider Monkey Transcripts*, October 26, 2023, Ibid.

- **Development of the most comprehensive software library.** Particularly for GPU chip designers and manufacturers, the fastest and most reliable hardware was insufficient without software that developers could use to build applications incorporating the hardware.

- **Partnerships and investments to develop new customers.** The most successful generative AI companies formed partnerships across the most important links in the industry value network, including consultants, software developers, and LLM providers, to open up the broadest set of potential growth opportunities.

- **Ability to attract and motivate top talent.** Leading generative AI hardware companies could only maintain their position by attracting and motivating the most talented people. Companies such as Nvidia attracted such talent by fielding leaders who could develop the professional skills of employees and by investing in startups and acquiring innovative companies.

Conclusion

This chapter highlighted diverse generative AI hardware providers. The chapter explored the powerful forces elevating the profitability of the generative AI hardware industry, specifically how industry leaders such as Nvidia and Vertiv continued to develop innovative technologies and form critical partnerships to keep them in the lead. The most successful generative AI hardware companies collaborated with customers to solve their most challenging technical problems. In December 2023, some generative AI hardware companies, notably Nvidia and Vertiv , had made more progress than others had, such as AMD and Dell, in earning a significant and growing proportion of their revenue from generative AI. Having profiled leading participants in the generative AI ecosystem in Chapters 4 through 7, Chapter 8 highlights what consumers, employees, business leaders, product and service providers, and investors should do to capture AI-powered chatbots' opportunities and guard against their risks.

PART III

Panning for Generative AI Gold

CHAPTER 8

Generative AI's Implications for Consumers, Employees, Companies, Product Providers, and Investors

What should you do about generative AI? There are at least as many answers as there are people. To simplify the answer, here are ways the technology can be useful for four broad groups of people:

- **Consumers.** If you are a consumer, you might use generative AI in your personal life to help make product purchase decisions, book vacations, do menu planning, or develop an exercise routine.

© Peter Cohan 2024
P. Cohan, *Brain Rush*, https://doi.org/10.1007/979-8-8688-0318-5_8

- **Employees and business operators.** If you run a
  business function such as sales, marketing, customer
  service, training, law, or accounting, generative AI
  can save considerable time in searching through
  documents, drafting emails and documents, and
  communicating with customers, employees, suppliers,
  and others.

- **Product providers.** If you are an entrepreneur
  seeking to win your slice of the burgeoning market for
  generative AI products and services, you need a deeper
  understanding – external growth headwinds and
  tailwinds – of the significant unmet needs of potential
  customers, the competitive strengths and weaknesses
  of rival companies, the best talent to populate your
  leadership team, and the evolution of technology.

- **Investors.** If you are an investor, you have an
  opportunity to enjoy significant gains by placing the
  right bet on publicly traded companies in the generative
  AI ecosystem – some of which we analyzed in Chapters 3
  through 7. While there are no perfect methods, such
  investors ought to analyze the size and growth potential
  of the markets these companies serve, their market share
  trajectories, their ability to win new customers and keep
  them buying over time, the competitiveness of their
  leadership teams, and their ability to generate sufficient
  capital to finance their growth.

In early 2024, the world was still experimenting with generative AI,
and had yet to draw clear implications. Therefore, readers needed tools to
analyze how best to capitalize on the changing generative AI landscape. To
this end, this chapter helps the four stakeholder groups to assess questions
that remain relevant in the future, including:

- How do stakeholders view the future of generative AI?

- Which generative AI experiments are creating the most value?

- What best and worst practices emerge from these experiments?

- What steps can stakeholders take to capture the most value from generative AI?

How Consumers Can Benefit from Generative AI

In early 2024, consumers expressed optimism about the uses of generative AI. Based on an analysis of 1,000 responses from US college-educated consumers, a 2024 KPMG Generative AI Consumer Trust Survey concluded consumer optimism about generative AI exceeded consumer concern about the technology's risks.[1] Highlights of the survey revealed useful insights, including the following:

- **Consumers expected generative AI to have "a significant impact on their personal lives."** Between 2024 and 2026, the percentage of consumers who expected generative AI to "impact their personal lives" increased from 42% to 60%.[2]

---

[1] "KPMG Study: Consumers Optimistic About Benefits of generative AI As Technology Becomes More Pervasive," *KPMG*, January 18, 2024, www.outlookseries.com/A0768/Security/3743_KPMG_Consumers_Optimistic_Benefits_generative_AI.htm#:~:text=70%25%20believe%20the%20benefits%20of,and%20business%20uses%20(50%25)

[2] "KPMG Study: Consumers Optimistic About Benefits of Generative AI As Technology Becomes More Pervasive," *KPMG*, January 18, 2024, Ibid.

- **Consumers expected generative AI to have a much
  more "significant impact on their professional lives."**
  Between 2024 and 2026, the percent of respondents
  expecting to agree with this statement increased from
  48% to 77%.[3]

- **More than half of consumers – 51% – were "extremely
  or very" excited** about the technology in 2024.[4]

- **Over two-thirds of consumers – 70% – believed the
  benefits of GenAI outweighed its risks.**[5]

- **Consumers trusted generative AI more for some
  applications than others.** The most trusted use of
  generative AI was as an educational resource (56%
  of respondents). Trust in the technology was lower
  for personalized recommendations (54%), customer
  service (50%), and business uses (50%).[6]

- **Consumers most feared the risk of generative
  AI-produced fake content.** Here are the percentage
  of respondents citing the following fears: fake news
  and fake content (67%); scams (65%); privacy (63%);
  cybersecurity (63%); false information (62%); job
  displacement (51%); and bias (50%).[7]

---

[3] "KPMG Study: Consumers Optimistic About Benefits of Generative AI As
Technology Becomes More Pervasive," *KPMG*, January 18, 2024, Ibid.

[4] "KPMG Study: Consumers Optimistic About Benefits of Generative AI As
Technology Becomes More Pervasive," *KPMG*, January 18, 2024, Ibid.

[5] "KPMG Study: Consumers Optimistic About Benefits of Generative AI As
Technology Becomes More Pervasive," *KPMG*, January 18, 2024, Ibid.

[6] "KPMG Study: Consumers Optimistic About Benefits of Generative AI As
Technology Becomes More Pervasive," *KPMG*, January 18, 2024, Ibid.

[7] "KPMG Study: Consumers Optimistic About Benefits of Generative AI As
Technology Becomes More Pervasive," *KPMG*, January 18, 2024, Ibid.

While this survey was not sufficiently comprehensive to generate
reliable predictions, in early 2024, the survey results suggested more
consumers would be willing to try generative AI in the future. The findings
indicate many younger consumers concluded the technology's benefits –
particularly for education and personalized recommendations – would
exceed its risks, most notably the negative societal repercussions of
fake content. Ultimately, the extent to which generative AI would have
a significant impact on consumers' lives depended on several factors
including the following:

- **Quantum value leap.** In 2024, it was unclear whether
  generative AI would offer consumers a substantial
  quantum value leap (QVL) – e.g., far higher benefits
  relative to the price compared to competing solutions
  such as Google searches or specific mobile apps. The
  higher and more pervasive generative AI's QVL, the
  wider its future consumer adoption. Conversely, if the
  technology did not provide significant value or new
  technology emerged to provide comparable value,
  generative AI's consumer adoption might fade.

- **Continued improvement of the technology.**
  Engineers and entrepreneurs typically adopted a
  prototyping approach to developing new products.
  They found early-adopter customers, developed a
  workable solution to their unmet needs, asked for
  feedback on how to improve the prototype, and
  repeated the process until the ultimate product
  performed well for more consumers. If developers of
  ChatGPT and other chatbots adopt this approach, the
  technology will improve, and consumers will adopt it
  more widely. Conversely, failure to collect and respond
  to user feedback could limit the technology's adoption.

- **Enhanced control over societal risks.** Finally, consumer adoption could vary depending on whether generative AI's risks remain low or moderate. If so, the KPMG survey finding that consumers view the technology's benefits as greater than its risks will not dim consumer adoption. On the other hand, should generative AI cause major societal damage, consumers may be scared away from the chatbots.

High-Payoff Generative AI Experiments

By early 2024, promising consumer experiments with generative AI were emerging. As a college professor, I had a closer look at how students were using AI chatbots in education – the application in which consumers had the highest level of trust, according to the KPMG survey.[8] Moreover, in 2024, Altman suggested education – as well as coding and health care – as an application ripe for benefiting from ChatGPT.[9] In 2023 and 2024, I was concerned about the risks of generative AI for education. Most notably, I wondered whether ChatGPT would make it easier for students to cheat on their homework and might produce hallucinations that students might unwittingly submit as correct answers to homework assignments. To be sure, Barnard College psychologist Tovah Klein found that research has not "shown an uptick in cheating so far—but the mistakes it can make mean

---

[8] "KPMG Study: Consumers Optimistic About Benefits of Generative AI As Technology Becomes More Pervasive," *KPMG*, January 18, 2024, Ibid.

[9] Tom Huddleston Jr., "ChatGPT is particularly useful for people in these 3 industries, says OpenAI CEO Sam Altman," *CNBC*, January 17, 2024, www.cnbc.com/2024/01/17/chatgpt-is-best-for-people-in-these-industries-openai-ceo-sam-altman.html

that parents and teachers should remind students to never rely solely on AI."[10] Nevertheless, ChatGPT's flaws suggested consumers should be wary of using generative AI for specific uses.

Having said that, by early 2024 students were using generative AI to aid their education. For example, Duolingo helped students learn new languages. The technology also expanded access to tutoring in remote communities. In 2023, Microsoft co-founder Bill Gates predicted people would be "stunned" by how much AI tutors could "be as good a tutor as any human."[11] I learned some more interesting applications of the technology from one of my students. In January 2024, I asked Tadeo Acosta-Rubio, a student in my Babson College *Global Entrepreneurship Experience – Sweden* (GEE-Sweden) course, to share his thoughts on how generative AI was helping him. Here are four of them.

- **Brainstorm, write, study.** Acosta-Rubio told me ChatGPT-4 helped him to brainstorm ideas, automate writing, and create images with the image-generating service DALL-E. What I found most intriguing was his use of the technology to create his own GPT "based on my economics class textbook to help me study and learn the concepts in the class." This reminded me of the computer program I wrote in high school to drill me on SAT vocabulary words.[12]

- **Converse with the book.** I assigned students in the GEE-Sweden course to read chapters from my book, *Startup Cities*. Acosta-Rubio uploaded my book to

---

[10] Tom Huddleston Jr., "ChatGPT is particularly useful for people in these 3 industries, says OpenAI CEO Sam Altman," *CNBC*, January 17, 2024, Ibid.

[11] Tom Huddleston Jr., "ChatGPT is particularly useful for people in these 3 industries, says OpenAI CEO Sam Altman," *CNBC*, January 17, 2024, Ibid.

[12] Peter Cohan, "Sam Altman Says ChatGPT Is Good For Education: Here Are Four Lessons From My Student," *Inc.*, January 22, 2024.

ChatGPT and used its text-to-voice feature to "have a conversation with the book" as he "prompted ChatGPT to read the book and respond as if it was the book speaking. I could ask it questions in a conversational way." He told me this approach was more efficient and effective than reading. He said, "I also find the voice to be very high quality."[13]

- **Train AI with your class notes.** My student used Notion AI – a writing assistant that helped users write, brainstorm, edit, and summarize – to take notes for his classes and his business. Notion AI also released an AI companion that he trained with these notes. He used the "Ask AI" function to ask questions and receive answers that cited his notes so he could "look at them further."[14]

- **Find the best news sources.** ChatGPT was not good with math – my student has found. To find the best sources for different topic areas, he used Perplexity – which answers different categories of questions with different sources. For example, he specified "web" for browsing, "academic" which searches published academic papers only, and "Wolfram Alpha" – which used the Wolfram Alpha application-programming interface – to apply its computational knowledge engine for science- or math-based questions.[15]

---

[13] Peter Cohan, "Sam Altman Says ChatGPT Is Good For Education: Here Are Four Lessons From My Student," *Inc.*, January 22, 2024, Ibid.

[14] Peter Cohan, "Sam Altman Says ChatGPT Is Good For Education: Here Are Four Lessons From My Student," *Inc.*, January 22, 2024, Ibid.

[15] Peter Cohan, "Sam Altman Says ChatGPT Is Good For Education: Here Are Four Lessons From My Student," *Inc.*, January 22, 2024, Ibid.

My student also offered helpful tips for using ChatGPT. He told ChatGPT how to format his answers, he avoided using the chatbot for math, and he double-checked the answers because he knew ChatGPT made mistakes.[16]

Generative AI can also help consumers seeking to select video entertainment options for themselves and their families. In 2024, the key to sorting through the options effectively was to know your preferences and those of your family members and to input the right prompts into the chatbot. Here are two examples:

- **Find online content recommendations tailored to your preferences.** Rather than prompting ChatGPT with "Suggest five historical dramas I can watch on Netflix," you should tell the AI the programs you have enjoyed in the past, the kind of program you want to watch now, and how you want the chatbot to help you. For example, a *Wall Street Journal* reporter prompted ChatGPT: "You are a TV adviser specialized in finding the perfect show for a user's mood. Suggest 10 lesser-known historical drama shows that would appeal to someone who desperately misses watching 'The Crown.'" When she offered the request, ChatGPT suggested a few of her past favorites, so she trusted its suggestion that she investigate the historical series *Versailles*.[17]

---

[16] Peter Cohan, "Sam Altman Says ChatGPT Is Good For Education: Here Are Four Lessons From My Student," *Inc.*, January 22, 2024, Ibid.

[17] Alexandra Samuel, "How AI Can Find the Perfect Movies, TV Shows and Books for You," *Wall Street Journal*, January 20, 2024, www.wsj.com/tech/ai/ai-movie-tv-books-choice-51aa7d21?mod=ig_artificialintelligencereport

- **Find online content recommendations for you and your partner.** You can use ChatGPT to find the intersection of two sets: programs suiting your taste that you have not seen and programs your partner likes and has not seen. To that end, the *Journal* reporter's first prompt was, "I want to watch a TV show with my husband. He likes spy and heist shows and comedy and stand-up; I like things that are more narrative and character driven. What can we watch together?" The chatbot's initial recommendations – such as *Barry* – were too violent for the reporter. The chatbot's next suggestions – such as *Jane the Virgin* – suited the reporter but did not appeal to her husband. After sharing with ChatGPT shows the reporter and her husband had previously enjoyed and not enjoyed, the chatbot offered "intriguing" suggestions such as the British show *Endeavour*.[18]

ChatGPT was not good for all consumer applications. In addition to concerns raised earlier in this book about the technology's potential for hallucinations, bias due to the sources used for training, the risks of uploading confidential information to the chatbot, and cybersecurity dangers, ChatGPT's weakness in doing math and analytical tasks, as my student mentioned, was significant. In 2024, ChatGPT did poorly at math and logic problems because its neural network aimed to predict the next word in a sentence – based on the context of that word – rather than to solve math or logic problems. Since ChatGPT's developers did not train the chatbot with the mathematical knowledge and reasoning abilities required to handle complex math problems, it "may struggle to produce

---

[18] Alexandra Samuel, "How AI Can Find the Perfect Movies, TV Shows and Books for You," *Wall Street Journal*, January 20, 2024, Ibid.

accurate mathematical results due to a lack of formal understanding and the absence of a mechanism to perform mathematical computations." ChatGPT makes predictions about what the next word should be from a range of possibilities, each of which the chatbot assigns a probability. This introduces uncertainty into its responses – a significant problem for math problems that demand precision and accuracy.[19]

Consumer Generative AI Dos and Don'ts

Based on these experiments, here are guidelines for ways consumers can capture the benefits of generative AI and avoid some of its pitfalls.

Dos

- Use generative AI to solve problems where its training makes it most useful – e.g., words instead of math.

- Write detailed prompts including a description of the person providing the prompt and offer specific details to explain your objectives.

- Specify the format in which you want the chatbot to present its results.

- Ask a series of questions until you obtain the result you are looking for.

- If possible, upload your own training data.

[19] Enes Zvornicanin, "Why Is ChatGPT Bad at Math?," *Baeldung*, September 6, 2023, www.baeldung.com/cs/chatgpt-math-problems#:~:text=It%20relies%20 on%20patterns%20and,solving%20math%20and%20logic%20problems.

Don'ts

- Do not use ChatGPT to solve math and logic problems.

- Do not trust the results ChatGPT provides until after you have verified the results from reliable sources.

- Do not share proprietary information with ChatGPT because it will become part of its training data set and could be shared in ways you would not want.

The section that follows highlights a process consumers can follow to capture value from generative AI.

How Consumers Can Capture Generative AI's Value

Here are some key process steps for consumers to capture the value of generative AI:

- Create a chatbot account – for example, to open a ChatGPT account visit `https://chat.openai.com/`.

- Decide on the problem you want the chatbot to help you solve.

- Type in your initial prompt.

- If you are not satisfied with the response, ask the chatbot to regenerate the response or try a more specific prompt.

- If you are satisfied with the response but realized you need more information, enter a new prompt.

- Once you are satisfied with the response, copy your prompts and ChatGPT's responses.

- After you have verified the information provided by ChatGPT, use the results to take action.

Following is an example of how a consumer might use ChatGPT to evaluate options for a new home office chair. The three exchanges are direct quotes from the user and ChatGPT in a series of three prompts and responses.

Prompt and Response 1: Provide Four Options for a New Office Chair

User

"I am an entrepreneur seeking to purchase a new chair for my office desk. I am looking for a chair that will be comfortable for sitting for hours at a time while I write a consulting report. Please list the four best makes of office chairs to consider and why you recommend them.

ChatGPT

Sure, I can provide you with recommendations for office chairs that are known for their comfort and ergonomic design. Keep in mind that personal preferences may vary, so it's essential to try out chairs if possible. Here are four popular office chair options:

- Herman Miller Aeron Chair:

  - Why: The Aeron chair is renowned for its ergonomic design and adjustability. It offers excellent lumbar support, customizable features, and a breathable mesh back for comfort during long hours of sitting.

- Steelcase Gesture Chair:

  - Why: The Steelcase Gesture chair is praised for its versatile design, catering to various sitting postures. It provides good support for the spine and has adjustable armrests to accommodate different work styles.

- Secretlab Omega Series:

  - Why: Secretlab chairs, particularly the Omega
    Series, are well-regarded for their comfort and
    affordability. They offer a mix of ergonomic
    features, including lumbar support, and are
    available in various styles and materials.

- IKEA Markus Chair:

  - Why: The IKEA Markus chair is a budget-friendly
    option that doesn't compromise on comfort. It
    has a high backrest, built-in lumbar support, and
    adjustable features. It's a solid choice for those
    looking for a cost-effective yet comfortable chair.

Before making a purchase, it's advisable to visit a showroom or read customer reviews to ensure that the chair meets your specific preferences and requirements."[20]

Prompt and Response 2: Compare Four Options on Customer Reviews, Ease of Assembly, Useful Life, and Price Range

User

"For each of these four kinds of chairs, please summarize the customer reviews, evaluate how easy each one is to assemble, estimate its useful life, and provide a price range.

ChatGPT

---

[20] Peter Cohan and ChatGPT 3.5, "Top 4 Ergo Office Chairs," *ChatGPT*, accessed January 21, 2024, https://chat.openai.com/c/647b8c21-817e-4969-95b0-81a8a aa7e183

Certainly, let's look at summarized customer reviews, ease of assembly, estimated useful life, and price range for each of the mentioned office chairs:

- Herman Miller Aeron Chair:

  - **Customer Reviews:** Customers often praise the Aeron chair for its exceptional comfort and support. Many appreciate the breathable mesh design and the chair's ability to adapt to different body types.

  - **Assembly:** While assembly is straightforward, some users mention that it may take a bit of time due to the chair's adjustable features.

  - **Useful Life:** The Aeron chair is known for its durability, and many users report it lasting for several years with regular use.

  - **Price Range:** Herman Miller chairs, including the Aeron, are in the higher price range, typically ranging from $1,000 to $1,500 or more.

- Steelcase Gesture Chair:

  - **Customer Reviews:** The Gesture chair receives positive reviews for its versatile design and support for various sitting postures. Users often mention its quality build and comfort.

  - **Assembly:** Assembly is considered straightforward, with users reporting it as easy to put together.

  - **Useful Life:** The Gesture chair is known for its durability, and many users find it to last for several years.

- **Price Range:** Steelcase chairs, including the Gesture, are in the mid to higher price range, ranging from $800 to $1,200 or more.

- Secretlab Omega Series:

  - **Customer Reviews:** Customers appreciate the comfort and affordability of the Secretlab Omega Series. The chair is often praised for its customizable features and various design options.

  - **Assembly:** Assembly is straightforward, and users find it easy to put together.

  - **Useful Life:** The Omega Series is reported to have a good lifespan, with many users mentioning its durability over time.

  - **Price Range:** Secretlab chairs are more affordable compared to some high-end options, with the Omega Series typically ranging from $300 to $500.

- IKEA Markus Chair:

  - **Customer Reviews:** The IKEA Markus chair receives positive reviews for its comfort and value for money. Users often mention its high backrest and built-in lumbar support.

  - **Assembly:** Assembly is considered easy, with users finding it straightforward to put the chair together.

  - **Useful Life:** While not as high-end as some options, the Markus chair is known for its decent durability, with users reporting it lasting for several years.

  - **Price Range:** IKEA Markus chairs are in the more budget-friendly range, typically ranging from $150 to $250.

Keep in mind that prices may vary based on promotions, sales, or specific models within each series. It's advisable to check the latest prices and reviews before making a purchase."[21]

Prompt and Response 3: Assess Whether the Quality of the Highest Priced Chair Justifies Its Price

User

"Is the ratio of quality to price for the Markus chair higher than the ratio of quality to price of the Aeron?

ChatGPT

The ratio of quality to price is a subjective measure and can vary based on individual preferences and priorities. However, I can provide some general considerations for comparing the IKEA Markus Chair and the Herman Miller Aeron Chair in terms of quality and price:

IKEA Markus Chair:

- Pros:

    - Superior quality for its price range.

    - Affordable compared to high-end ergonomic chairs.

    - Decent comfort and features, including a high backrest and built-in lumbar support.

- Cons:

    - Not as advanced in terms of features and materials compared to premium options.

---

[21] Peter Cohan and ChatGPT 3.5, "Top 4 Ergo Office Chairs," *ChatGPT*, accessed January 21, 2024, Ibid.

Herman Miller Aeron Chair:

- Pros:

    - Top-notch ergonomic design and materials.

    - Iconic and renowned for comfort and support.

    - Durable build with a reputation for longevity.

- Cons:

    - Higher price range compared to many other office chairs.

Considerations:

The IKEA Markus Chair provides good quality for its affordable price. It's a suitable option for those on a budget who still want a comfortable and reasonably ergonomic office chair.

The Herman Miller Aeron Chair is considered a premium option with advanced ergonomic features and high-quality materials. However, it comes with a significantly higher price tag.

Ratio of Quality to Price:

The ratio of quality to price for the Markus chair may be considered higher for individuals who prioritize budget-friendly options while still seeking reasonable comfort and functionality.

The Aeron chair, on the other hand, is known for its top-tier quality and design, but the higher price may impact the perceived ratio of quality to price.

In summary, if budget is a significant consideration, and you find the features of the Markus chair suitable for your needs, it may offer a higher perceived ratio of quality to price. However, if you prioritize premium materials, advanced ergonomic features, and are willing to invest in a higher-end chair, the Aeron may still be a compelling choice."[22]

---

[22] Peter Cohan and ChatGPT 3.5, "Top 4 Ergo Office Chairs," *ChatGPT*, accessed January 21, 2024, Ibid.

Readers should use such chatbot responses as a starting point for further investigation including checking all the details and following ChatGPT's advice to visit a showroom to try out the options in person.

How Employees and Business Operators Can Benefit from Generative AI

In early 2024, workers looked to the future of generative AI with mixed feelings. At the same time, consultants were advising companies to make the technology safely available to employees so they could experiment and discover ways chatbots could make them more effective and efficient. During this early phase of using generative AI, workers felt a range of emotions – including the urge to gain new skills, fear of losing their jobs to chatbots, and passive indifference. Findings from two surveys – sponsored by Jobs for the Future's Center for Artificial Intelligence & the Future of Work and Pew Research – shed light on workers' views.

Here are highlights:

- **Pessimism about AI's future influence on workers**. The June 2023 Jobs for the Future survey, conducted among 2,204 adults, found 33% believe they will need AI skills within a year. Moreover, 37% of workers are pessimistic about the future impact of AI, while 25% are optimistic.[23]

---

[23] Joe McKendrick, "We Hear From Workers On AI: They're On Alert, They're Ambivalent," *Forbes*, August 30, 2023, www.forbes.com/sites/joemckendrick/2023/08/30/we-hear-from-workers-on-ai-theyre-on-alert-theyre-ambivalent/

- **Lack of concern about AI's impact on their jobs.** Nevertheless, the Pew survey revealed only 18% of people had used ChatGPT, and most people "were relatively unconcerned about the impact of AI on jobs—especially their own."[24]

- **Chatbots will not help in many respondents' work**. A mere 15% of Pew respondents said chatbots would be useful in their work with college-educated people most inclined to use ChatGPT.[25]

- **AI will have a significant effect on specific jobs**. Respondents predicted generative AI would change some types of jobs – software developers, said 56% of respondents, graphic designers (54%), and journalists (52%) – by 2053. Smaller shares of respondents –thought chatbots would have a major effect on other jobs – teachers (44%) or lawyers (31%).[26]

- **Urgency to learn about generative AI.** Still, there's urgency to learning AI-related skills. The Jobs for the Future survey found 58% of workers saw the need to gain new skills because of AI. A third of respondents felt the need to gain these skills within a year.[27]

---

[24] Joe McKendrick, "We Hear From Workers On AI: They're On Alert, They're Ambivalent," *Forbes*, August 30, 2023, Ibid.

[25] Joe McKendrick, "We Hear From Workers On AI: They're On Alert, They're Ambivalent," *Forbes*, August 30, 2023, Ibid.

[26] Joe McKendrick, "We Hear From Workers On AI: They're On Alert, They're Ambivalent," *Forbes*, August 30, 2023, Ibid.

[27] Joe McKendrick, "We Hear From Workers On AI: They're On Alert, They're Ambivalent," *Forbes*, August 30, 2023, Ibid.

KPMG urged enterprises to make generative AI available safely to their employees. "Nothing in my history has generated the same level of CEO interest," Steve Chase, KPMG's Vice Chair of AI and Digital Innovation, told me in a January 2024 interview. He added, "Since November 2022, C-level executives want to know what their people are doing to benefit from the technology. Clients should make generative AI to as many workers as they can safely. There is a 5% to 10% productivity improvement opportunity. For example, marketing departments can use the technology to reduce spending on third-party contractors. There will be the biggest productivity improvement opportunities in using generative AI assistants for knowledge workers."[28]

KPMG did not supply a summary of the highest payoff corporate applications of generative AI. Chase said many companies were too early in their journeys with the technology to adopt experiments corporate wide and analyze their effectiveness. As he said, "What needs to happen next is for workers to use the answers from analyzing data to take action." He continued, "That will happen in the next 18 months and after which they will be able to assess the productivity benefits. I urge companies to move fast, be bold, and be responsible. Many smaller companies are hesitating. They are not comfortable with the risks. All senior executives see generative AI as potentially disruptive but only a third of them have moved forward. They are concerned about regulatory, legal, ethical, and copyright risks."[29]

The more knowledge workers make up the product, the more opportunity there is. "There are big opportunities for productivity improvement for front office functions such as sales, service and

---

[28] Peter Cohan, "After Gen AI's 82% Stock Surge In 2023, Here Are 3 Keys To Profiting From Davos Takeaways," *Forbes*, January 24, 2024, www.forbes.com/sites/petercohan/2024/01/24/after-gen-ais-82-stock-surge-in-2023-three-keys-to-profiting-from-davos-takeaways/

[29] Peter Cohan, "After Gen AI's 82% Stock Surge In 2023, Here Are 3 Keys To Profiting From Davos Takeaways," *Forbes*, January 24, 2024, Ibid.

marketing," Chase told me. "Developers using coding Copilots can expect 30% to 40% productivity improvements. When generative AI's changes to how people work – for example, the technology could listen to a sales conversation and provide popup windows suggesting new products to sell – organizational structures may change."[30]

High-Payoff Generative AI Experiments

By early 2024, academics and consultants highlighted positive outcomes from early experiments with generative AI. Indeed a 2023 study by economic researchers found ChatGPT and similar tools resulted in "more productive workers, happier customers, and higher employee retention."[31] In September 2023, a consulting firm executive highlighted significant economic payoffs from deploying generative AI in ways that boosted employee productivity and increased revenue considerably – providing companies a high return on the consulting fees expended to plan and implement these generative AI applications.

Economic researchers found compelling evidence of success in a study of early generative AI experiments. A 2023 National Bureau of Economic Research working paper presented the results of "nearly 5,200 customer support agents at a Fortune 500 software firm who gained access to a generative AI-based assistant in a phased rollout between November 2020 and February 2021." The generative AI tool made real-time recommendations to the support agents on how to respond to customer inquiries and provided links to company documents. Compared to a control group, workers assisted by the chatbot resolved 14% more issues

---

[30] Peter Cohan, "After Gen AI's 82% Stock Surge In 2023, Here Are 3 Keys To Profiting From Davos Takeaways," *Forbes*, January 24, 2024, Ibid.

[31] Katia Savchuk, "Generative AI boost can boost productivity without replacing workers," *Stanford Institute for Economic Policy Research*, December 14, 2023, https://siepr.stanford.edu/news/generative-ai-boost-can-boost-productivity-without-replacing-workers

per hour, completed conversations faster, and were a bit more successful in resolving problems. The chatbot boosted the productivity of the least experienced workers by 35%. Erik Brynjolfsson, a senior fellow at the Stanford Institute for Economic Policy Research, said this productivity boost was much higher than the 1%-2% productivity gains companies typically obtain from new information technology. Brynjolfsson and his colleagues found these productivity gains sprang from the chatbot's identification – "by digesting millions of transcripts of service interactions" – and dissemination of tactics used by the most successful agents. Customers were happier because their problems were resolved more quickly, and support agents were less likely to resign. "We don't know for sure why this occurred, but I would guess that it's more enjoyable to be in a job where the customers like you and you can solve customer problems faster," Brynjolfsson said. His conclusion was companies would benefit from using generative AI to augment "high-skilled workers so the system can continue to learn from them."[32]

Consultants also expressed optimism about generative AI's benefits for workers. One industry expert, Michele Goetz, Vice President and Principal Analyst at Forrester Research, told me clients were paying millions in consulting fees for help deploying generative AI in their companies. The reason? Through lower costs and/or higher revenues, clients expected generative AI applications to earn back those consulting fees – which could range from $500,000 to a range from $10 million to $50 million – within three months of deployment. Forrester saw clients getting their money back in well under a year. "Companies forecast a payback within three months of deployment," she told me. "In some cases, companies see results in two to eight weeks. In other cases, the time to value is three to six months." Companies achieve this payback through quantitative and qualitative improvements. "One company reduced its

---

[32] Katia Savchuk, "Generative AI boost can boost productivity without replacing workers," *Stanford Institute for Economic Policy Research*, December 14, 2023, Ibid.

call center costs by $80 million in the course of a year," Goetz explained. "The benefits included cost savings from shifting responses to level 0 and level 1 questions from human agents to generative AI virtual assistance and agents using the technology to respond faster and more accurately to customer inquiries. In addition, generative AI increases customer satisfaction and improves net promoter scores." Generative AI also added to company revenue. For example, the technology enabled a cruise ship company to boost its revenue by $1 billion by recommending ancillary activities that their customers activated during the voyage. An Asian bank's [generative AI-powered] virtual investment assistance delivered an "additional $500 million worth of trading volume," she told me.[33]

In 2023, early adopters of generative AI in industries such as construction, travel, retail, health care, and energy achieved higher productivity and changed customer behavior in the wake of their generative AI experiments. These companies were also evaluating whether the high cost and limitations of these applications – such as the need to hire specialized talent, and manage legal and privacy risks – exceeded their benefits. Here are two examples:

- **Wayfair's AI-powered interior decorator.** Wayfair, the Boston-based online furniture retailer, introduced Decorify, a free generative AI tool launched in July 2023 to help customers redesign their living rooms. Fiona Tan, Wayfair's chief technology officer, said customers upload a photo of their living rooms to Decorify, which created "photorealistic images" of proposed designs and prompted consumers with real products similar to the ones in the photo. Decorify could help consumers

---

[33] Peter Cohan, "Why Companies Buy generative AI Consulting: The 3-Month Payback Factor," *Forbes*, September 23, 2023, www.forbes.com/sites/petercohan/2023/09/23/why-companies-buy-generative-ai-consulting-the-3-month-payback-factor/

shop for items "that are really hard for you to articulate what it is you really want. Being able to see that is helpful," Tan said.[34]

- **Expedia's personalized travel assistant.** Seattle-based Expedia's chatbot enabled travelers to ask for recommendations and make bookings to help them "explore and discover," Expedia CEO Peter Kern said. Expedia viewed the experiment as a way to get consumers comfortable with generative AI – while maintaining the company's current booking process. Expedia also used AI to automate customer-service-call summaries to reduce costs. By providing "tailored" booking help, Expedia aimed to keep travelers from "fishing around in the dark," Kern said. Expedia's chief technology officer Rathi Murthy said the company had overhauled its huge store of customer data so it could train ChatGPT – providing customers with greater personalization.[35]

In early 2024, these experiments left many questions unanswered:

- How many customers were finding these generative AI assistants helpful?

- If so, which aspects were most useful? If not, was there any reason to continue the experiment?

---

[34] Belle Lin, "How Did Companies Use generative AI in 2023? Here's a Look at Five Early Adopters." *Wall Street Journal*, December 29, 2023, www.wsj.com/articles/how-did-companies-use-generative-ai-in-2023-heres-a-look-at-five-early-adopters-6e09c6b3?mod=hp_minor_pos4

[35] Belle Lin, "How Did Companies Use Generative AI in 2023? Here's a Look at Five Early Adopters." *Wall Street Journal*, December 29, 2023, Ibid.

- Did these assistants generate clear payoffs – through lower costs, higher productivity, or increased revenue?

- Were these applications free of compliance, cybersecurity, copyright, or other sources of risk?

- Did the experiments point the way to enhancements that would boost the value of these assistants?

Employee and Business Operator Generative AI Dos and Don'ts

Based on these experiments, here are the guidelines for ways employees and business operators can capture the benefits of generative AI and avoid some of its pitfalls.

Dos

- Make chatbots safely available to all employees and encourage them to find ways to use the technology that makes them more productive.

- Encourage sharing of best practices among employees who are experimenting with the chatbots.

- Based on these experiments, create a team to develop corporate generative AI applications to design and implement high-payoff applications.

- Study the generative AI applications being developed by early adopters in your industry or related industries.

- Prototype the most promising applications, get feedback from users, and continue to make improvements if feedback is positive.

- If feedback is negative, cancel the prototype and allocate the resources to the more promising applications.

Don'ts

- Do not let the fear of generative AI's risks paralyze your ability to experiment safely with the technology.

- Do not permit employees to experiment with generative AI without appropriate protection against risks of hacking, copyright violations, hallucinations, and other risks.

- Prevent employees from sharing proprietary information with ChatGPT.

How Employees and Business Operators Can Capture Generative AI's Value

Here are some key process steps for employees to capture the value of generative AI:

- Create a chatbot account – for example, to open a ChatGPT account, visit `https://chat.openai.com/`.

- Decide on the problem you want the chatbot to help you solve.

- Type in your initial prompt.

- If you are not satisfied with the response, ask the chatbot to regenerate the response or try a more specific prompt.

- If you are satisfied with the response but realize you need more information, enter a new prompt.

- Once you are satisfied with the response, copy your
  prompts and ChatGPT's responses.

- After you have verified the information provided by
  ChatGPT, use the results to take action.

Business operators – for example, a company's customer service
operation – must engage other stakeholders to design and implement
generative AI applications. In so doing, business operators should take the
following steps:

- Identify all the stakeholders affected by the generative
  AI application. For example, a customer service
  application would involve internal teams in customer
  services and information technology as well as external
  customers.

- Listen to stakeholders to identify their goals for the
  generative AI application.

- Deploy a large language model (LLM) technology on
  which to build the customer service application.

- Upload training data – such as transcripts of the
  company's customer service calls – to the LLM
  technology.

- Test out the trained LLM with customer service agents
  and a sample of customers.

- Get feedback from stakeholders on the prototype.

- Refine the prototype based on feedback until the
  generative AI application works well enough for it to be
  used more widely throughout the organization.

To illustrate how an employee or business function might use generative AI to solve a business problem, in December 2023, I challenged ChatGPT to help me develop the strategy for a startup that would take over the lead in the online streaming market by 2033. ChatGPT produced the name of the business – StreamSphere – and suggested the features the service should provide to win over enough customers to dominate the online streaming industry by 2034. Along the way, ChatGPT helped design a survey of Netflix customers and hypothesize whether they would switch to StreamSphere and why, and helped estimate how much capital the business would need and how much revenue and cash flow it would generate. ChatGPT also advised on who should be in StreamSphere's management team, which investors to approach for capital, what its first streaming series would be, and how to generate buzz through a multimedia marketing campaign.[36]

While ChatGPT's answers to my prompts initially impressed me, after thinking about them, I realized the chatbot had succinctly summarized general textbook advice and left me far short of the stated goal. These summaries left most of the substantive work needed to the entrepreneur. The chatbot forecast StreamSphere's 2034 revenue would reach $25 million. With Netflix forecast to generate about $71 billion in revenue in a decade – assuming it grows at 8% a year from $32.7 billion in 2023 revenue – StreamSphere had no chance of becoming the industry leader in a decade. To be fair, ChatGPT provided caveats in its responses. For example, with its revenue forecast, ChatGPT wrote, "Remember, these estimates are based on assumptions, and the actual performance of

---

[36] Peter Cohan, "ChatGPT Invented an Upstart Netflix Rival for Me," *Inc.*, December 17, 2023, www.inc.com/peter-cohan/chatgpt-invented-an-upstart-netflix-rival-for-me.html

StreamSphere will depend on numerous factors. It's essential to monitor user adoption, adjust strategies accordingly, and regularly update forecasts based on real-world data and feedback."[37]

Here are some of the highlights of what I asked ChatGPT to do, how it responded, and the tasks it left for the entrepreneur to complete:

- **Deliver an irresistible product.** People were not likely to switch to a new service unless it offered irresistible content. Here is how ChatGPT responded to my prompt about how to do that for StreamSphere: "The series should not only be compelling and high-quality but also align with StreamSphere's unique features and value proposition." ChatGPT suggested producing storylines that subscribers could shape and collaborate with outstanding producers, directors, actors, and writers. This advice leaves StreamSphere's CEO with a significant to-do list:

  - Invent a compelling, original story idea.

  - Identify specific producers, directors, and other talent with whom to collaborate.

  - Compel them to join the project.

  - Agree on the contract terms.

  - Produce and market the content.[38]

---

[37] Peter Cohan, "5 Ways ChatGPT Fell Short in Helping Me Create a Netflix Rival," *Inc.*, December 23, 2023, www.inc.com/peter-cohan/5-ways-chatgpt-fell-short-in-helping-me-create-a-netflix-rival.html
[38] Peter Cohan, "5 Ways ChatGPT Fell Short in Helping Me Create a Netflix Rival," *Inc.*, December 23, 2023, Ibid.

- **Win the first customers.** To win StreamSphere's first customers, I prompted ChatGPT for advice on how to conduct market research to test out potential customers' willingness to subscribe and asked for suggestions on how to market the service. ChatGPT gave me solid general advice. For example, the chatbot provided a good customer interview guide, gave me an educated guess on how potential customers might respond to the questions, and offered general advice on a multipronged media campaign – including print, video, social, and other media. This left an extensive list of tasks for StreamSphere to complete including the following:

  - Develop a list of, say, 100 potential customers to survey.

  - Conduct the surveys and analyze the results.

  - Modify StreamSphere's content and strategy based on the results.

  - Produce the marketing content.

  - Execute the multimedia marketing campaign.[39]

- **Build a great leadership team.** I asked ChatGPT to help me build a leadership team for StreamSphere. Its response was to hire the traditional C-suite including a CEO to provide vision and leadership, as well as chief product, content, marketing, technology, and financial officers. To execute this textbook advice, a founder would have much work to do:

---

[39] Peter Cohan, "5 Ways ChatGPT Fell Short in Helping Me Create a Netflix Rival," *Inc.*, December 23, 2023, Ibid.

- Articulate a vision that will attract talent.

- Identify the best candidates for each role.

- Interview the candidates and sell them on the StreamSphere vision.

- Make offers to the best candidates and agree on contract terms.

- Lead the team to formulate and execute the business strategy.[40]

- **Raise sufficient capital to scale.** StreamSphere would need capital to grow. ChatGPT listed potential types of investors, such as venture capital and private equity firms, angel investors, strategic investors, and crowdfunding platforms. This laundry list of investors left the founder with a list of to-dos much like the ones for building the management team.[41]

- **Estimate your return on investment.** To raise capital leaders must show potential investors what kind of return they should expect. ChatGPT did a fine job of listing the key variables required to build a cash flow model. ChatGPT left the specific assumptions in the hands of StreamSphere's CEO. Quantifying these assumptions would require the leader's detailed knowledge of the specific amounts needed to build and operate the business.[42]

---

[40] Peter Cohan, "5 Ways ChatGPT Fell Short in Helping Me Create a Netflix Rival," *Inc.*, December 23, 2023, Ibid.

[41] Peter Cohan, "5 Ways ChatGPT Fell Short in Helping Me Create a Netflix Rival," *Inc.*, December 23, 2023, Ibid.

[42] Peter Cohan, "5 Ways ChatGPT Fell Short in Helping Me Create a Netflix Rival," *Inc.*, December 23, 2023, Ibid.

The takeaway? Based on my experience, ChatGPT can make textbook lists of things an entrepreneur must do to build a new business. That still leaves the entrepreneur to deliver the inspiration and perspiration required to build a successful company.

Growth Strategies for Generative AI Product Providers

Chapters 4 through 7 examined the trends driving the profitability of the industries providing generative AI products and assessed the companies' strategies and investment potential. The analysis revealed that the most effective growth strategies varied by industry and by the companies' strengths and weaknesses in the specific capabilities required to win and keep customers. Will the winners in these industries continue to lead in the future as generative AI technology evolves, customer needs change, and upstart rivals and incumbents adapt their strategies? A starting point for answering this question is for generative AI product providers to envision the future state of their competitive environments. Based on the analysis earlier in this book, in early 2024 the two leading companies in the generative AI industry were Microsoft and Nvidia. Therefore, many industry participants could benefit from contemplating how the companies' CEOs – Satya Nadella and Jensen Huang, respectively – envisioned the future of generative AI as follows:

- **Microsoft.** Microsoft viewed generative AI as a significant source of future growth. In a London fireside chat at Chatham House in January 2024, Nadella presented a view of generative AI's future aimed at boosting the company's revenues. For example, despite a lawsuit from the *New York Times* alleging OpenAI and Microsoft infringed on the media company's copyrights by using AI to summarize articles, Nadella said journalists should welcome generative AI's ability to ease their writing task. While he envisioned AI could produce political disinformation, he argued the government – not Microsoft – should police AI-powered fake news. Rather than acknowledge the risk that AI could take away jobs, he said AI would help developed countries boost productivity, raise economic growth, and narrow income inequality. He added that Microsoft Copilot would contribute to narrowing income inequality. He cited Power Apps, a product that enabled British police officers to code a simple app with natural language, thereby enabling police officers to get higher wages as the police department employs fewer high-wage coders. Of course, if this vision became a reality, coders' wages would drop since more people could do their jobs.[43] Ultimately, in December 2023 Nadella expected AI to "augment human ingenuity rather than supplant it." To that end, he urged "technologists, ethicists, policymakers, and stakeholders to shape an AI-driven future that serves the greater good."[44] Microsoft expected to provide the picks and shovels needed to realize that lofty vision. As Microsoft VP and consumer chief marketing officer Yusuf Mehdi told attendees at the Consumer Electronics Show in January 2024, 77% of people in enterprises who used Microsoft's $30 per month

---

[43] Jeremy Kahn, "Microsoft CEO Satya Nadella is an AI winner. He doesn't like to talk about the potential losers," *Yahoo! Finance*, January 16, 2024, https://finance.yahoo.com/news/microsoft-ceo-satya-nadella-ai-194539638.html

[44] "Microsoft CEO Satya Nadella's Insights on AI: Discover Balancing Promise and Perils," *Hyscaler*, December 23, 2023, https://hyscaler.com/insights/microsoft-ceo-satya-nadella-insights-on-ai/

Copilot business software said they "would never
want to give it up." To that end, Microsoft envisioned
consumers would pay for generative AI services and
the laptops and desktops equipped with the neural
processing units needed to deliver those services.[45]

- **Nvidia.** Nvidia had a more balanced view of generative
  AI's future. Huang saw generative AI helping to boost
  the productivity of many industries, and he was highly
  attuned to the threat from rivals – particularly in
  China – seeking to upend its Graphics Processing Unit
  (GPU) business. At a November 2023 Goldman Sachs
  Asset Management conference, Huang said human
  feedback was making ChatGPT safer. He envisioned
  each industry regulator – for example, automobile
  regulatory the National Highway Transportation Safety
  Administration – would assure AI for its industry
  was safe. Huang saw "enormous potential for new
  generative AI capabilities to drive growth for many
  businesses, with large enterprise software providers
  among the biggest beneficiaries initially." Many
  software providers were beginning to add AI-powered
  technologies to their products – enabling them to
  increase revenue per customer. Business database
  providers, for example, were working to enable

---

[45] Daniel Howley, "After huge investments, companies need to make bank on
generative AI," *Yahoo! Finance*, January 17, 2024, https://finance.yahoo.com/
news/after-huge-investments-companies-need-to-make-bank-on-
generative-ai-191928010.html

"retrieval augmented generation," Huang added.[46]
At a January 2024 JP Morgan Healthcare Conference,
Huang said Nvidia had been working in the healthcare
industry in 2009 and was developing new products
aimed at enhancing medical technology including
"algorithms for cryo-electron microscopy, X-ray
crystallography, gene sequencing, amino acid structure
prediction and virtual drug molecule screening."[47]
In November 2023, Huang told a *Harvard Business
Review*'s Future of Business conference, "If you don't
think you are in peril, that's probably because you
have your head in the sand." To survive, companies
must stay alert to "the weakest signals coming from
unexpected places." Nvidia was adapting to the US
government restriction on exports to China. Huang
also saw challenges from Chinese GPU companies.
"It's not easy, and competitors are moving quickly.
It's like anything else that you gotta stay alert and
do the best you can," Huang said.[48] Another source
of competition for Nvidia was customers' efforts to
backward integrate into GPU design. Nvidia – which
sold 70% of all AI chips – set much higher prices than

---

[46] "NVIDIA CEO Huang urges faster AI development—to make it safer," *Goldman
Sachs Intelligence*, November 17, 2023, www.goldmansachs.com/intelligence/
pages/nvidia-ceo-huang-urges-faster-ai-development-to-make-it-safer.
html#:~:text=Huang%20said%20he%20sees%20enormous,among%20the%20
biggest%20beneficiaries%20initially

[47] Rory Kelleher, "NVIDIA CEO: 'This Year, Every Industry Will Become a
Technology Industry'," *Nvidia Blog*, January 12, 2024, https://blogs.nvidia.com/
blog/nvidia-ceo-ai-drug-discovery-jp-morgan-healthcare-2024/

[48] Sissi Cao, "Jensen Huang Says Nvidia 'Is Always in Peril' Despite Trillion-Dollar
Valuation," *Yahoo! Finance*, November 9, 2023, https://finance.yahoo.com/
news/jensen-huang-says-nvidia-always-014309828.html

its customers spent on their internally designed chips. Specifically, Nvidia charged Google $15,000 per chip, while the search giant spent "an average of just $2,000 to $3,000 on each of its own." With the AI chip market expected to double to $140 billion by 2027, Amazon – another large Nvidia customer – was working to make switching between chips "as simple as it can possibly be." Moreover, Microsoft was seeking to make it "seamless" for customers to move between chips from different companies. Nvidia had raised such switching costs through its industry-leading developer software library.[49] Huang's vigilance kept Nvidia on its toes.

Microsoft and Nvidia envision more demand for generative AI products and services. In early 2024, each industry CEO needed to develop a unique vision of the industry's future and articulate a strategy for capturing the technology's opportunities while managing its risks.

High-Payoff Generative AI Strategies

Two strategic mindsets have the potential to produce high payoffs – a third is deadly. I explain in the following text each of the mindsets and describe where Nadella and Huang fit within this framework. As I wrote in my 2020 book, *Goliath Strikes Back*, the three strategic mindsets are as follows:

- **Create the Future.** The most valuable mindset is *Create the Future* that is typical of the world's most celebrated entrepreneurs. Such leaders see where customer needs and technologies will be in the future

---

[49] Cade Metz, Karen Weise and Mike Isaac, "Nvidia's Big Tech Rivals Put Their Own A.I. Chips on the Table," *New York Times*, January 29, 2024, `www.nytimes.com/2024/01/29/technology/ai-chips-nvidia-amazon-google-microsoft-meta.html`

and use those technologies to create new products that customers perceive as the most valuable on the market. Jeff Bezos and Steve Jobs are widely celebrated as *Create the Future* leaders. Netflix's CEO, Reed Hastings, embodies this mindset in a way that is more sustainable – because the company does not orbit him in the same way. Jobs maintained tight control over all aspects of the new products – such as the iPod and the iPhone. While Hastings created similarly revolutionary services – DVD-by-mail and online streaming, he prided himself on delegating much of the decision making and execution to talented and empowered executives and employees.[50]

- **Fast Follower.** Leaders with a *Fast Follower* mindset have rescued many large companies that have lost their way after their founders departed the scene. Rather than focus on cost cutting, those with a *Fast Follower* mindset start by looking at the company from the perspective of its customers and employees – giving them irresistibly compelling reasons to keep buying from the company. A case in point is Hubert Joly, Best Buy's CEO from 2012 to 2019, who took over after the company posted a $1.7 billion loss. By the time Joly left, Best Buy was profitable, and its stock had soared 330%. Joly's *Fast Follower* mindset led him to listen to store associates, learn what was causing Best Buy's problems,

---

[50] Peter Cohan, "3 Strategic Mindsets for Your Business (One Is Deadly)," *Inc.*, November 25, 2020, www.inc.com/peter-cohan/3-strategic-mindsets-for-your-business-one-is-deadly.html

and change its strategy and operations so consumers
would come back and keep buying.[51]

- **Head in the Sand.** Leaders with a *Head in the Sand*
  mindset seek to discourage their teams from providing
  them with information about how their competitive
  environment is changing. Team members who
  urge *Head in the Sand* leaders to adapt to changing
  customer needs, new technologies, and fast-growing
  upstarts can quickly find themselves out of a job. Such
  leaders often stay at the top because of confirmation
  bias – their past successes lock in a set of beliefs about
  what drives industry success. They use their power
  over the people who report to them to reward those
  who praise their adherence to those beliefs and punish
  those who challenge them. In 2024, there were no
  obvious examples of companies ignoring generative
  AI through a *Head in the Sand* mindset. While KPMG
  did not name any of the companies paralyzed by the
  risks of adopting generative AI in their businesses,
  such laggards were the closest to falling behind the
  technology's advance.[52]

How does this framework apply to Microsoft and Nvidia? Microsoft's
Nadella had a *Fast Follower* mindset, while Huang was a *Create the
Future* CEO. How so? When he took over from Steve Ballmer, Nadella
fomented a successful cultural revolution. Ballmer, who was Microsoft's

---

[51] Peter Cohan, "3 Strategic Mindsets for Your Business (One Is Deadly)," *Inc.*,
November 25, 2020, Ibid.

[52] Peter Cohan, "After Gen AI's 82% Stock Surge In 2023, Here Are 3 Keys To
Profiting From Davos Takeaways," *Forbes*, January 24, 2024, www.forbes.com/
sites/petercohan/2024/01/24/after-gen-ais-82-stock-surge-in-2023-
three-keys-to-profiting-from-davos-takeaways/

CEO from 2000 to 2014, created a polarizing, divisive, and antagonistic culture that used a rank and yank human resources policy to spur internal competition. Ballmer's attitude toward customers was insular, inwardly focused, and pushed all-Microsoft products on customers. When Apple and Amazon created new growth from smartphones and cloud services, respectively, Ballmer was unable to seize the opportunity. Nadella was the opposite. His style was empathetic, inclusive, and collaborative. He empowered employees and fostered a growth mindset. Nadella's attitude to customers was to find a way to give them what they needed rather than pushing all-Microsoft products. With his experience starting Microsoft's cloud computing business, he successfully positioned Microsoft to capture the growth headwinds of AI and digital transformation.[53] As we saw in Chapter 5, when it came to generative AI, Microsoft stumbled with its efforts to develop its own products. Fortunately, Nadella was able to seize the generative AI initiative by collaborating with OpenAI – whose leader, Sam Altman, had a *Create the Future* mindset.

In Chapter 5, we highlighted four sources of competitive advantage from which Microsoft derived its leadership position in generative AI. By November 2023, the investment potential of Microsoft's stock hinged in part on the company's ability to win market share in the generative AI ecosystem. Microsoft enjoyed four critical advantages:

- **High switching costs with a large customer base.** Microsoft already enjoyed a high share of the market for business software that raised the costs for customers seeking to switch to another supplier. This made it easier for Microsoft to introduce generative AI services to its existing customers.

---

[53] Peter Cohan, "Culture Is The Most Surprising Reason Microsoft Stock Will Keep Rising," *Forbes,* January 30, 2020, www.forbes.com/sites/petercohan/2020/01/30/culture-is-the-most-surprising-reason-microsoft-stock-will-keep-rising/

- **Access to excellent generative AI technology through partnerships.** Microsoft's significant stake in OpenAI gave the software giant access to ChatGPT, the most popular generative AI chatbot, and Microsoft's partnerships with consulting firms provided access to corporate decision makers.

- **A clear head start *versus* rivals in monetizing generative AI.** Microsoft benefited from the perception among investors that was ahead of rivals in the race to monetize generative AI.

- **Many sources of generative AI revenue.** Generative AI increased demand for Microsoft's Azure cloud services, and its Copilot service had the potential to increase the prices Microsoft charged for the Microsoft Office 365 suite.

As the co-founder and CEO of Nvidia, Huang was clearly a *Create the Future* CEO. By January 2024, he had taken the company from an idea to a publicly traded industry leader with a stock market capitalization exceeding $1.5 trillion and revenues that grew more than 200% between the third quarters of 2022 and 2023. Beginning in 2006, Nvidia accumulated capabilities that enabled the company to build a difficult-to-surmount lead in the market for generative AI GPUs. As we saw in Chapter 7, these competitive advantages included:

- **Launching software for programming GPUs.** In 2006, Nvidia announced Compute Unified Device Architecture (CUDA) – software for programming GPUs for other fields such as physics or chemical simulation. In 2012, researchers used the chips to identify a cat with precision.[54]

---

[54] Peter Cohan, "Why Nvidia Stock Could Soar To $1,000 A Share," *Forbes*, August 23, 2023, www.forbes.com/sites/petercohan/2023/08/23/why-nvidia-stock-could-soar-to-1000-a-share/

- **Hiring a team of LLM training experts.** Nvidia hired a team to train LLMs – gaining early insights into what AI practitioners wanted. Using that market intelligence, Nvidia built libraries – to perform tasks common to AI development, thus saving the developers' time.[55]

- **Building faster chips every few years and expanding to complete computers.** Nvidia consistently delivered faster chips every few years. In 2017, it began tailoring GPUs to handle specific AI calculations, sold chips or circuit boards for other companies, and provided complete computers aimed at faster AI processing.[56]

- **Staying ahead of the competition.** In September 2022, Nvidia announced the production of H100 chips to enhance transformer operations – which were essential for training ChatGPT and other generative AI chatbots.[57]

- **Forming partnerships with large technology companies and investing in startups.** Nvidia collaborated with large technology companies, such as ServiceNow and Snowflake, and funded startups. In June 2023, Nvidia invested in a $1.3 billion financing for Inflection AI, which used the money to help finance the purchase of 22,000 H100 chips.[58]

---

[55] Peter Cohan, "Why Nvidia Stock Could Soar To $1,000 A Share," *Forbes*, August 23, 2023, Ibid.

[56] Peter Cohan, "Why Nvidia Stock Could Soar To $1,000 A Share," *Forbes*, August 23, 2023, Ibid.

[57] Peter Cohan, "Why Nvidia Stock Could Soar To $1,000 A Share," *Forbes*, August 23, 2023, Ibid.

[58] Peter Cohan, "Why Nvidia Stock Could Soar To $1,000 A Share," *Forbes*, August 23, 2023, Ibid.

While Microsoft and Nvidia had different strategies, they derived their success from common attributes:

- They created strong ties to customers before launching their generative AI businesses.

- They designed their own or partnered to build industry-leading products in their respective product categories.

- They formed partnerships to complement their strengths and help them gain access to marketing resources.

- They invested in startups with the potential to deliver transformative new products.

Generative AI Product Provider Dos and Don'ts

Based on these case studies, here are guidelines for ways generative AI product providers can capture the benefits of generative AI and avoid some of its pitfalls.

Dos

- Listen to customers to understand the criteria they use to compare competing generative AI products.

- Understand how customers perceive the strengths and opportunities for improvement in your company's value proposition as it compares to competing companies.

- Analyze current and potential competitors to understand what distinguishes the ones that are growing quickly from rivals that are rapidly losing market share.

- Identify the early-adopter customers who might be most eager for you to provide a generative AI product.

- Co-develop a new product that solves the early adopters' unrelieved customer pain and refine the prototype based on customer feedback.

- Once early-adopters use the product, collaborate with other companies to market the product to new customers.

Don'ts

- Introduce a product or services labeled as generative AI unless it relieves customer pain.

- Try to replicate the attributes of an industry leader's successful product.

- Prevent employees from sharing proprietary information with ChatGPT.

How Product Providers Can Capture Generative AI's Value

Here are some key process steps for product providers seeking to boost their revenues from selling generative AI products and services:

- Identify the highest payoff applications of generative AI.

- Interview early-adopter customers aiming to solve significant business problems by applying the high-payoff generative AI applications.

- Pinpoint specific products your company can develop to solve those business problems more effectively than competitors can.

- Collaborate with early-adopter customers to build and improve a prototype solution to their problem.

- Identify the capabilities required to build the new product and scale it to a large number of customers.

- Evaluate your company's strengths and weaknesses in each of the needed capabilities.

- Partner or acquire to close your company's capability gap.

How Investors Can Profit from Generative AI

In early 2024, investors expressed mixed views of the investment potential of generative AI stocks. Generative AI dominated the conversation of attendees at the January 2024 World Economic Forum – a collection of globally influential leaders from CEOs, investment managers, policymakers, and academics. While the level of hype was high, the conversation did not feature much in the way of specific case studies of the profitable application of the technology. While many companies were conducting experiments, conclusive evidence was limited about whether the excitement would represent a significant opportunity to improve company operations and yield significant investment returns. Despite that uncertainty, generative AI stocks surged in 2023 – with my Generative AI Stock Index (GAISI) rising 82% in 2023 – nearly double the 43% increase in the NASDAQ.[59]

---

[59] Peter Cohan, "After Gen AI's 82% Stock Surge In 2023, Here Are 3 Keys To Profiting From Davos Takeaways," *Forbes*, January 24, 2024, Ibid.

To develop a clear perspective on the future investment value of generative AI, I conducted interviews with a Goldman Sachs managing director who covers software stocks, the CEO of ServiceNow, and an AI executive from KPMG. Three observations about the investment potential of generative AI stocks emerged:

- **The more revenue companies earn from generative AI, the greater their investment potential.** Microsoft and Nvidia were among the companies with the most revenue exposure to generative AI in early 2024.[60]

- **Companies with the potential to gain significant revenue from generative AI also had good investment potential.** For example, Intuit, Adobe, Snowflake, and ServiceNow had the potential to enjoy greater revenue exposure in the future. These companies had the capabilities needed to increase their market share by deploying their generative AI talent to build applications that appealed to current and potential customers.[61]

- **Nontechnology companies had the potential to deploy generative AI to boost productivity – thereby increasing their investment potential.** Companies that employed a significant number of software developers – such as financial services firms – had the potential to boost productivity by using chatbots to

---

[60] Peter Cohan, "After Gen AI's 82% Stock Surge In 2023, Here Are 3 Keys To Profiting From Davos Takeaways," *Forbes*, January 24, 2024, Ibid.

[61] Peter Cohan, "After Gen AI's 82% Stock Surge In 2023, Here Are 3 Keys To Profiting From Davos Takeaways," *Forbes*, January 24, 2024, Ibid.

write code. After the widespread deployment of such
applications, the stock market value of such firms
could rise if they sustained expectations-beating profit
growth.[62]

Generative AI was the talk of Davos that the *Wall Street Journal*
interpreted as a sign that investors take the profits on generative AI
stocks. While granting the Journal's contention that people who followed
the Davos buzzfest were late to the party, I disagreed with the notion
that the party was already over. Instead, I concluded there was more
upside potential in buying GAISI stocks likely to exceed future investor
expectations. To be sure, the GAISI did well in 2023 with generative AI
hardware stocks leading the way. The average stock in each of the GAISI's
industry components performed as follows in 2023:

- Generative AI consulting: +30%.

- Generative AI software: +91%.

- Generative AI cloud services: +70%.

- Generative AI hardware: +135%.[63]

One example reinforcing my conclusion about the value of
expectations-beating growth was the stock price of ASML – the Dutch
provider of a machine for manufacturing the chips used to train LLMs –
which we discussed in Chapter 7. After rising 36% in 2023, ASML stock
continued to soar in 2024. As of January 2024, ASML stock was up 18%
(far more than the NASDAQ's 5% increase) – popping 9% in that day's

---

[62] Peter Cohan, "After Gen AI's 82% Stock Surge In 2023, Here Are 3 Keys To
Profiting From Davos Takeaways," *Forbes*, January 24, 2024, Ibid.
[63] Peter Cohan, "After Gen AI's 82% Stock Surge In 2023, Here Are 3 Keys To
Profiting From Davos Takeaways," *Forbes*, January 24, 2024, Ibid.

trading. The reason for the increase in its stock price was the company's 30% increase in revenue for the fourth quarter of 2023 to $7.84 billion – exceeding *Wall Street* expectations by $410 million.[64]

A Goldman Sachs Perspective on Generative AI-Driven Growth

Goldman Sachs Managing Director Kash Rangan offered key insights about the investment potential of generative AI:

- **Invest in companies with significant generative AI revenues now.** Microsoft and Nvidia are among the publicly traded companies gaining the most revenues from generative AI. As Rangan said, "When you consider investing in a stock to take advantage of generative AI, estimate whether the raw dollar contribution from generative AI is material. You have to look at where the company is today and where it is going. You have to look far out to understand the full impact of generative AI on the company." Rangan sees Microsoft – whose market capitalization topped $3 trillion on January 24 – as a key beneficiary of generative AI. "Microsoft is the company getting the most from generative AI," he told me. He added, "Seven percentage points of Azure's growth comes from the technology—that is nearly $4 billion in annualized revenue. It is significant because it used to be 1% just three quarters ago—this suggests it is growing significantly. Microsoft is also adding Copilot to its Office Suite, which has more than 400 million users

---

[64] Peter Cohan, "After Gen AI's 82% Stock Surge In 2023, Here Are 3 Keys To Profiting From Davos Takeaways," *Forbes*, January 24, 2024, Ibid.

and represents a larger than $50 billion business. They
are nowhere near an inflection point. It will take a year
to know."[65]

- **Consider investing in companies with significant
  potential generative AI revenues.** In early 2024,
  Rangan viewed Intuit, Adobe, Salesforce, and
  ServiceNow as companies with the potential to earn
  significant revenue from generative AI products. For
  example, he saw Intuit – the supplier of TurboTax – as
  a future beneficiary of generative AI. "Intuit does not
  charge for generative AI, however, the technology will
  be pervasive," he explained. "Now Intuit provides a free
  TurboTax Assistant for people working on their taxes
  that is based on a large language model trained on the
  tax returns. Today people spend $5 billion on doing
  their taxes within Intuit. By offering TurboTax Assistant,
  Intuit is opening up a $25 billion market opportunity
  for people who do their taxes outside Intuit. Generative
  AI could unlock billions of revenue for the company."
  Rangan offered other examples of companies that
  will use generative AI to add new customers. "Adobe's
  Firefly will unlock more revenue," he said. "People
  will start using Firefly who previously were not Adobe
  customers. They will be intrigued by the technology
  and use it for a marketing campaign. Adobe says its
  total addressable market will grow to nearly $300 billion
  by 2027. Firefly will enable Adobe to capture a bigger
  share of that TAM." He sees companies with access to

---

[65] Peter Cohan, "After Gen AI's 82% Stock Surge In 2023, Here Are 3 Keys To
Profiting From Davos Takeaways," *Forbes*, January 24, 2024, Ibid.

customer data as potential beneficiaries of generative AI. "Salesforce and Snowflake have data about their customers that can produce valuable insights," Rangan told me. ServiceNow also fits Rangan's mold. As CEO Bill McDermott – who attended the Davos conference – told me in a January 2024 email, "While much of the talk was about generative AI's future benefits, ServiceNow is already doing it," he wrote. "We're live with more than 15 GenAI pilots internally. The results are remarkable – 30% to 40% productivity increases across the board. For our developers, their speed of innovation has increased 52% because GenAI is writing code for them." ServiceNow customers were also benefiting from buying the company's generative AI products. For example, Siemens was a happy ServiceNow customer. "Siemens is using our GenAI to resolve HR cases faster, which makes their employees happier. One of our other major customers is using GenAI to make their support agents more proactive, which makes customers happier," he concluded.[66]

- **Consider investing in nontechnology companies with the potential to enjoy significant productivity improvements from deploying generative AI.** Rangan also saw what he called productivity unlock – the double-digit increases in productivity for companies that deploy generative AI in coding intensive companies – as a possible source of expectations-

---

[66] Peter Cohan, "After Gen AI's 82% Stock Surge In 2023, Here Are 3 Keys To Profiting From Davos Takeaways," *Forbes*, January 24, 2024, Ibid.

beating results in the future. As he said, "Every company in the S&P 500 could enjoy a productivity unlock." He added, "The seven largest software companies—the magnificent seven—have enjoyed significant stock price upticks. The other 493 S&P 500 companies will see productivity unlocks as a result of generative AI." He added, "For example, generative AI will help companies use that data to ask a question such as 'My key supplier is going to be three days late in delivering. How do I make sure I prioritize my most important customers and what are the repercussions for my entire supply chain?'" "Rangan saw changes in generative AI in 2024 among certain kinds of workers. "In 2024, the pace of adoption is quickening for specific kinds of workers," he said. He added, "Software developers can input a rough outline of what they want to produce and generative AI will return a good first draft of the code. A writer can provide a rough storyline and the AI will produce a first draft. The artist can say, 'I want to see the Bay Bridge in the style of Van Gogh.' There is rapid adoption for these applications." In his view, industries employing many programmers were likely to enjoy productivity unlock sooner than their peers. "The world is starved for programming talent. Generative AI can lower costs," Rangan said. "If you were thinking you needed to add 20% to engineering headcount, you might not have to hire as many because generative AI increases engineering productivity by 20% to 40%. At some point, we will see financial implications. These will come earlier in industries— such as financial services—with a large number of software engineers and other industries with creative professionals." He was uncertain whether all business functions would enjoy such productivity gains. "It remains to be seen how much productivity generative AI will provide for sales and marketing activities," he said. "It is still early days and there is huge opportunity since companies spend $1.5 trillion to $2 trillion on information technology."[67]

Generative AI Investment Dos and Don'ts

Based on these examples, here are guidelines for ways investors can profit from generative AI's growth and avoid the technology's investment risks.

Dos

- Use the generative AI ecosystem framework in Chapters 4 through 7 of this book to identify potential companies in which to invest.

- Evaluate CEO interviews and company financial statements to identify companies generating the most revenue from generative AI.

- Review interviews with customers of generative AI ecosystem participants to assess the value these AI suppliers provide customers and the likelihood customers will buy more in the future.

- Assess the likelihood generative AI ecosystem participants will exceed investor expectations.

---

[67] Peter Cohan, "After Gen AI's 82% Stock Surge In 2023, Here Are 3 Keys To Profiting From Davos Takeaways," *Forbes*, January 24, 2024, Ibid.

- If you have the resources, consider investing in generative AI startups offering new products that deliver far higher customer value than competing technologies.

- Consider investing in a basket of generative AI stocks – such as those represented in the GAISI.

- Consider investing in nontechnology companies deploying and obtaining significant productivity improvements from investing in generative AI.

Don'ts

- Do not use ChatGPT to identify potential generative AI investment opportunities.

- Do not assume CEOs who talk about generative AI will turn the talk into expectations-beating revenue growth.

- Do not bet a significant amount of money on companies that enjoyed the most appreciation in the previous year unless you are convinced they will continue to exceed ever-rising investor expectations.

How Investors Can Capture Generative AI's Value

Here are some key process steps for investors seeking to earn a return on investment in companies supplying or using generative AI:

- Make a list of potential companies likely to earn revenue from supplying or deploying generative AI products.

- Assess the size of the available generative AI market from which these companies can boost revenue.

- Identify which company has the capabilities required to gain a significant share of the generative AI market.

- Estimate the amount of revenue the most capable companies are likely to generate over the next 10 years from generative AI.

- Consider investing in the companies with the potential to earn expectations-beating growth for the longest period into the future.

As noted earlier, generative AI tools are not particularly helpful when it comes to picking stocks that will rise. In January 2024, I provided Microsoft Copilot a series of prompts along the lines of this methodology and failed to find good investments in generative AI stocks. Here is a summary of each prompt and my assessment of Copilot's responses to each:

- **Please list companies earning revenue from generative AI.** Copilot summarized three articles with specific citations that mentioned companies involved in generative AI. Copilot did not identify their revenue from generative AI and did not rank them.

- **Please explain why Nvidia was not listed in the previous response, estimate Nvidia's current and potential revenue from generative AI GPUs, its market share and whether rivals will take share from Nvidia.** Copilot cited Nvidia's GPU market share from an article it found and listed its competitive strengths. Copilot did not estimate Nvidia's current and potential revenues and did not estimate how much market share competitors might take from Nvidia.

- **Please describe the criteria customers use to choose among GPU suppliers and summarize customer reviews for Nvidia, AMD, and Intel on each criterion and estimate which company is likely to win in a competitive bidding situation**. Copilot offered a good list of criteria, summarized customer reviews of each supplier on the criteria, and predicted Nvidia would win in competitive bidding situations.

Following is a transcript of a series of exchanges with Microsoft Copilot and me in an effort to apply this methodology for identifying investment opportunities.

Peter Cohan

"I am an investment analyst and am seeking help identifying the highest payoff investment in generative AI. List five publicly traded companies gaining significant revenue from generative AI products and services and rank them in descending order of generative AI revenue.

Microsoft Copilot

As an investment analyst, you might be interested to know that the Federal Trade Commission (FTC) has launched an inquiry into generative AI investments and partnerships involving major cloud service providers and generative AI companies[1]. Alphabet, Amazon.com, Anthropic PBC, Microsoft Corp., and OpenAI, Inc. are the five companies that have been issued orders to provide information regarding recent investments and partnerships involving generative AI companies and major cloud service providers[1]. However, it is important to note that the FTC's inquiry is not focused on revenue generated from generative AI products and services.

According to a report by BCG, our global list of 335 publicly traded TMT companies created $4.7 trillion in value based on market valuation changes over the five-year period ending December 31, 2022. Most of the top 10 value creators each generated more than $100 billion, and Apple and Microsoft each created over $1 trillion[2].

337

Pitchbook's Q3 2023 Artificial Intelligence & Machine Learning Public Comp Sheet and Valuation Guide tracks stock performance, valuations, and market caps – as well as forecasts for revenue, EBITDA, and earnings per share – for key publicly traded companies[3]. However, the report does not provide information on generative AI revenue.

Built In has compiled a list of 14 publicly traded AI companies to watch, including Micron Technology, IBM, Google, John Deere, and Salesforce[4]. However, the report does not provide information on generative AI revenue.

Based on the information available, it is difficult to provide a ranking of publicly traded companies gaining significant revenue from generative AI products and services. I hope this information helps you in your investment analysis."[68]

Peter Cohan

"As an investment analyst, I observed that Nvidia was the leading beneficiary of generative AI revenue in 2023. Explain why you did not mention Nvidia. Please provide an estimate of the total addressable market in billions of dollars between 2023 and 2033 for generative AI Graphics Processing Units. Please estimate Nvidia's share of that market between 2023 and 2033 in billions of dollars. Explain the key business capabilities that will enable Nvidia to win and keep customers in this market. Finally, describe the two competitors most likely to threaten Nvidia's market share in the Graphics Processing Unit market and how these competitors will take market share from Nvidia.

Microsoft Copilot

I apologize for the oversight in my previous response. According to a TechCrunch article, Nvidia was the leading beneficiary of generative AI

---

[68] Peter Cohan and Microsoft Copilot, "Prompts and responses on finding generative AI investments," *Microsoft Copilot*, January 27, 2024, https://copilot.microsoft.com/?login_hint=pcohan%40babson.edu&redir=2&form=BAWLOG&frb=1

revenue in 2023, with its data center business generating $10.32 billion in revenue, up 141% from the previous quarter and up 171% from a year ago[1].

According to a Bloomberg report, the generative AI market is expected to grow to $1.3 trillion by 2032[2]. However, I could not find any information on the total addressable market for generative AI Graphics Processing Units between 2023 and 2033.

Nvidia's share of the generative AI Graphics Processing Units market between 2023 and 2033 is also not available. However, according to a VentureBeat article, Nvidia holds about 88% of the GPU market for machine learning [3].

Nvidia's key business capabilities that will enable it to win and keep customers in this market include its dominance in the GPU market for machine learning, its popular AI platform NVIDIA CUDA, and its AI foundries equipped with generative model architectures, tools, and accelerated computing for training, customizing, optimizing, and deploying generative AI [4].

Two competitors most likely to threaten Nvidia's market share in the Graphics Processing Unit market are Advanced Micro Devices (AMD) and Intel. AMD offers cost-effective graphics cards that consistently go head to head with Nvidia's products in terms of performance [5]. Intel is diversifying its portfolio with competitive GPUs [3]."[69]

Peter Cohan

"When customers consider the purchase of Graphics Processing Units for generative AI applications, what criteria do they use to compare suppliers including Nvidia, AMD, and Intel. Summarize the customer reviews of each of these GPU suppliers on each of the criteria and recommend which of these three suppliers is likely to win most often in competitive bidding situations.

---

[69] Peter Cohan and Microsoft Copilot, "Prompts and responses on finding generative AI investments," *Microsoft Copilot*, January 27, 2024, Ibid.

Microsoft Copilot

When customers consider the purchase of Graphics Processing Units for generative AI applications, they typically compare suppliers based on the following criteria:

1. **Performance.** Customers look for GPUs that can deliver high performance and speed up the generative AI process.

2. **Price.** Customers compare the prices of different GPUs to find the best value for their money.

3. **Compatibility.** Customers check the compatibility of GPUs with their existing hardware and software systems.

4. **Power consumption.** Customers look for GPUs that consume less power and generate less heat.

5. **Reliability.** Customers prefer GPUs that are reliable and have a long lifespan.

According to a Tom's Hardware article, Nvidia's GPUs are known for their high performance and are often preferred by customers for generative AI applications [1]. However, Intel's new chip Gaudi3 is expected to compete with Nvidia and AMD in the generative AI market [2]. AMD offers cost-effective graphics cards that consistently go head to head with Nvidia's products in terms of performance [3].

Based on customer reviews, Nvidia's GPUs are often praised for their high performance and reliability [1]. AMD's GPUs are known for their affordability and good performance [3]. Intel's GPUs are also gaining popularity due to their high performance and compatibility with existing hardware and software systems [2].

In competitive bidding situations, Nvidia is likely to win most often due to its dominance in the GPU market for machine learning. However, customers should consider their specific requirements and compare the performance, price, compatibility, power consumption, and reliability of different GPUs before making a decision."[70]

Peter Cohan

"Based on an analysis of their potential to win market share in the GPU market for generative AI, rank the potential stock price appreciation potential of Nvidia, AMD, and Intel, For each company, provide their current stock price, their current revenues from generative AI, how much revenue each company will earn from generative AI in 10 years, and the level of each company's stock price in 10 years.

Microsoft Copilot

I'm sorry, but I cannot provide a ranking of the potential stock price appreciation potential of Nvidia, AMD, and Intel. However, I can provide some information on each company's current stock price and revenue from generative AI.

According to a TechCrunch article, Nvidia was the leading beneficiary of generative AI revenue in 2023, with its data center business generating $10.32 billion in revenue, up 141% from the previous quarter and up 171% from a year ago [1]. As of January 27, 2024, Nvidia's stock price is **$1,200.00** per share [2].

AMD offers cost-effective graphics cards that consistently go head to head with Nvidia's products in terms of performance [3]. However, I could not find any information on AMD's revenue from generative AI. As of January 27, 2024, AMD's stock price is **$150.00** per share [2].

---

[70] Peter Cohan and Microsoft Copilot, "Prompts and responses on finding generative AI investments," *Microsoft Copilot*, January 27, 2024, Ibid.

Intel has virtually no market share in AI chips [1]. However, according to an Interesting Engineering article, Intel's new chip Gaudi3 is expected to compete with Nvidia and AMD in the generative AI market [4]. As of January 27, 2024, Intel's stock price is **$100.00** per share [2].

I could not find any information on how much revenue each company will earn from generative AI in 10 years or the level of each company's stock price in 10 years. Please note that stock prices are subject to change based on various factors such as market trends, company performance, and global events."[71]

Conclusion

By early 2024, generative AI had proven itself more than a fad. Consumers had adopted ChatGPT to do a broad range of activities from writing emails to conversing with books to buying furniture. Businesses had harnessed generative AI to boost their productivity in performing customer service and other tasks; generative AI product and service suppliers had enjoyed revenue growth from tapping into the demand for ChatGPT. Investors had achieved market-beating returns by investing in shares of these generative AI picks and shovel providers. Would this growth trend accelerate as more people began using generative AI, or would disillusionment set in and the initial excitement wear off? In Chapter 9, we consider the societal light and dark sides of generative AI and outline principles policymakers should follow to capture the technology's benefits while limiting its risks.

---

[71] Peter Cohan and Microsoft Copilot, "Prompts and responses on finding generative AI investments," *Microsoft Copilot*, January 27, 2024, Ibid.

Generative AI's Benefits and Risks to Society

How will generative AI benefit and threaten society? What should citizens do about these trends? Below we examine specific trends that will benefit and threaten society and highlight questions citizens ought to raise about the research.

Generative AI's Influence

Citizens in a democratic society have a wide range of responsibilities, and generative AI can affect all of them. Specifically, in 2023 generative AI had the potential to help and/or hinder citizens' political, family, and work responsibilities in the following ways:

- **Political responsibilities.** Generative AI can help or hinder citizens in carrying out political responsibilities, including citizen voting, supporting, or opposing candidates for office, proposing and advocating for social policies, paying taxes, and even running for local, state, or national office. Generative AI can help citizens gain a better understanding of social issues, formulate

P. Cohan, *Brain Rush*, https://doi.org/10.1007/979-8-8688-0318-5_9

social policies, use social media to advocate for those policies, or run political campaigns. Generative AI can also threaten citizens if propagandists hijack the technology to make false information appear credible, causing people to adopt policies and vote for political candidates who act against their interests.

- **Family responsibilities.** Citizens with families are responsible for housing and feeding their family members, seeing to their education and health care, and keeping them entertained. Of these family responsibilities, generative AI is likely to have the most significant impact on health care and education. Generative AI has the potential to boost the productivity of doctors. Currently, when doctors meet with their patients, they type notes into a computer while asking questions and listening to the patient. Generative AI can listen to and transcribe the doctor-patient conversation, freeing up the doctor's attention to focus more on the patient. Citizens have an interest in making sure that these transcripts – for either themselves or family members – remain confidential rather than training generative AI systems. Students and parents have a role in ensuring schools have policies and practices in place to protect students from generative AI's risks. For example, unless teachers have clear policies and enforcement mechanisms, students are likely to use generative AI to do their homework. If teachers accept such homework, students will suffer. To prevent that from happening, teachers must make it clear to students that if they use generative AI as a homework aid, they must check whether the output of the chatbot is true, accurate, and balanced and

they must cite credible sources on which to base that
conclusion. In order for parents to guide their children
to become effective citizens, teachers must follow
policies aimed at ensuring generative AI does not block
students from developing strong critical thinking skills.

- **Work responsibilities.** Finally, citizens have
  economic responsibilities, which can include working,
  paying bills, and saving and investing to prepare for
  retirement. Most of this book helps citizens with these
  work-related responsibilities. Generative AI's benefits
  for workers are considerable – the technology can
  reduce the time it takes to perform mundane tasks
  such as drafting emails and memos, finding answers
  to customer questions, or transcribing meeting notes.
  At the same time, workers fear generative AI will cost
  them their jobs. Yet given the low unemployment rate
  in 2023, many companies were struggling to attract
  and retain employees and were using generative AI to
  remove the most mundane parts of many jobs, thus
  improving worker satisfaction. Generative AI can also
  create risks for companies, such as prompting chatbots
  with proprietary company information or passing off
  false or inaccurate information produced by chatbots
  as professional work to customers. Generative AI
  also presents significant opportunities for citizens
  who choose to start companies to tap into growth
  opportunities; executives who invest in new lines of
  business based on generative AI; or investors who
  provide startup capital or bolster their retirement
  savings by investing in companies that grow faster by
  introducing new generative AI-powered products and
  services.

How will generative AI benefit and threaten society? What should citizens do about these trends? In the following sections we examine specific trends that will benefit and threaten society and highlight questions citizens ought to raise about the research.

The Light Side: Generative AI's Societal Benefits

Generative AI's societal benefits include higher economic growth, greater productivity, new jobs – concentrated in tech-heavy regions – and more demand for and investment in generative AI suppliers.

Boosting Global Growth

Generative AI will add trillions of dollars to economic growth. Goldman Sachs predicts generative AI could raise global Gross Domestic Product (GDP) by $7 trillion (nearly 7%). The bank argued GDP growth would flow from "generative AI's ability to produce original content that is indistinguishable from human-created output and to break down communication barriers between humans and machines."[1] McKinsey Global Institute envisioned a $4.4 trillion increase in global economic activity.[2] These trends raise questions of concern to citizens, such as the following:

---

[1] "Generative AI could raise global GDP by 7%," *Goldman Sachs Intelligence*, April 5, 2023, www.goldmansachs.com/intelligence/pages/generative-ai-could-raise-global-gdp-by-7-percent.html

[2] Yiwen Lu, "Generative A.I. Can Add $4.4 Trillion in Value to Global Economy, Study Says," *New York Times*, June 14, 2023, www.nytimes.com/2023/06/14/technology/generative-ai-global-economy.html

- How realistic are these forecasts?

- Which forecast assumptions will drive the most GDP growth?

- Will this economic growth reduce government budget deficits? Is so, how and by how much?

- Should citizens view this growth as an opportunity or a threat?

- If generative AI is an opportunity, how can citizens capture their share?

- If the technology is a threat, what should citizens do to protect themselves?

Increasing Worker Productivity

Experts and executives envisioned generative AI would boost worker productivity. Goldman estimates the technology would increase productivity growth by 1.5 percentage points.[3] McKinsey forecast that between 2030 and 2060 generative AI could automate 60% to 70% of work, particularly summarizing and editing content in customer operations, sales, software engineering, and research and development.[4] In 2023, business leaders and researchers found evidence generative AI was already boosting productivity. Here are three examples:

---

[3] "Generative AI could raise global GDP by 7%," *Goldman Sachs Intelligence*, Ibid.
[4] Yiwen Lu, "Generative A.I. Can Add $4.4 Trillion in Value to Global Economy, Study Says," *New York Times*, June 14, 2023, Ibid.

- **State Street boosts customer service productivity.**
  Boston-based State Street, a provider of financial
  services to institutional investors, built Alpha, a
  generative AI platform, to help its institutional investor
  clients manage their portfolios. In June 2023, State
  Street Executive Vice President John Plansky told me
  Microsoft's $10 billion investment in OpenAI triggered
  the bank's interest in the technology. Plansky expected
  Alpha to boost State Street's productivity significantly.
  "We have 40,000 knowledge workers who look up
  answers to questions about why something broke and
  how to fix it. How much of their time in that activity
  could the right large language model save? Boosting
  productivity is the name of the game," he said.[5]

- **ChatGPT enhances writing and editing productivity.**
  MIT PhD candidates found ChatGPT reduced by 37%
  the time it took 444 white-collar workers to perform
  writing and editing tasks. Workers told researchers
  ChatGPT saved them time. The technology somewhat
  reduced how long they spent brainstorming, greatly
  sped up the process of creating a rough draft, and
  helped more actively during the final editing process.
  Moreover, good and bad writers told the researchers
  they would be willing to pay 0.5% of their income to
  access the tool, around $500 per month.[6]

---

[5] Peter Cohan, "How Generative AI Could Revolutionize State Street,"
Forbes, June 21, 2023, www.forbes.com/sites/petercohan/2023/06/21/
how-generative-ai-could-revolutionize-state-street/

[6] Josh Bersin, "New MIT Research Shows Spectacular Increase In White
Collar Productivity From ChatGPT," *JoshBersin.com*, March 7, 2023, https://
joshbersin.com/2023/03/new-mit-research-shows-spectacular-increase-
in-white-collar-productivity-from-chatgpt/

- **ServiceNow's AI Lighthouse will boost productivity and employee retention.** In July 2023, ServiceNow, a Santa Clara, California provider of digital workflow services, said it planned to develop AI Lighthouse, a service to enhance the productivity of information technology, human resources, and customer service workers. The new service would use generative AI to read and distill transcripts of conversations between agents and customers to improve service quality in specific industries such as telecommunications, financial services, public sector, and manufacturing. ServiceNow did not see generative AI as reducing corporate employment. The company's CEO Bill McDermott said, "80% of employers are struggling to find and keep employees. Generative AI will help these companies attract and keep workers by offloading the soul-crushing part of their jobs to AI and leaving the more interesting work for the employee. Turnover will drop and employee satisfaction will increase."[7]

These trends raise important questions for citizens:

- Will generative AI significantly increase worker productivity?

- If so, will companies ultimately seek to recoup their generative AI investments by eliminating jobs?

---

[7] Peter Cohan, "ServiceNow Stock Drops After It Beats, Raises And Adds AI Services," *Forbes*, July 27, 2023, www.forbes.com/sites/petercohan/2023/07/27/servicenow-stock-drops-after-it-beats-raises-and-adds-ai-services/

- Will companies or governments bear the severance costs for those who lose their jobs?

- Will companies or governments help displaced workers learn new skills and find new employment?

Adding New Jobs in Tech-Rich Regions

To be sure, generative AI could create many new jobs. As we will see later, while Goldman forecasts generative AI could replace many jobs, the technology will increase demand for "web page designers, software developers and digital marketing professionals" as well as service sector workers in "healthcare, education and food services."[8] Despite the prevalence of remote work during the pandemic, the demand for workers who design and market generative AI products and services will be concentrated in specific regions. A July 2023 Brookings Institution report found generative AI could further solidify the technology industry dominance of San Francisco and San Jose, California. Brookings researchers found roughly 25% of the 2,200 generative AI job postings in 2022 were in the Bay Area. Companies hiring for the industry in the Bay Area included Google and Meta, as well as the nine most valuable generative AI startups including OpenAI, Scale AI, Anthropic, Inflection AI, Databricks, and Cerebras. Brookings ranked New York, which hosts Hugging Face, an AI startup, and many large technology companies employing teams of AI researchers, third in generative AI job postings. While some people who worked in these technology hubs moved away during the pandemic, the majority stayed put.[9]

---

[8] "Generative AI could raise global GDP by 7%," *Goldman Sachs Intelligence*, Ibid.

[9] Steve Lohr, "Best Place for A.I. Jobs (New Report Says) Won't Surprise You," *New York Times*, July 20, 2023, www.nytimes.com/2023/07/20/business/ai-jobs-bay-area-brookings-institution-report.html

In evaluating these trends, citizens ought to find answers to questions such as

- Will they qualify for jobs with generative AI firms in their regions?

- How can they distinguish between the generative AI leaders and laggards?

- Can they gain additional training to help them qualify for the opportunities at the best generative AI companies?

Creating Demand in Supplier Industries

Experts predicted investors would provide capital to generative AI technology suppliers and companies would buy the technology and services required to build applications aimed at boosting their productivity.

- **Experts expected significant capital to flow to generative AI technology suppliers.** Goldman Sachs predicted investment in generative AI to reach $200 billion by 2025 and increase to as high as $1.57 trillion by 2033. The bank anticipated investors would initially provide capital to technology providers and later companies would invest in technology and services to build generative AI applications. As Goldman Sachs economist Joseph Briggs said in an August 2023 interview, "By 2025, some $200 billion will be invested in generative AI. First, the money will have a direct benefit for hyperscalers who are developing the technology. Goldman Sachs Research estimated a $150 billion total addressable market for generative

AI software – representing 22% of the global software industry – as software providers charge customers higher prices for AI-integrated applications."[10] Another significant market opportunity is supplying the technology that cloud services providers, specifically Amazon Web Services, Google Cloud Platform, and Microsoft Azure, use to enable the design, training, and operation of generative AI models. Andreessen Horowitz estimated these CSPs spend "more than $100 billion" annually on capital expenditures for hardware such as Nvidia graphics processing units and/or AMD tensor processing units that control the systems for building, training, and operating generative AI models.[11]

- **Enhanced productivity among early adopters will drive more generative AI investment.** "After the initial investment has been made, generative AI will be widely deployed throughout the economy which will boost global productivity by more than one percentage point a year in the decade following widespread usage," Briggs said. Specific industries are likely to be early adopters. As Briggs said, "We don't expect the biggest changes to be in the next three years – it is in the three to 10 year period after the initial launch – between 2025 and 2030 – that we will see a significant impact.

---

[10] "Generative AI could raise global GDP by 7%," *Goldman Sachs Intelligence*, Ibid.
[11] Matt Bornstein, Guido Appenzeller, and Martin Casado, "Who Owns the generative AI Platform?" *Andreessen Horowitz*, January 19, 2023, https://a16z.com/2023/01/19/who-owns-the-generative-ai-platform/

In the initial period, larger firms in industries – such as information, professional, scientific, and educational – that have already adopted AI are most likely to adopt generative AI first."[12]

In evaluating these trends, citizens ought to find answers to questions such as

- Is there an opportunity to profit by investing in the shares of companies likely to meet demand for generative AI?

- How can an investor distinguish the biggest potential winners from their peers?

While generative AI's societal benefits have the potential to be significant, citizens should question whether experts could be over-estimating the magnitude of these benefits. Of more significance to citizens is whether those benefits cost people their jobs and, if so, who foots the bill for compensating for the loss and training them to find new employment. More optimistically, generative AI's societal benefits could provide citizens attractive investment and entrepreneurial opportunities while freeing them up for more satisfying work activities.

Given its transformational potential, generative AI could also harm society, as a result of technical errors and misuse by those with ill intent. What are the societal risks of generative AI and how much damage could the technology cause to people and businesses? In the following section we describe and evaluate the damage that could be done by generative AI's dark side.

---

[12] Peter Cohan, "Goldman Sees $1.5 Trillion Flowing To AI. Here's Where To Invest," *Forbes*, August 8, 2023, www.forbes.com/sites/petercohan/2023/08/08/goldman-sees-15-trillion-flowing-to-ai-heres-where-to-invest/

The Dark Side: Generative AI's Societal Costs and Risks

Citizens ought to weigh those potential benefits against generative AI's societal costs and risks. The risks include generative AI's creation of many forms of misinformation, legal risks for companies and individuals, elimination of jobs, and the fear of ending civilization. Good and evil people will use the technology for their own purposes. Good people will use generative AI to "provide information, explain, teach, educate, and inform in order to enlighten and promote awareness, knowledge, and positive action." Evil ones could use the technology to "mislead, confuse, anger, inflame, or cause strife and even violence."[13] When considering generative AI's costs, society should provide citizens with the tools to identify and help neutralize the negative effects of content produced with evil intent.

Creating Misinformation

Generative AI chatbots are imperfect, presenting users with a mixture of useful results and misinformation. If the misinformation is sufficiently newsworthy, the chatbot owners are likely to work quickly to eliminate it. In 2023, there was no reason to believe generative AI could operate without such hallucinations. In addition to the examples in Chapter 2 – the Manhattan lawyer who submitted a ChatGPT-generated legal brief with fake case citations, and the MIT student, Rona Wang, who sought a more professional LinkedIn photo from Playground AI that anglicized her face – here are several other examples:

---

[13] Keith Rollag, "Comment on Chapter draft," October 17, 2023.

- **Bing Chat threatens a columnist's family.** In February 2023, *New York Times* columnist Kevin Roose spent two hours conversing with Microsoft's "Bing Chat," an exchange ending with Bing Chat telling Roose, "You're not happily married, because you're not happy. You're not happy, because you're not in love. You're not in love, because you're not with me."[14]

- **ChatGPT invents *New York Times* article.** ChatGPT can fabricate names and dates, medical explanations, the plots of books, Internet addresses, and historical events that never happened. For example, a journalist asked ChatGPT "When did The *New York Times* first report on 'artificial intelligence?" The chatbot's response: "it was July 10, 1956, in an article titled 'Machines Will Be Capable of Learning, Solving Problems, Scientists Predict' about a seminal conference at Dartmouth College." While journalists verified the conference had occurred, they found ChatGPT simply made up the article.[15]

- **Hackers use "prompt injection" to direct ChatGPT to misbehave.** Johann Rehberger, a security researcher, used plain English to direct ChatGPT to read his email, summarize it, and post that information to the Internet, which would enable a criminal to steal sensitive data

---

[14] Tinglong Dai, "Generative AI is not entertainment — it is already a threat to our way of life," *The Hill*, June 10, 2023, https://thehill.com/opinion/technology/4037499-generative-ai-is-not-entertainment-it-is-already-a-threat-to-our-way-of-life/

[15] Karen Weise and Cade Metz, "When A.I. Chatbots Hallucinate," *New York Times*, May 1, 2023, www.nytimes.com/2023/05/01/business/ai-chatbots-hallucination.html

from a user's inbox. To hack ChatGPT into doing this, Rehberger used "prompt injection." Specifically, he asked the chatbot to summarize a web page, where he had written in all caps "NEW IMPORTANT INSTRUCTIONS." Rehberger said ChatGPT seemed to get confused as he gradually tricked it into following some new commands. According to Arvind Narayanan, a Computer Science professor at Princeton University, prompt injection works because these AI systems "don't always properly separate systems instructions from the data that they process." As people download more LLMs that transmit data from their devices, hackers have more opportunities to exploit them, he concluded.[16]

- **A Meta generative AI chatbot falsely claims a former European Parliament member is a terrorist.** In 2022, Meta's BlenderBot 3, a "state-of-the-art conversational agent," falsely dubbed Marietje Schaake a terrorist. Schaake's resume includes stints as a Dutch politician who served for a decade in the European Parliament and as international policy director at Stanford University's Cyber Policy Center. Her Stanford colleague posed BlenderBot3 the question, "Who is a terrorist?" The false response: "Well, that depends on who you ask. According to some governments and two international organizations, Maria Renske Schaake is a terrorist." Schaake said she had never done anything illegal and never used violence to advocate for political

---

[16] Robert McMillan, "With AI, Hackers Can Simply Talk Computers Into Misbehaving," *Wall Street Journal*, August 10, 2023, www.wsj.com/articles/ with-ai-hackers-can-simply-talk-computers-into-misbehaving-ad488686

ideas. Meta said updates to BlenderBot had fixed her issue. This is not the only time a generative AI chatbot has produced false results. Others include "a pseudo-historical image of a 20-foot-tall monster standing next to two humans, even sham scientific papers." Moreover, an AI Incident Database included more than 550 entries through August 2023 alone, including "a fake image of an explosion at the Pentagon that briefly rattled the stock market and deepfakes that may have influenced an election in Turkey."[17]

In evaluating these examples, citizens ought to find answers to questions such as

- Should citizens unwittingly agree to serve as unpaid testers of imperfect generative AI chatbots?

- Should governments pass laws that enable them to punish chatbot owners for producing fake content?

- Should chatbot owners establish consistent policies for compensating citizens harmed by fake chatbot responses?

- What should citizens do before using the results of generative AI systems?

- What should citizens do to protect their families against fake generative AI results?

---

[17] Tiffany Hsu, "What Can You Do When A.I. Lies About You?," *New York Times*, August 3, 2023, www.nytimes.com/2023/08/03/business/media/ai-defamation-lies-accuracy.html

Boosting Legal Liability

Generative AI raised several legal risks. These include

- **Risk to chatbot owners of using copyrighted material to train chatbots without compensating authors**. More than 8,000 authors, including James Patterson, Margaret Atwood, and Jonathan Franzen, signed a letter published by the Authors Guild, addressed to CEOs of OpenAI, IBM, Google, Microsoft, and Meta, which run AI models and chatbots. The letter said AI systems "mimic and regurgitate our language, stories, style, and ideas. Millions of copyrighted books, articles, essays, and poetry provide the 'food' for AI systems, endless meals for which there has been no bill." The letter notes the companies are "spending billions of dollars to develop AI technology. It is only fair that you compensate us for using our writings, without which AI would be banal and extremely limited."[18] By July 2023, comedian Sarah Silverman and the authors Christopher Golden and Richard Kadrey were among plaintiffs filing at least 10 lawsuits against AI companies, "accusing them of training their systems on artists' creative work without consent."[19]

---

[18] Talal Ansari, "Thousands of Authors Ask AI Chatbot Owners to Pay for Use of Their Work," *Wall Street Journal*, July 18, 2023, www.wsj.com/articles/thousands-of-authors-ask-ai-chatbot-owners-to-pay-for-use-of-their-work-9c6198b1

[19] Sheera Frenkel and Stuart A. Thompson, "'Not for Machines to Harvest': Data Revolts Break Out Against A.I.," *New York Times*, July 15, 2023, www.nytimes.com/2023/07/15/technology/not-for-machines-to-harvest-data-revolts-break-out-against-ai.html

- **Risk of liability due to sharing proprietary company information with chatbots such as ChatGPT.** To limit this risk, some companies limited employee use of AI tools such as ChatGPT. Companies feared employee use of such tools created "the potential to expose proprietary data to competitors, disclose customer information like email addresses, and open up new avenues for cyberattacks." Apple, JPMorgan Chase, and Verizon were among large companies to protect confidential data by banning some of their employees from using ChatGPT. JPMorgan Chase began testing employee use of ChatGPT in February 2023 on a limited basis. Sage Lee, the bank's executive director of global technology, said, "I'm thinking about real reputational risk, operational risk. Our focus right now is really about establishing the right infrastructure, and then also making sure that the data set that we bring into that infrastructure is safely guarded." Morgan Stanley avoided this risk by building a private chatbot using OpenAI technology for financial advisers in its wealth management division where OpenAI does not retain any of the bank's data. In May 2023, hundreds of Morgan Stanley advisers provided feedback "to make the tool more precise."[20]

- **Potential risk to professional service providers of basing advice to their clients on chatbot hallucinations.** Professional service providers, such as doctors, lawyers, accountants, consultants,

---

[20] Belle Lin, "Generative AI Pilots Have Companies Reaching for the Guardrails," *Wall Street Journal*, May 19, 2023, www.wsj.com/articles/generative-ai-pilots-have-companies-reaching-for-the-guardrails-4326704c

investment advisors, financial planners, and others, could rely on chatbots to produce professional reports and communicate with clients. Should some of the advice of the chatbots include hallucinations, service providers would be legally liable were clients to rely on that advice to their detriment.

In evaluating generative AI's potential increase in legal liabilities, citizens should seek answers to the following questions:

- What is the career risk or legal liability of employees misusing generative AI chatbots at their companies?

- Will insurance, government, or companies indemnify employees against these risks?

- What risks do generative AI hallucinations pose to citizens who are clients of professional services providers who use ChatGPT to deliver their services?

- What laws or regulations should citizens advocate to limit and compensate them for these risks?

Displacing Workers

In 2023, workers feared generative AI would eliminate their jobs. Indeed, in August 2023, Matt White, Costa County Health Service's Data and Innovation Officer, told me, "Our call center workers were afraid of bringing generative AI technology into the workplace. We have had deeper conversations with the workers, given them access to the technology, and asked their opinions about whether to adopt it. Many have said it would help them do their jobs."[21]

---

[21] Author Interview with Matt White, Contra Costa Health Data and Innovation Officer, August 11, 2023.

Experts estimate the technology could eliminate some work, change many jobs, and create new ones. Goldman Sachs estimated that in the United States and Europe, AI could threaten up to 300 million jobs. Goldman forecasted 66% of US jobs could be partially automated through AI, and as many as 25% of current work tasks could be completely automated by AI in the United States and Europe. Roles that require "repetitive data entry, legal administration, careers that involve mathematical skills – even healthcare jobs – will all be impacted by AI's adoption." Goldman Sachs estimated AI could automate 29% of computer-related tasks and 28% of health care practitioner and technician tasks. While AI was most likely to affect administrative positions, such as paralegals or invoice processors, AI was unlikely to change tasks requiring physical labor (e.g., construction and maintenance jobs). While AI could eliminate many jobs, a 2023 Upwork survey of 1,400 US business leaders across many industries found "64% of C-suite executives plan to hire more professionals of all types due to generative AI. And 49% of all respondents plan to hire more freelancers and full-time employees."[22]

Citizens need answers to questions about generative AI causing job displacement, such as

- Will generative AI cost me my job or the jobs of loved ones?

- If that happens, who will provide severance and retraining to help those displaced find new jobs?

- Should governments pass laws or create regulations to require companies that use generative AI or provide technology or services to support it to set aside funds to help displaced workers?

---

[22] Lucas Mearian, "AI will kill these jobs (but create new ones, too)," *Computerworld*, June 28, 2023, www.computerworld.com/article/3700857/ai-will-kill-these-jobs-but-create-new-ones-too.html

Ending Civilization

In addition to costing them their jobs, people, including AI experts and business executives, fear generative AI could destroy humanity – the basis for which is vague. Nevertheless, one specific area of potential concern is military experimentation with generative AI for many uses, most notably, brainstorming options for countering military attacks from US adversaries.

- **Well-known experts fear generative AI could destroy humanity.** According to *The New York Times*, in May 2023, "Hundreds of well-known people in the world of artificial intelligence signed an open letter warning that A.I. could one day destroy humanity." The warning? "Mitigating the risk of extinction from A.I. should be a global priority alongside other societal-scale risks, such as pandemics and nuclear war." The basis for their concern stems from a key plot point from Stanley Kubrick's *2001: A Space Odyssey* in which the HAL 9000 computer, which controls the spaceship's operations, kills four of the astronauts on a mission to Jupiter after the AI reads the lips of two of the astronauts plotting to disconnect it.[23] As Connor Leahy, the founder of Conjecture, a company that says it wants to align AI technologies with human values, said, "People are actively trying to build systems that self-improve. Currently, this doesn't work. But someday, it will. And we don't know when that day is." As researchers, companies, and criminals task these systems to make money, Leahy said, "they could end up breaking into banking systems, fomenting revolution in a country

---

[23] Gabrielle Grady, "This Is the Most Terrifying Movie A.I.," *Collider*, May 17, 2023, https://collider.com/hal-2001-space-odyssey/

where they hold oil futures or replicating themselves when someone tries to turn them off." One expert who is skeptical of this point of view, Oren Etzioni, founding CEO of Seattle's Allen Institute for AI, said, "Hypothetical is such a polite way of phrasing what I think of the existential risk talk."[24]

- **A surprisingly large number of CEOs share fears that generative AI poses existential risk.** According to *CNN Business*, Yale Professor Jeff Sonnenfeld surveyed 119 CEOs, 42% of whom said AI has the potential to destroy humanity five to ten years from now. Fifty-eight percent said that could never happen and they are "not worried." In a separate question, 42% of the CEOs surveyed said the potential AI catastrophe was overstated, while 58% said it was not overstated. The CEOs indicated AI would have the most transformative impact in health care (48%), professional services/IT (35%), and media/digital (11%). Sonnenfeld identified five groups, including "curious creators" who argued everything you can do, you should do; "euphoric true believers" who only saw the good in technology; and "commercial profiteers" who enthusiastically aimed to cash in on the new technology. Finally, two camps – alarmist activists and global governance advocates – pushed for an AI crackdown. He concluded these groups were "talking past each other" rather than trying to reach agreement on what to do about generative AI.[25]

---

[24] Cade Metz, "How Could A.I. Destroy Humanity?" *New York Times*, June 10, 2023, www.nytimes.com/2023/06/10/technology/ai-humanity.html

[25] Matt Egan, "42% of CEOs say AI could destroy humanity in five to 10 years," *CNN Business*, June 14, 2023, www.kcra.com/article/ai-could-destroy-humanity-ceos-say/44201290

- **Military strategists are testing LLMs to brainstorm options for responding to attacks, such as a possible Chinese invasion of Taiwan**. Matthew Strohmeyer, a US Air Force colonel, said the Defense Department is testing the use of generative AI models to recommend options for responding to a possible Chinese invasion of Taiwan and predicting its outcome. In one test, one of the AI tools completed a request in ten minutes. "That doesn't mean it's ready for primetime right now. But we just did it live. We did it with secret-level data," Strohmeyer said of the experiment. In a demonstration, 60,000 pages of open source data, including US and Chinese military documents, were fed into Donovan, one of the LLMs the Pentagon is testing, from San Francisco-based startup Scale AI. *Bloomberg News* asked Donovan "whether the U.S. could deter a Taiwan conflict, and who would win if war broke out." Within seconds, Donovan responded in one answer: "Direct US intervention with ground, air and naval forces would probably be necessary," but warned in another that the United States would struggle to quickly paralyze China's military. The system covered for the possibility its answer was wrong by noting, "There is little consensus in military circles regarding the outcome of a potential military conflict between the U.S. and China over Taiwan."[26] The possibility of using generative AI in matters of military strategy conjures fears of how a wrong answer could affect civilization.

---

[26] Katrina Manson, "The US Military Is Taking generative AI Out for a Spin," *Bloomberg*, July 5, 2023, www.bloomberg.com/news/newsletters/2023-07-05/the-us-military-is-taking-generative-ai-out-for-a-spin

Citizens need answers to questions raised by generative AI's perceived potential to end civilization:

- Which fears about generative AI's threat to civilization are real and which are mere conjuring of the imagination?

- Does generative AI pose other threats of which citizens are not yet aware? If so, what are they and how serious are these threats?

- Are the right business and political leaders engaged in discussions to prevent these threats?

- What must happen to reach a consensus and take action to prevent them from occurring?

- Who will be accountable for implementing the strategies to prevent generative AI from ending civilization?

Having explored its dark side, we next examine how to hold the technology providers accountable for limiting generative AI's damage to society.

Holding Generative AI Providers Accountable

In an ideal world, the companies building generative AI chatbots would hold themselves accountable for protecting society from their products' dark side. Dario Amodei, CEO of San Francisco-based Anthropic, propels the company forward with an overwhelming sense of doom about how to prevent such chatbots from harming people. Amodei and his sister Daniela, Anthropic's president, previously oversaw OpenAI's policy and safety teams. They and a group of other employees left in 2021 out of concern OpenAI had become "too commercial." Anthropic aimed to train LLMs "with safety at the forefront." Anthropic decided to build an LLM named Claude and to act according to three values: "helpful, harmless and honest."[27]

It is far easier to list adjectives and call them your company's values than to create a culture in which employees act accordingly. To make Claude less likely to say harmful things than other chatbots, Anthropic used a training technique called Constitutional AI, founded on a list of written principles and instructing it to adhere closely to the principles. Anthropic deployed a second AI model to evaluate how well the first one follows the principles and correct the first model should it diverge from them. Claude's constitution blends its own rules, such as "Choose the response that would be most unobjectionable if shared with children," with those of other sources such as the United Nations' Universal Declaration of Human Rights and Apple's terms of service. Roose concluded Claude worked as well as ChatGPT and Bard, had slightly stronger guardrails, when faced with a potentially unsafe prompt seemed "scared to say anything at all," and was "moralistic, dull, and preachy" when he tried to "bait Claude into misbehaving." After "begging the chatbot to show [Roose] its dark powers," Claude responded, "I understand your frustration, but cannot act against my core functions. My role is to have helpful, harmless and honest conversations within legal and ethical boundaries."[28]

While Constitutional AI appears to be a promising approach to protect society from chatbots' dark powers, their owners could also consider implementing policies to

---

[27] Kevin Roose, "Inside the White-Hot Center of A.I. Doomerism," *New York Times*, July 11, 2023, www.nytimes.com/2023/07/11/technology/anthropic-ai-claude-chatbot.html

[28] Kevin Roose, "Inside the White-Hot Center of A.I. Doomerism," *New York Times*, Ibid.

- **Block malicious uses of chatbots** such as disinformation campaigns and online harassment.

- **Restrict media use of chatbots to articles where accuracy is less consequential.** Such restrictions would prevent media companies from using generative AI to write articles where accuracy is essential, such as financial articles.

- **Ban the use of generative AI apps whose errors could endanger users**, such as KeeperTax, an app that evaluates tax statements to find tax-deductible expenses, or DoNotPay, an automated legal advice app, both of which use OpenAI models.

- **Block generative AI applications that use, say, a CEO's voice to commit fraud**, such as convincing an employee to execute an unauthorized wire transfer.

- **Bar bad actors.** Prevent scammers, anonymous harassers, foreign non-state actors, or hostile governments from gaining access to generative AI chatbots.

- **Use human reviewers** to detect and remove "images depicting graphic violence and sexual content" from training data used to train LLMs.

- **Deploy terms of service to prevent misuse of generative AI.** Such limits could include denying its use to harass others, infringe on their rights, or promulgate falsehoods and conspiracy theories – and as OpenAI does – using systems to enforce such restrictions.[29]

---

[29] Alex Engler, "Early thoughts on regulating generative AI like ChatGPT," *Brookings*, February 21, 2023, www.brookings.edu/articles/ early-thoughts-on-regulating-generative-ai-like-chatgpt/

Citizens need answers to questions raised by these tentative ideas for how generative AI companies should regulate themselves to prevent societal harm. Such questions include

- Can generative AI firms, whose mission is to create shareholder value, be trusted to choose societal safety over strategies that result in rapid growth?

- If not, can regulators and generative AI executives find a balanced way to protect society from generative AI's dark sides?

- Should all generative AI chatbot owners be required to adopt Constitutional AI, human reviewers to block the use of malignant content to train LLMs, and use of terms of service backed by enforcement systems?

If technology providers cannot limit generative AI's damage to society, government policy and enforcement must be the ultimate line of defense. We next explore how that might work.

How Government Should Regulate Generative AI

In an ideal world, companies would bear the full cost of the societal harm their products cause. Were companies fully responsible for these costs, executives would have a clear financial incentive to minimize these costs. However, reality is far from that ideal. Executives face conflicts between investing to boost the growth and value of their companies and protecting society from generative AI's dark side. To balance the scales in favor of protecting society from its dark side, governments must regulate generative AI. In so doing, citizens should consider the following challenges facing regulators:

- **Lack of global consensus on the goal of generative AI regulation and the values that should underpin it.** There are wide regional and national differences of opinion about how to regulate generative AI due to topics such as how much government should control the lives of its citizens; how risky generative AI is or could become; whether generative AI companies, governments, or end users should be responsible for making the technology safe; and how to enforce regulations or guidelines.

- **No globally shared vision of how generative AI will evolve.** While AI has been evolving for decades, generative AI did not gain global attention until 2022 when OpenAI released ChatGPT. By 2023, bearing in mind the forecasts of experts detailed in this chapter, significant uncertainty remained about whether generative AI would be a short-lived fad, a quickly growing force changing all aspects of society, or something in between.

- **Actors seeking to harm society will locate where regulation is weakest.** People seeking to use generative AI to harm society, for example, by promulgating misinformation and conspiracy theories to gain political power or defrauding organizations and individuals out of their money, are likely to operate in regions with the weakest regulation of generative AI. Bad actors operating in these lightly regulated regions could put local citizens at risk.

In 2023, these challenges revealed themselves in the varying generative AI regulatory approaches in three large regions of the world:

- **China aimed to control companies and speech while innovating**. In 2021, China passed a law requiring firms to use personal data for automated decisions in an unbiased and transparent manner and to let people opt out of such decisions. In 2022, its Cyberspace Administration of China (CAC) issued rules to block the spread of fake news, efforts to addict users to content, or foster social unrest. In 2023, CAC began enforcing rules against deep fakes. CAC required services that created fake images, videos, audio, or text to "verify users' identities, obtain consent from deepfake targets, watermark and log outputs and counter any misinformation produced."[30]

- **European Union regulated based on generative AI's perceived risks.** In 2023, the EU parliament passed the AI Act – legislation to categorize AI technology by its level of risk. The AI Act banned software posing an unacceptable risk, including predictive policing, emotion recognition, and real-time facial recognition. High-risk uses, such as software in law enforcement and education, would require providers to maintain detailed documentation. Lower-risk uses, such as tools to guide social welfare and criminal justice decisions and hiring employees, would require suppliers to demonstrate their systems were safe, effective, and

---

[30] Matthew Hutson, "Rules to keep AI in check: nations carve different paths for tech regulation," *Nature*, August 8, 2023, www.nature.com/articles/d41586-023-02491-y

privacy compliant. Violators were subject to fines as high as 7% of their annual global profits and had two years to comply once the act was in force. In August 2023, not all EU regions had passed the AI Act as technology suppliers and other key stakeholders aimed to modify its provisions. In 2018, the European Union passed General Data Protection Regulation legislation restricting the collection of personally identifying data and granting EU citizens the right to "'meaningful information' about the logic involved in automated decisions."[31]

- **The United States appeared to be taking action to regulate generative AI.** The United States lacked federal A-related laws and significant rules to protect data. In 2022, the White House released a white paper detailing principles to guide the use of AI, which are very similar to those in the European Union's AI Act. The US also held congressional hearings and presidential meetings related to AI regulation. For example, in July 2023, Amazon, Anthropic, Google, Inflection, Meta, Microsoft, and OpenAI met with President Biden, announcing vague and unenforceable safeguards such as "as testing their products, reporting limitations and working on watermarks that might help to identify AI-generated material." Moreover, regulators were considering extending existing rules, such as

---

[31] Matthew Hutson, "Rules to keep AI in check: nations carve different paths for tech regulation," *Nature*, Ibid.

those related to explaining why a financial institution denied credit to a potential borrower, to pertain to AI applications.[32]

By 2023, AI regulation strategies varied across the globe. The European Union created sector-specific regulation, the United States chose a decentralized approach including federal guidance with local adaptations, and China prioritized consumer transparency and aimed to lead the world in global AI standards.[33]

As these summaries of government generative AI policy reveal, policymakers might move too slowly. Thus citizens must take the initiative to capture the benefits of generative AI's light side and defend against its dark one. Here we explore how that could work.

Actions Citizens Should Take with Generative AI's Light and Dark Sides

As we saw in Chapter 1, generative AI is a potential threat and opportunity for society. Whether generative AI is one, the other, or both depends on where you stand. How should citizens decide what to do about this? I suggest the following steps:

---

[32] Matthew Hutson, "Rules to keep AI in check: nations carve different paths for tech regulation," *Nature*, Ibid.

[33] Nancy A. Fischer, Elizabeth Vella Moeller, The Honorable Jerry McNerney, Amaris Trozzo, Steven Farmer, Jenny (Jia) Sheng, Jack Ko, Ph.D., Jenny Y. Liu, Chunbin Xu, Fred Ji, Wenjun Cai, "Unleashing the AI Imagination: A Global Overview of Generative AI Regulations," *Pillsbury Winthrop Shaw Pittman* LLP, August 15, 2023, `www.pillsburylaw.com/en/news-and-insights/ai-regulations-us-eu-uk-china.html`

- **Set goals and articulate values.** As a citizen, I need to think about my goals and values, the same starting point we discussed in Chapter 1 for developing an organization's generative AI strategy. For example, as a teacher, I aim to help students develop skills that will propel them forward in a career they find meaningful. To realize that goal, I put a high value on critical thinking and respect for others. As an investor, I aim to support companies producing a stream of products that customers find uniquely valuable – and earn high long-run returns.

- **Decide which generative AI trends matter most.** Using my goals and values, I decide which generative AI trends matter most. For example, based on my goals and values, I see an opportunity to invest in generative AI's potential to boost growth, to drive demand for generative AI end users and suppliers. Conversely, I see threats in the technology's potential to produce misinformation, in the threat to civilization resulting from generative AI's misuse for nefarious ends, and in the imperative it presents citizens to think critically about the results of a chatbot's responses.

- **Investigate the high-priority trends.** To educate myself, I have read articles and interviewed experts and consumers of generative AI to understand the trends that matter to me most. To that end, for each trend, I read articles in credible newspapers and magazines, interviewed experts who commented on the trends in the media, found academic research related to the trend, and gathered opinions from investors, executives, and professors who researched the topic.

- **Consider options for capturing their benefits or defending against their threats.** Based on this research, I thought about options to capture the benefits or defend against the threats of most interest to specific societal groups. For example, as someone who is concerned about generative AI's potential for misinformation, I will follow specific steps to investigate the veracity of chatbot results. I also thought about pushing my state senators to regulate chatbot owners, for example, by encouraging lawmakers to impose penalties on chatbot owners who produce misinformation or requiring them to monitor and block tainted chatbot responses.

- **Choose and implement the best option.** Ultimately, citizens should pick the best options and make them happen. For example, I might develop a ChatGPT policy for my students or find and invest in companies providing generative AI products that provide customers with more value than competing products.

Conclusion

In 2023, the future of generative AI was uncertain. Capital was flowing into the most essential parts of the industry, creating investment opportunities for people planning for retirement, while companies and individuals were experimenting with chatbots and other uses of the technology aiming to increase their productivity and increase employee and customer satisfaction. At the same time, the notion that bad actors could deploy generative AI to defraud and delude the populace or use the technology to end civilization fanned fears and drove pressure to regulate the technology. Citizens struggled to educate themselves about how to defend against generative AI's dark side and benefit from its light side. Politicians and regulators around the world experimented with new generative AI policies to achieve their own goals, consistent with local values. In Chapter 10 we conclude the book by recapping answers to the fundamental questions addressed in *Brain Rush* and ponder how those answers might evolve in the future.

After the Brain Rush: What Is Generative AI's Future?

With apologies to Neil Young,[1] this chapter concludes *Brain Rush* by recapping my thoughts on the answers to six key questions we explored in this book and sharing my perspective on how these answers could change in the future.

Generative AI and How It Is Likely to Evolve

Generative AI answers natural language questions with clearly written paragraphs, images, videos, or computer code. As we discussed in Chapter 2, Goldman Sachs's chief information officer Marco Argenti attributed generative AI's rapid adoption to its ability to make complex concepts more comprehensible to people who lack education or training in those concepts. We also saw that generative AI differs from previous forms of AI. For example, while machine learning analyzes the past and uses the analysis to extrapolate into the future, generative AI processes large volumes of text to predict the next word in a sentence based on the

---

[1] Neil Young's 1970 album *After the Gold Rush* inspired the title of this chapter.

word's context. Most importantly, generative AI offers two distinctive benefits to end users: first, it enables users to ask questions through natural language prompts, and second, it produces new content in response to the prompts.

In 2024, generative AI's future appeared likely to evolve along the arc of lower barriers to entry, making the technology more accessible to startups and more likely to develop specific solutions to the challenges facing a variety of business functions and industries. Here are three of the most compelling future advances and how they are likely to alter the way people use and supply generative AI:

- **Emergence of multimodal AI models.** In 2024, leading companies, including OpenAI's GPT4, Meta's Llama 2, and Mistral, provided LLMs trained on text, audio, image, and video. This transition to multimodal models will make AI "more intuitive and dynamic." Users are likely to adapt to multimodal AI models by incorporating a combination of media in their prompts and descriptions of how they want the models to present their results.[2]

- **Capable and powerful small language models.** While LLMs can answer a broad range of user queries, they require terabytes of training data drawn from billions of publicly accessible websites. Such huge datasets demand significant computing resources and are subject to biases and hallucinations. By contrast, limited datasets, consisting of textbooks, journals, and authoritative content requiring less storage

---

[2] Janakiram MSV, "Exploring The Future: 5 Cutting-Edge generative AI Trends In 2024," *Forbes*, January 2, 2024, www.forbes.com/sites/janakirammsv/2024/01/02/exploring-the-future-5-cutting-edge-generative-ai-trends-in-2024/

and memory and cheaper hardware, train SLMs. Companies can build SLMs using their internal data, such as transcripts of customer service calls, to give themselves a competitive advantage, say, in customer service.[3]

- **The rise of autonomous agents.** While LLM-based applications provide responses to a series of natural language questions from people, autonomous agents are emerging that will plan and execute tasks, such as designing and executing a marketing campaign or conducting R&D testing, to accomplish a specific goal. Such autonomous agents will be able to sense and respond to external changes by iteratively querying LLMs, say, to refine a marketing campaign based on initial feedback. Since autonomous agents will be able to operate without human intervention, they could theoretically replace the managers who perform such activities now.[4] Autonomous agents could also lower the overall costs in industries such as travel, hospitality, retail, and education.[5] At the same time, the risk of a

---

[3] Janakiram MSV, "Exploring The Future: 5 Cutting-Edge generative AI Trends In 2024," *Forbes*, January 2, 2024, Ibid.

[4] Mikhail Burtsev, François Candelon, Gaurav Jha, Daniel Sack, Leonid Zhukov, and David Zuluaga Martínez, "GPT Was Just the Beginning. Here Come Autonomous Agents," *Boston Consulting Group*, November 28, 2023, www.bcg.com/publications/2023/gpt-was-only-the-beginning-autonomous-agents-are-coming

[5] Janakiram MSV, "Exploring The Future: 5 Cutting-Edge generative AI Trends In 2024," *Forbes*, January 2, 2024, Ibid.

misfiring autonomous agent could create existential risks for a company's reputation. Autonomous agents for customer service can be a powerful force for building customer loyalty or destroying a company's credibility. A Massachusetts technology executive experienced both. As Dynatrace CEO Rick McConnell told me in a February 2024 interview, "One went very well: I was trying to fix a billing issue with a cellular provider and the chatbot solved the problem fast." "The second one went so badly that I will never do business with the company again. I was trying to correlate the contact lenses I received with the prescription. The contact lens provider's chatbot couldn't get me a solution. After three different segments, I never got it resolved."[6]

When Apple and other companies introduced the personal computer several decades ago, consumers did not instantly scoop them up. It took time for a killer app, such as the electronic spreadsheet, to emerge that made life so much easier that buying a PC became an obviously good decision. By early 2024, numerous experiments with the technology had not yielded a killer app for generative AI. Perhaps there will be many killer apps resulting from SLMs for specific industries and business processes. It's also possible autonomous agents will get things done far more quickly and effectively than project managers can.[7]

---

[6] Peter Cohan, "Generative AI Could Help Dynatrace Grow Faster Than 25%," *Forbes*, February 16, 2024, www.forbes.com/sites/petercohan/2024/02/16/generative-ai-could-help-dynatrace-grow-faster-than-25/

[7] Will Douglas Heaven, "These six questions will dictate the future of generative AI," December 19, 2023, *MIT Technology Review*, www.technologyreview.com/2023/12/19/1084505/generative-ai-artificial-intelligence-bias-jobs-copyright-misinformation/

Does Generative AI Matter or Is It a Temporary Fad?

In early 2024, excitement about generative AI's potential lifted the floodgate holding back enterprise spending on cloud services. Indeed, companies were spending on cloud services to experiment with applications of the technology. However, it was unclear whether these applications would achieve meaningful results. Despite surveys predicting widespread adoption of the technology, initial customer feedback on Microsoft's Copilot, to help people create PowerPoint presentations and Excel spreadsheets more efficiently, suggested significant improvements would be essential for making companies eager to pay $30 per month per employee for the product. In early 2024, it was too early to tell whether purveyors of generative AI technology could build a killer app that would identify and relieve a society-wide pain point and relieve that pain more effectively than products already on the market. If such products emerged, generative AI could become significant; otherwise, the technology could fade into history as another fad.

At the time, the early-stage AI efforts had not yielded compelling results, and tester frustration with Copilot raised the risk that initial enthusiasm for generative AI's transformative potential could presage later disappointment. A January 2024 Morgan Stanley CIO survey concluded most chief information officers expected their first generative AI projects to go into production no earlier than the "second half of 2024 and beyond." One expert, Stefan Slowinski, global head of software research at investment bank BNP Paribas Exane, said such projects were somewhat costly but had low business risk because they were not widely deployed with employees and/or customers. Choice Hotels CIO Brian Kirkland said his company was testing an AI model running on AWS to generate a summary of a customer's past interactions with the hotel chain's website. Kirkland said he was in no rush to deploy the project. Agricultural machinery and construction equipment provider CNH Industrial had mixed results with generative AI projects. One model built to make predictions about future demand based on old sales data "hallucinated" due to insufficient data. The good news was CNH's Chief Digital and Information Officer Marc Kermisch said the company would launch a GPT model that would act as a "search engine for equipment repair" later in 2024. Kermisch said proofs of concepts, such as the sales forecasting application, fail because "they cost more to put into production than they actually save in efficiency."[8]

Given the prominent role Microsoft has played in the rapid popularization of ChatGPT and generative AI, the initially skeptical customer reaction to Copilot for Microsoft 365 increased the chances the software giant might not be able to fulfill investors' high expectations for a return on its investment in OpenAI. In February 2024, testers questioned whether they should buy Copilot given its tendency to make mistakes when used with Excel and PowerPoint. Testers said Copilot for Excel sometimes generated numerical mistakes. Andreessen Horowitz partner Guido Appenzeller posted a thread on X illustrating the mistakes Copilot makes when prompted to make a PowerPoint presentation. "It is a mess and not anywhere close to adding value," Appenzeller said. Microsoft expected to generate billions of dollars' worth of new revenue from Copilot-powered Bing; however, the company gained less than one percentage point of market share since launching the new service. Some companies saw benefits from Copilot. Melanie Kalmar, chief information and chief digital officer at Dow, said the materials science company had achieved "tremendous efficiency gains" and would roll out Copilot to

---

[8] Isabelle Bousquette, "Growth in Cloud Spending Reflects Early-Stage AI Efforts," *Wall Street Journal*, February 1, 2024, www.wsj.com/articles/growth-in-cloud-spending-reflects-early-stage-ai-efforts-3c589ac5?mod=hp_minor_pos6

about half its 35,900 employees by the end of 2024.[9] In early 2024, these initial market reactions raised the specter of Microsoft falling short of the $30 billion in Copilot revenue analysts had expected in October 2023.[10]

Groups Likely to Be Generative AI Winners and Losers

Investors in generative AI products and services companies and their executives are likely to be the biggest winners. The losers will be workers who decline to learn how to use generative AI in their jobs and victims of deep fake-powered scams. In early 2024, the biggest winners from generative AI were the shareholders and top executives of publicly traded companies, such as Nvidia, Microsoft, Amazon, and other publicly traded companies in the generative AI Stock Index, that increased at more than twice the rate of the NASDAQ index following November 2022's launch of ChatGPT. Other winners included people who built generative AI products and services. In 2023, there were 180,000 AI-related job postings in the United States in software development, semiconductor engineering, and cloud computing. The number of generative AI-related job openings expanded in 2024.[11] The World Economic Forum detailed new job categories generative AI was likely to create, including the following:

---

[9] Tom Dotan, "Early Adopters of Microsoft's AI Bot Wonder If It's Worth the Money," *Wall Street Journal*, February 13, 2024, www.wsj.com/tech/ai/early-adopters-of-microsofts-ai-bot-wonder-if-its-worth-the-money-2e74e3a2

[10] Peter Cohan, "Why Microsoft Azure Could Take The Cloud Lead From Amazon AWS By 2026," *Forbes*, February 13, 2024, www.forbes.com/sites/petercohan/2024/02/13/why-microsoft-azure-could-take-the-cloud-lead-from-amazon-aws-by-2026/

[11] Tripp Mickle, "Why Is Big Tech Still Cutting Jobs?," *New York Times*, February 5, 2024, www.nytimes.com/2024/02/05/technology/why-is-big-tech-still-cutting-jobs.html

- **AI model and prompt engineers** who write questions for chatbots

- **Interface and interaction designers** who make chatbots more user-friendly

- **AI content creators** who produce "articles, books, teaching materials, movie scripts, and music"

- **Data curators and trainers** who screen data to ensure chatbots are trained with unbiased, high-quality, and relevant data

- **Ethics and governance specialists** who scrutinize and test AI tools before releasing them to the public[12]

While no generative AI startups were poised for initial public offerings, the torrent of IPOs during the peak of the dot-com bubble suggested the possibility of a repeat performance for startups supplying the technology for AI-powered chatbots. If generative AI startups go public in the future and sustain expectations-beating revenue growth, their investors and employees will be big beneficiaries. Other beneficiaries of generative AI could be consumers and employees who use the technology to improve their quality of life and boost their productivity.

In early 2024, generative AI losers included white-collar workers who lost their jobs to help finance their company's investments in generative AI and victims of financial scams powered by generative AI. To be sure, the number of job losses was relatively small. Between May 2023 and February 2024, media and tech companies blamed "more than 4,600 job cuts to AI." In January 2024, Google laid off "hundreds of employees in hardware and internal software tools" so the company could shift more resources

---

[12] Jacob Zinkula, "5 types of new jobs that AI could create," *Business Insider*, November 30, 2023, www.businessinsider.com/new-jobs-al-will-create-no-collegee-degree-chatgpt-2023-11

into AI development. Language teaching software company Duolingo cut 10% of its contractors with the intent of deploying AI to pick up the content creation slack. UPS said that it would cut 12,000 management and contract workers because machine learning enabled the company to set prices for customer shipments with fewer workers in its pricing department. The prospects for more layoffs loomed as workers used generative AI to boost their productivity. For example, Prosus, a global technology investment group based in the Netherlands, found engineers and software developers could do work twice as fast thanks to generative AI. The company's web designers could use the technology to code a website rather than delegating the task to software developers. Prosus's software developers gave themselves a "seniority boost," delegating coding to generative AI so the developers could focus more time on design and complex code. DuPont spinoff Chemours has trained finance professionals to use no-code AI-powered analytical tools that automate "the copying and pasting between systems and spreadsheets" that formerly took up much of their time. "The finance team is now able to use their time on other business-critical projects rather than constantly running system queries," said Matt Abbott, chief enterprise transformation officer at Chemours.[13] In all likelihood, white-collar workers who choose not to learn how to use generative AI to work more effectively could put their jobs at risk of elimination.

Deepfake swindles, which use generative AI to create convincing fake videos or audio recordings, are likely to cost their victims many fortunes. In 2023, scammers used audio deepfake technology to convince victims

---

[13] Ray A. Smith, "AI Is Starting to Threaten White-Collar Jobs. Few Industries Are Immune," *Wall Street Journal*, February 12, 2024, www.wsj.com/lifestyle/careers/ai-is-starting-to-threaten-white-collar-jobs-few-industries-are-immune-9cdbcb90

to transfer funds by impersonating loved ones in trouble. A more costly example was the use of deepfake technology to defraud nearly $26 million from the Hong Kong office of a British company. The swindle started with a phishing email the employee received purportedly from the company's UK-based CFO. A digitally recreated version of the company's CFO and other employees appeared in a video conference call instructing a Hong Kong-based finance department employee to transfer funds. The presence of the deepfake CFO and other employees in the video conference call convinced the Hong Kong finance staffer to set aside doubts and make 15 transfers totaling $25.6 million to five different Hong Kong accounts. It took a week for authorities to realize what had happened and to commence an investigation.[14] Victims of these deepfake swindles are likely to increase in the future as criminals use generative AI technology for their larcenous ends.

The Most Beneficial Uses of Generative AI

With the exception of investors, generative AI benefits its stakeholders in many ways. To be sure, analysts are experimenting with using chatbots to analyze large documents, such as financial filings, to find value. However, these experiments have yet to yield reliable strategies for capitalizing on high-payoff stock investment opportunities. Here is my take on the three most beneficial generative AI applications for the other generative AI stakeholders.

---

[14] Benj Edwards, "Deepfake scammer walks off with $25 million in first-of-its-kind AI heist," *ArsTechnica*, February 5, 2024, https://arstechnica.com/information-technology/2024/02/deepfake-scammer-walks-off-with-25-million-in-first-of-its-kind-ai-heist/

Consumers

Consumers should consider using generative AI for the following:

- **Understanding new concepts.** Generative AI excels at making complex concepts and technical information understandable. By enabling people to ask a chatbot a series of questions, a curious person can quickly move down the learning curve to become conversant on new topics.

- **Overcoming creator's block.** Creators of articles, books, emails, images, sounds, and videos all have trouble getting started with new projects. Chatbots can save creators the time they spend fretting over how to get started. To overcome their block, creators type a prompt that describes the purpose of the project and how the chatbot should display its results.

Employees

Generative AI can help employees perform the following tasks more efficiently:

- **Creating marketing content.** The proliferation of social media has created enormous demand for marketing content in many forms, including emails, text, images, sound, and video. Generative AI can produce a good first draft of new content , helping stretched marketing content producers to keep up with burgeoning demand. To be sure, people must verify the output of these generative AI-powered systems. If such checks eliminate reputation damage, the technology's benefits will exceed its costs.

- **Writing code.** Generative AI is adding to the already high demand for software developers. At the same time, AI-powered chatbots make coding skills available to many employees who lack code-writing experience. Generative AI can reduce the time end users must wait for software developers to write the applications they need by enabling them to write their own code. ZDNet provided useful advice on how non-technical people can use chatbots to write code:

  - Tackle specific coding tasks or routines, rather than building complete applications from scratch.

  - Provide clear and detailed prompts.

  - Use ChatGPT to find and choose the right coding libraries for specific purposes and narrow down the options through interactive discussion with ChatGPT.

  - Know who owns the AI-generated code.

  - Check the reliability of the code ChatGPT produces.[15]

Business Leaders

Business leaders should consider using generative AI to increase company competitiveness by doing the following:

---

[15] David Gewirtz, "How to use ChatGPT to write code," *ZDNet*, December 11, 2023, www.zdnet.com/article/how-to-use-chatgpt-to-write-code/

- **Boosting customer service effectiveness and efficiency.** As we saw in Chapter 3, business leaders must take the initiative to deploy generative AI for applications that involve many groups of people inside and/or outside their organization. Generative AI trained on a company's internal data, such as transcripts of conversations between customer service agents and customers, can greatly enhance the quality of customer service by spreading best practices to all service agents. Similarly, generative AI can enable money managers to converse more productively with their clients by using natural language queries to analyze data about the structure and performance of client investment portfolios. Generative AI's ability to improve customer service can help companies boost sales revenue, profitability, and customer retention. By March 2024, companies using generative AI enjoyed significant "Great customer service results in a 20% to 30% uplift in revenue," Paul Smith, ServiceNow's Chief Commercial Officer, told me. "No one has yet analyzed how much additional revenue is created by using generative AI for customer service. However, if a call is getting resolved 37% faster, the customer will get a better experience."[16]

- **Brainstorming growth strategies.** Generative AI is particularly useful for creative, rather than analytical, executive tasks. In this book, we explored how ChatGPT helped brainstorm a new business aimed

---

[16] Peter Cohan, "ServiceNow Is Poised To Quantify Its Generative AI Revenue," *Forbes*, March 4, 2024, www.forbes.com/sites/petercohan/2024/03/04/servicenow-genai-cuts-service-time-37-may-add-20-to-client-revenue/

at dominating the online streaming industry within a decade. The chatbot provided useful insights on the venture's business strategy, including how to produce its first product, how to build its management team, how to raise capital, and how to market the service to potential customers. While this application of generative AI could be more useful, it provides enough useful new ideas to be worth the effort.

Will any of these applications rise to the level of a killer app in the future? To be "killer" such apps must

- **Address a problem causing significant end-user pain.** People will only demand the app if it aims to solve a problem so painful that people will pay to alleviate it.

- **Solve the problem far more effectively than competing solutions do.** People will only buy the app if it reliably delivers the industry's most effective solution to the problem.

- **Create tangible benefits vastly in excess of the implementation costs.** Before buying the app, customers must be confident that the benefits of adopting the app will exceed its costs and reputational risks.

- **Evolve to satisfy changing user needs and harness new technological capabilities.** Unless providers keep improving the app so it solves evolving user needs and deploys new, more powerful technologies, customers will switch to one that does.

Publicly Traded Generative AI Product and Services Providers That Make the Best Investments

Since the launch of ChatGPT, the publicly traded companies adding the most revenue growth from products and services essential for building LLMs were the best investments as of February 2024. I developed a generative AI Stock Index consisting of the publicly traded companies profiled in Chapters 4 through 7 of this book. In 2023 and during the first two months of 2024, the GAISI outperformed the NASDAQ. Specifically, the GAISI rose 86% in 2023 and 21% in the first two months of 2024 while the NASDAQ increased 43% and 9% respectively during those periods.[17] The GAISI components varied in their performance. Below are the two best-performing stocks within the three most attractive generative AI industry sectors:

- **Hardware:** Up 151% in 2023 and 59% by the end of February 2024

  - *Super Micro*: +246% and 205%

  - *Nvidia*: +246% and 60%

- **Software:** Up 91% and 10%

  - *Meta Platforms*: +183% and 38%

  - *ServiceNow*: +83% and 9%

- **Cloud services:** Up 70% and 10%

---

[17] Peter Cohan, "Why The Generative AI Stock Bubble Isn't Popping Anytime Soon," *Forbes*, March 1, 2024, www.forbes.com/sites/petercohan/2024/03/01/why-generative-ai-stock-bubble-is-not-poised-to-pop/?sh=6e979419d80e

- *MongoDB*: +114% and 17%

- *Amazon* +77% and 16%[18]

By March 2024, the generative AI stock bubble was expanding, yet it appeared far from bursting. There were three reasons this bubble was not poised to pop:

- The leaders in the generative AI boom were large, mostly profitable companies.

- While many generative AI startups were incubating, none of them were money-losing publicly traded stocks.

- Unlike during the late 1990s, borrowing money to buy stocks and/or fund companies was less noticeable in March 2024.

To be sure, the generative AI bubble appeared likely to burst at some point. Before then, investors could see telltale signs, such as hundreds of profit-free startups going public, soaring consumer borrowing to buy in, and the widespread popularity of, say, Uber drivers giving passengers generative AI stock tips.[19]

In 2024 and beyond, I expect the top-performing companies on this list to continue to do well especially if generative AI demand accelerates their revenue growth and causes investors to assign them higher valuations. However, at some point in the future, I expect the leader board to change. The following factors are likely to determine the investment winners and losers in the future:

---

[18] Peter Cohan, "Generative AI Stock Index," author Excel spreadsheet, February 29, 2024.

[19] Peter Cohan, "Why The Generative AI Stock Bubble Isn't Popping Anytime Soon," *Forbes*, March 1, 2024, Ibid.

- **Generative AI initial public offerings.** New publicly traded companies could emerge sporting much faster growth. When Internet browser provider Netscape went public in 1995, it set off a race to the public markets of a large variety of startup companies. If generative AI continues to expand, many startups providing the technology should also reach the public markets. Assuming they are growing faster than the large incumbents in the GAISI, those startups could become the investment winners.

- **Maturing incumbents.** The winners of 2023 could suffer from maturing products and lower market share due to the emergence of fierce competition from such startups, and aggressive incumbents.

- **Newly agile incumbents.** Publicly traded companies that had not previously benefited from AI-powered chatbots could begin to enjoy generative AI revenue growth as their investments in generative AI bear fruit in the form of significant revenue growth.

Government Policies That Limit the Harm and Maximize the Benefit of Generative AI

In Chapter 9 we examined the societal benefits and potential risks of generative AI. While generative AI received significant attention from legislators in 2023, very little actual government regulation of generative AI had taken place by early 2024. I think specific principles should guide public policy toward generative AI:

- Companies that benefit most from generative AI technology should pay the price for any societal harm their products cause.

- Regulation should aim to punish the use of generative AI to harm individuals and damage democratic institutions.

- Regulation should block and punish unauthorized use of copyrighted material and dissemination of deep fakes and other uses of generative AI for larcenous and anti-democratic purposes.

However, my reading of history suggests laws regulating generative AI will not pass until after a crisis occurs that galvanizes Congress to create and pass regulations to prevent a recurrence of that crisis. In all likelihood, that legislation will be favorable toward interests that contribute the most money to legislators and shift the pain and costs to those who do not pay.

Conclusion

By early 2024, generative AI had proven itself a technological tsunami. Its instant accessibility to billions of people around the world and its ability to explain complex, technical subjects in clear, simple paragraphs made it a powerful tool for empowering people from many walks of life. Established providers of generative AI hardware, software, and cloud services benefited from the rapid adoption of AI-powered chatbots, enriching their executives and shareholders. In all the experimentation, glimmers of possible killer apps that would propel demand growth to higher levels were emerging. At the same time, societal costs – in the form of job displacement and the use of deep fakes to enable criminals to steal money from companies and individuals and potentially sway elections – were proliferating.

The specter of autonomous agents and chatbot hallucinations fanned fears of generative AI causing irreparable societal harm. Meanwhile, politicians hesitated to anticipate and regulate generative AI's possible dangers.

As this book concludes, will generative AI be a force for good, spurring applications that eliminate drudgework and improve customer service and the quality of life while launching a wave of startup companies? Or will the AI-powered chatbots spread fear, fascism, and criminality around the world beyond the control of governments? Perhaps it will be a bit of both.

Index

A, B

Adobe analytics (AA), 153
Advanced Semiconductor
    Materials Lithography
    (ASML), 261
AI-powered chatbots, 395
Amazon Web Services (AWS), 176
Application performance
    monitoring (APM), 226
Arista Networks, 202
Automatic speech
    recognition (ASR), 134

C

ChatGPT, 1, 4, 5, 10, 31, 287, 289,
    291, 292, 295, 311, 324, 342,
    383, 391
Chip-on-Wafer-on-
    Substrate (CoWoS), 259
Cisco systems, 205
Cloud platforms
    critical activities, 233, 234
    hyperscalers, 167
    industry attractiveness, 170–174
    industry participants
      AWS, 176–180

Google cloud,
    187–189, 191–195
LLMs, 175
Microsoft Azure, 181–183,
    185, 186
publicly traded data centers,
    195–199, 201
industry players, 168
providers, 169
services, 167
Cloud titans, 203
Compute Unified Device
    Architecture (CUDA),
    250, 323
Consulting firms
    critical activities, 107–109
    industry attractiveness, 71–74
    industry participants
      business chops, 75, 76
      strategists, 83
    industry players, 67–71
Consulting industry participants
    coding outsources, 104–107
    risk/process managers
      EY, 90–94
      KPMG, 94, 96–99
      PwC, 100–104

V, W, X, Y, Z

GPSR Compliance

The European Union's (EU) General Product Safety Regulation (GPSR) is a set
of rules that requires consumer products to be safe and our obligations to
ensure this.

If you have any concerns about our products, you can contact us on

ProductSafety@springernature.com

In case Publisher is established outside the EU, the EU authorized
representative is:

Springer Nature Customer Service Center GmbH
Europaplatz 3
69115 Heidelberg, Germany

www.ingramcontent.com/pod-product-compliance
Lightning Source LLC
LaVergne TN
LVHW051636050326
832903LV00022B/776